BLACK AMERICA SERIES

VANCE COUNTY
NORTH CAROLINA

BLACK AMERICA SERIES

VANCE COUNTY
NORTH CAROLINA

Andre D. Vann

ARCADIA
PUBLISHING

ISBN 978-0-7385-0663-0

Published by Arcadia Publishing
Charleston, South Carolina

Printed in the United States of America

Library of Congress Catalog Card Number: 00-108143

For all general information contact Arcadia Publishing at:
Telephone 843-853-2070
Fax 843-853-0044
E-Mail sales@arcadiapublishing.com
For customer service and orders:
Toll-Free 1-888-313-2665

Visit us on the Internet at www.arcadiapublishing.com

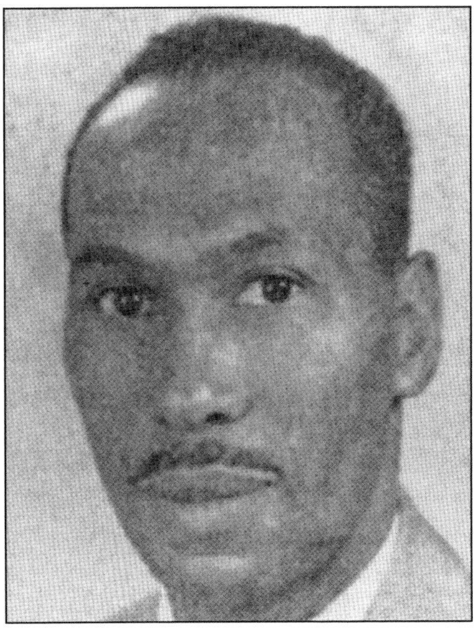

John Joseph Eisbey.

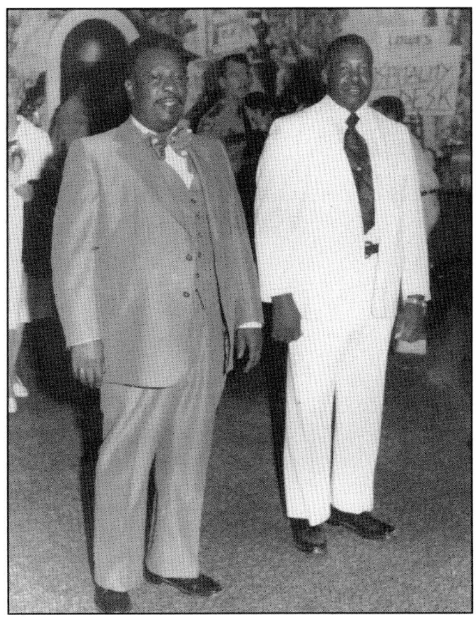

Edward Cecil Vann (left).

*This work is dedicated in memory of John Joseph Eisbey (1915-1971),
an educator, early photographer in Vance, Granville and Warren Counties,
and faithful member of my fraternity, the Alpha Phi Alpha Fraternity, Inc.;
and my father, Edward Cecil Vann (1930-1998), on the left of the photo,
who was a union organizer for the Local 337 T
of the Bakery, Confectionery and Tobacco Workers Union
and owner of Vann's Grocery and Fish Market,
who reminded me always to remember my heritage
and to give something back to my race and my community.*

Contents

Introduction

"The formation of Vance County was accomplished largely as a political expediency. It was in 1881 when Negroes in large numbers were voting solidly Republican, Granville and Franklin Counties were nip and tuck, Democratic or Republican. From the Democratic standpoint Warren County was hopelessly Republican. But by taking from Granville, Franklin and Warren, those sections that were heavily Republican and out of these sections forming the new county of Vance, the Democratic party could lose Vance to the Republicans and save Granville and Franklin for the Democrats. [U.S.] Senator [Zebulon Baird] Vance was a Democrat. He took kindly to this move and thanked the [North Carolina] Legislature for honoring him with naming the new county after him. At the same time Senator Zebulon Baird Vance showed his humor by always referring to Vance County as 'Zeb's Black Baby.' "

—Samuel Thomas Peace Sr., from *Zeb's Black Baby* (1955, Henderson, NC)

This pictorial history of African Americans in Vance County is a salute to the important role that they have played in the social, political, and economic life of the county. It is a celebration of the rich vibrant history and culture of a proud southern American people. Throughout the periods of slavery, Jim Crowism, and segregation, blacks looked inward and to themselves as they built sturdy institutions and neighborhoods that survive today with many of the original families still living on land owned by their forefathers and foremothers.

Much like a cherished family photo album, passed down from one generation to the next, *Vance County, North Carolina* preserves the memory of the generation who came before: morticians, barbers, shop keepers, doctors, soldiers, homemakers, teachers, ministers, and public servants who built durable institutions that survive like homes, churches, and schools, that were built for blacks and by blacks in Vance County from the 1880s to the 1990s.

This work represents a life-long quest to document the lost pages of history in regards to the African-American presence in the county. In its earliest stages citizens and residents in such neighborhoods as Mobile, Flint Hill, West End, and other rural communities like Williamsboro, Townsville, Kittrell, and Greystone actively sought to resurrect their communities through the tools of oral history and picture reproduction. These individuals much like members of my own family guided this work through its earliest stages until it was totally written. The commitment on the part of Mark Berry, Katie White, and Arcadia Publishing to tell for the first time in pictorial documentation the story of blacks living in Vance County, a rural southern community, attests to their willingness to blaze a new trail in the publishing industry.

Vance County has long been a major center of economic, political, religious, and social advancement for its blacks residents. Collective financial advancement and cooperation among black business and the masses gave rise to other black businesses and led to the founding of numerous civic, social, fraternal, and philanthropic organizations. During the late 19th and early 20th centuries an industrious community was formed. The story of Vance County can largely be seen as a "Tale of Two Cities": on one hand you have a white society with every privelege imaginable and on the other hand you have small black communities almost like islands that are segregated, poorer, and places where residents were treated as second-class citizens. Black residents worked hard to refute many of the old stereotypical images that were vestiges of slavery by becoming industrious institution builders who owed no allegiance except to their families and their communities.

Black neighborhoods served as great centers of social, economic, and religious endeavors for African Americans in Vance County. Mobile, Flint Hill, and West End typified the separateness that was evident throughout the entire South. In these neighborhoods one could find houses of worship, medical facilities, educational institutions, businesses, and various leisure activities. Doctors often lived next door to domestic workers, and everyone realized that they had a shared history and collective past.

One of the most important institutions that has endured and maintained collectivism and served as a social welfare agency is the black church. Churches served as vehicles of change as they lifted the spirits of the congregants on Sunday and provided self sustaining nurturance for their day-to-day activities. Churches also established nursing homes for the aged and sponsored many activities like nurseries, kindergartens, meeting halls, and social and literary clubs.

Another outgrowth of the struggle against Jim Crow was the growth and influence of numerous fraternal and civic societies, sororities, and organizations that were committed to helping African Americans. There were numerous organizations in Vance County such as the Elks, Masons, Shriners, and the Alpha Phi Alpha Fraternity that served where they were needed. The expressed purpose of these institutions that pre-dated state-sponsored social welfare institutions was to help the undeserved and underprivileged. Like the churches, they contributed to orphanages and the Jubilee Hospital. The hospital was the only institution in a 40-mile radius that was integrated and that cared for blacks needing medical assistance. It had an integrated staff and had a black nursing staff.

Education was another important facet of black life and culture. The Henderson Normal and Industrial Institute was opened in 1891 as the only school for blacks until the Central Colored Graded School was opened in 1899 to offer African-American children an education and opportunity to succeed. In 1935, the State of North Carolina assumed responsibility for operating all public elementary and high schools in Vance County. Blacks living in rural areas attended Rosenwald Schools (which were funded by northern philanthropist Julius Rosenwald) and rural black communities. Kittrell College was formed in Kittrell, NC, in 1886 by the board of bishops of the African Methodist Episcopal Church.

African Americans were involved in every imaginable vocation known to man from being well diggers to educators. Many were employed as domestics, tobacco factory workers, educators, morticians, physicians, and insurance agents. Others operated beauty salons, barbershops, restaurants, law practices, contractor companies, and grocery stores. These businesses provided service and employed countless blacks and helped to create a modest middle class in the African-American community in Vance County and surrounding areas.

Lastly, many African Americans worked with organizations that were determined to fight for civil rights and economic opportunity. Many worked to destroy segregation, to equalize educational opportunities and the enforcement of equal voting rights legislation. Such organizations as the Civic League, the Assembly of Vance, the NAACP, the SCLC, and the Gateway Community Development Corporation had memberships that numbered in the hundreds throughout the county. Some sought to show their loyalty, allegiance, and patriotism by serving as soldiers in World War I and World War II and supporting the war efforts by purchasing thrift stamps and liberty bonds.

This collection of photos traces the growth and development of a committed people from my hometown who played an important role in every aspect of Vance County. Moreover, *Vance County, North Carolina* is the positive result of a committed few who felt that such a work was needed and long overdue. It is hoped that this book will lead to a greater appreciation and understanding of African-American life, culture, and neighborhoods. May the next generation of African-American youth in the county continue to walk with their heads held high as a result of the contributions made by their ancestors who were Americans that—by historic and divine intervention—just happened to be from the continent of Africa.

One

Family Snapshots

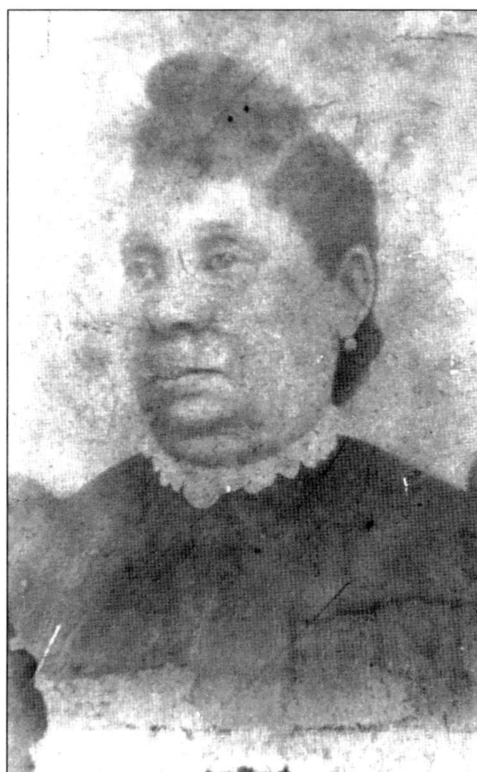

This is an 1890s photo of Rebecca Hawkins (1826–1901). A founder of the Mobile community, she was a slave on the Hawkins estate and a descendant of English navigator John Hawkins. She was married to Mingo Hawkins, who was a field hand and a skilled carpenter. By 1870, he owned a 40-acre farm in Vance County where he lived with Rebecca and their children. That land included the current streets of Hawkins Drive, Yancey Lane, Wilkins Lane, and Skenes Avenue. Rebecca had 21 children in all, but only 11 are known. Her children include Benjamin Hawkins, Lewis Hawkins, Lucy Alston, Carrie Hawkins Willis, Grant W. Hawkins, Thomas Hawkins, Robert Hawkins, Bettie H. Crutchfield, Florence Williams, Janie Burwell, and Ella Hawkins Brice. After emancipation, Rebecca owned a beautiful home on what is now Hawkins Drive in South Henderson. At the time of her death in 1901, she owned $500 in real estate and $500 in personal property. (Courtesy of Andre D. Vann.)

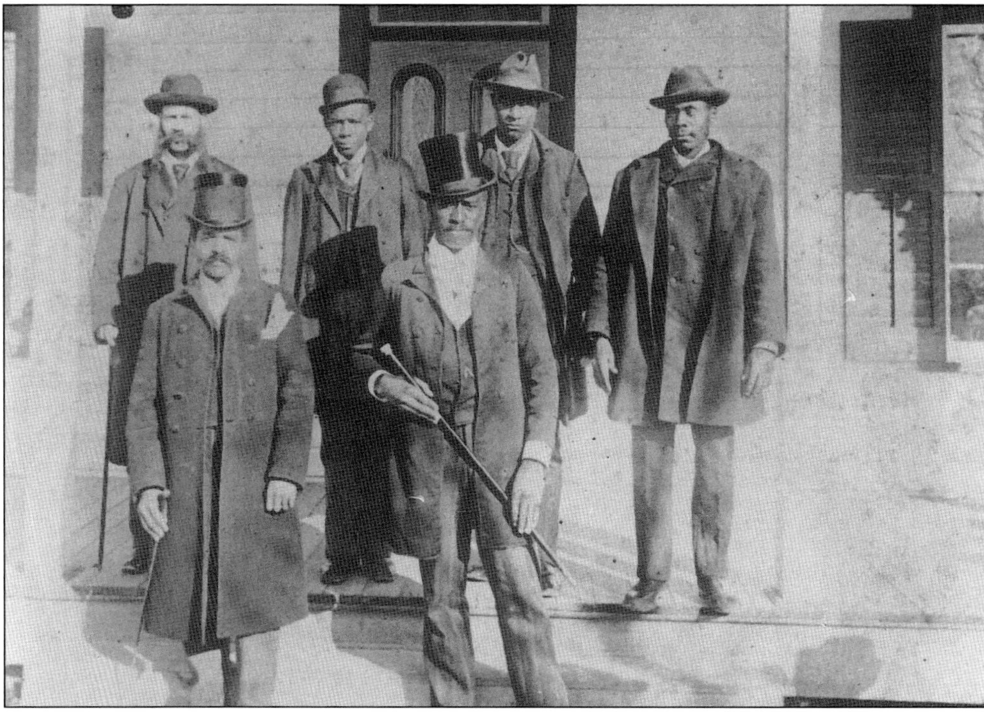

This early 1900s photo shows the sons of Rebecca and Mingo Hawkins Sr. on the steps of the home of Grant Hawkins Sr. All brothers were either building contractors, brick masons, or businessmen. Pictured, from left to right, are (front row) Lewis Hawkins and Thomas Hawkins; (back row) Benjamin Hawkins, Robert Hawkins, unidentified, and Grant W. Hawkins. (Courtesy of Andre D. Vann.)

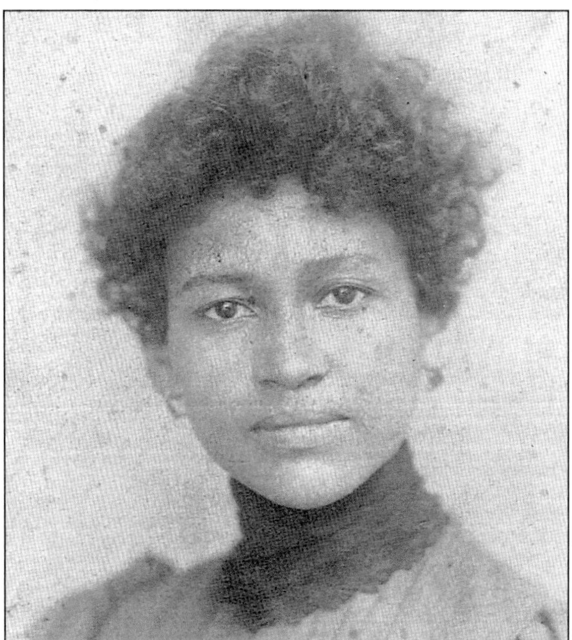

Amanda Moss Davis (1874–1969), the daughter of Richard and Narcissus Moss, was born in Granville County to parents who were of black and Saponi Indian heritage. In the 1880s her parents moved to Henderson. They joined the First Baptist Church (now Shiloh Baptist Church), and she was baptized by the late Dr. Richard I. Walden. She was united in marriage to W. Sherman Davis Sr. (1870–1927), a self-employed manufacturer of tobacco on Winder Street who later worked for the J.P. Taylor Tobacco Company. In the early 1900s the Davises built a home at 517 Winder Street, where they reared 10 children. Amanda is interred in the Davis family plot in the Blacknall Cemetery. (Courtesy of Otelia E. Barnwell.)

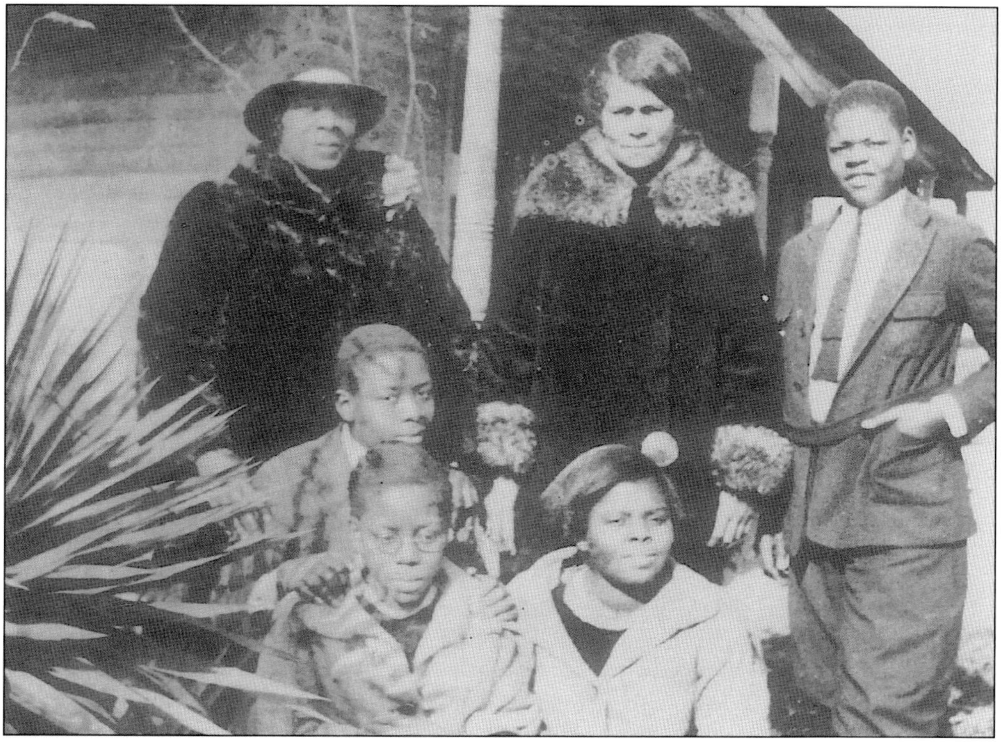

Members of the Brice and Hawkins family assembled *c*. 1935 in front of the home of Thomas and Cora Crutchfield in Mobile, on the South Williams Street extension, which is now St. Nicholas Street. They are as follows, from left to right: (seated) Eugene Brice, Lolita Brice Bluford, and Carol Brice Carey; (standing) Ella Hawkins Brice, Cora Crutchfield Hawkins, and Jonathan Brice. (Courtesy of Andre D. Vann.)

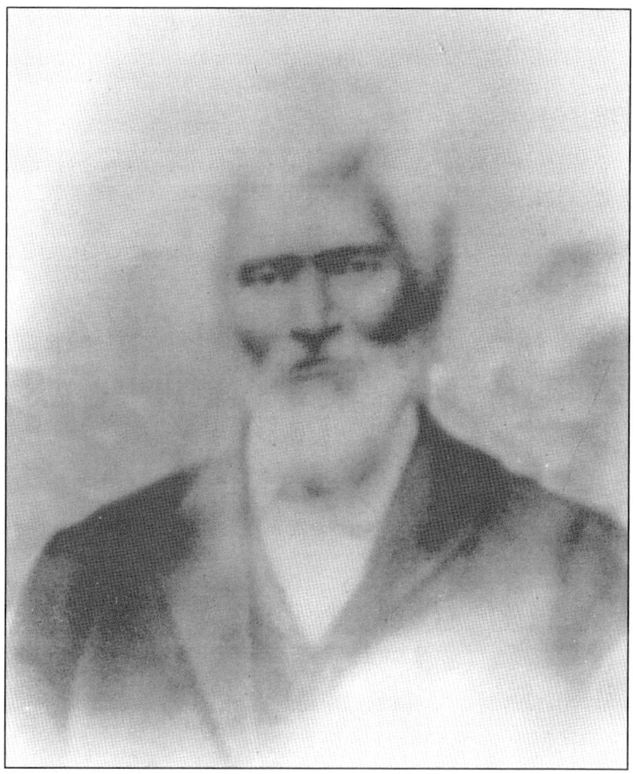

This is an 1890s pencil etching of Thomas Kemp Bullock. (Courtesy of Thomas Brown.)

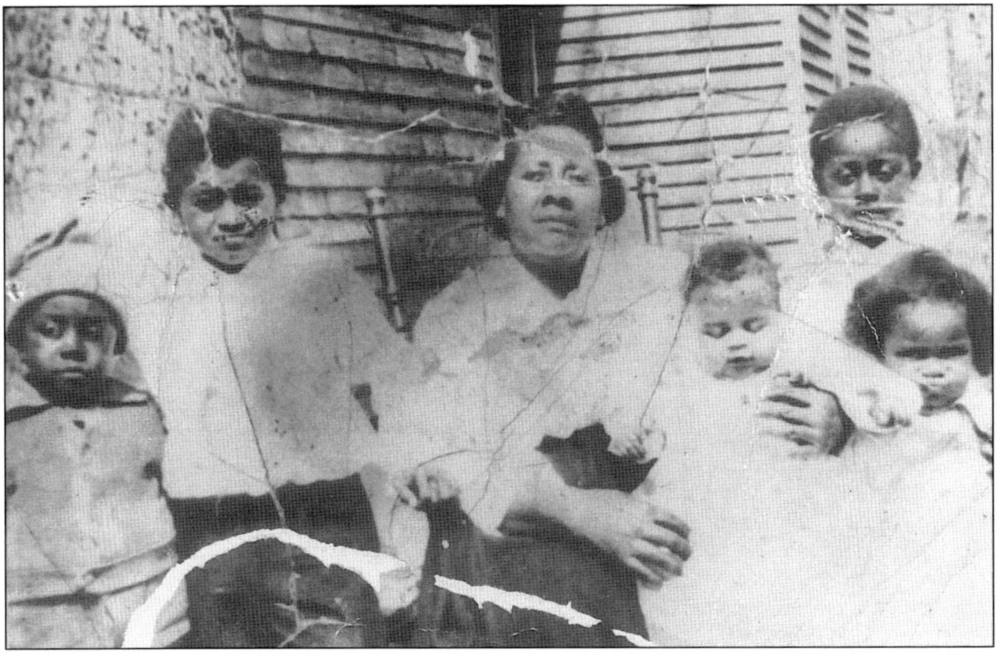

Mary Francis Turner Yarborough (1872–1933) is surrounded by her grandchildren *c.* 1925. From left to right are Eddie G. Yarborough, James "Mike" Yarborough, Mary F.T. Yarborough holding Albert Yarborough, Sam Yarborough, and Annie Yarborough Cunningham. (Courtesy of Andre D. Vann.)

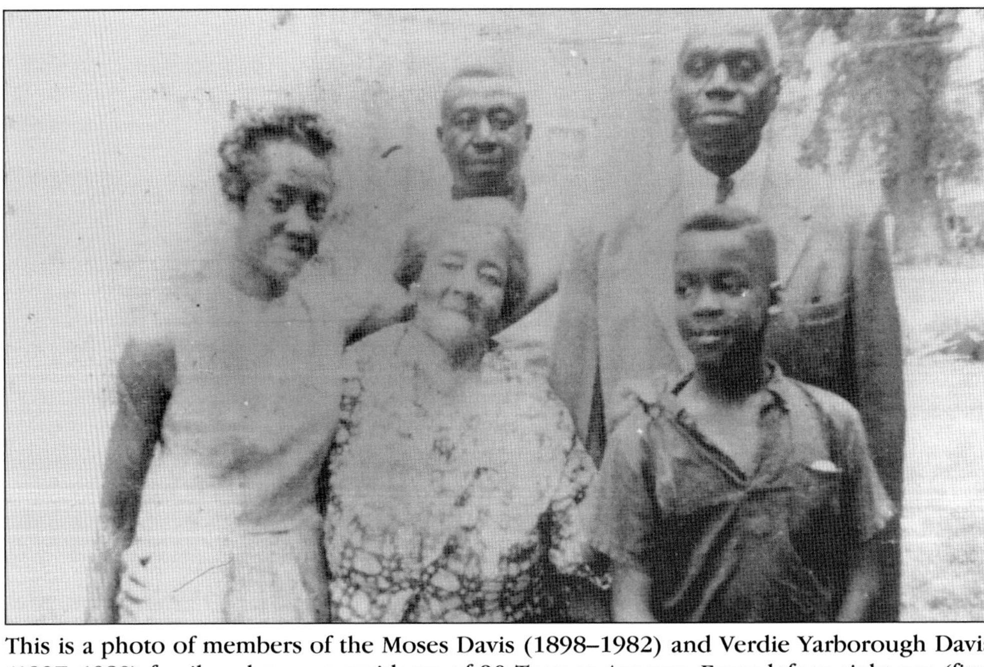

This is a photo of members of the Moses Davis (1898–1982) and Verdie Yarborough Davis (1897–1980) family, who were residents of 90 Terrace Avenue. From left to right are (first row) Annie Mae Davis, Verdie Yarborough Davis, and Morgan Davis; (back row) Clarence Wilbert Davis and his father, Deacon Moses Davis Sr. (Courtesy of Andre D. Vann.)

Catherine Hills Hawkins (1880–1942) of Mobile is pictured in 1940. She was the wife of Grant Washington Hawkins (1873–1921), who was a general contractor and real estate broker in Henderson. She was the mother of Grant Hawkins Jr., Charlie Hawkins, Robert Hawkins, Thurston Hawkins, Clarence Hawkins, Willie Hawkins Jefferies, Gertrude H. Granton, Louise H. Kinlock, Hattie H. Lyons, Mattie Hawkins, and Nannie H. Clements. A housewife for a considerable portion of her life, she also dabbled in real estate, and owned over 21 lots in South Henderson and several lots on Horner Street, which was a main thoroughfare for black residents in the county. She is interred in the Hawkins family plot of Blacknall Cemetery. (Courtesy of Andre D. Vann.)

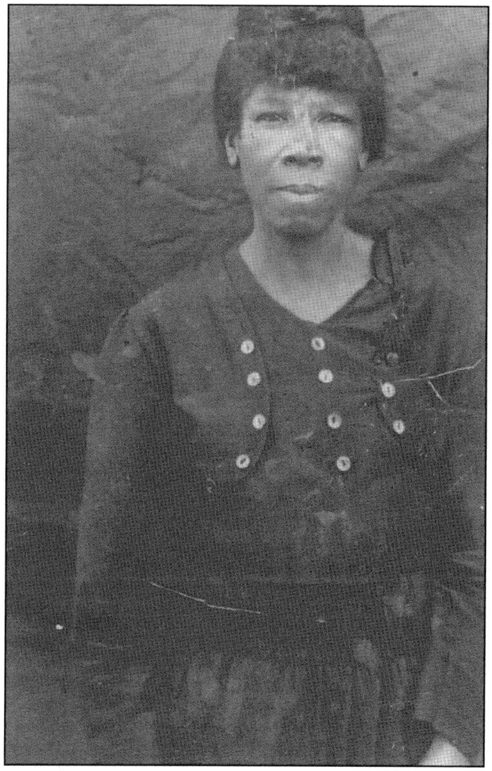

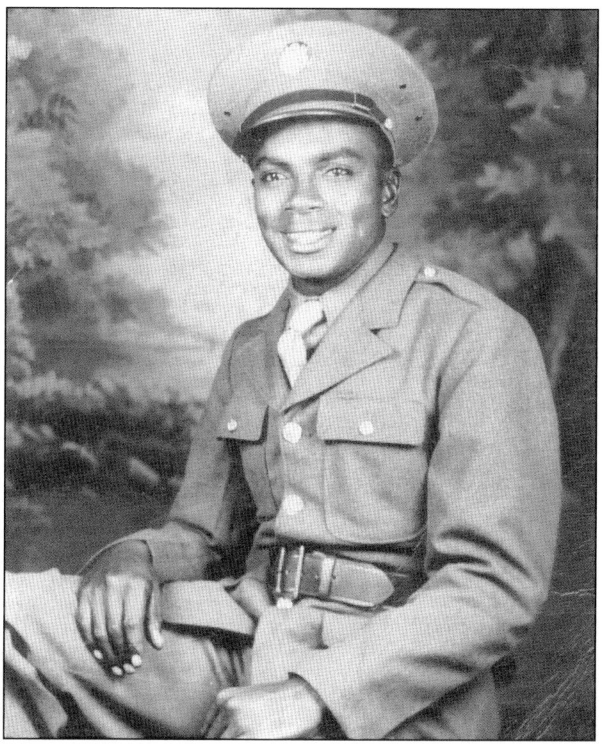

This is a 1940s Army photo of Fletcher W. Brodie, a resident of Flint Hill. (Courtesy of Johnnie Y.M. Brodie.)

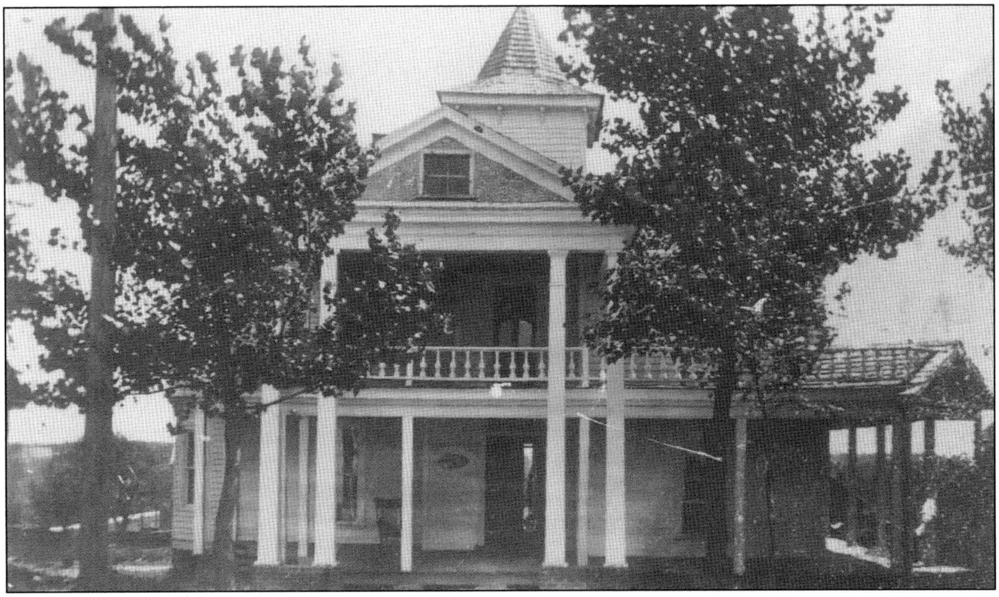

An early 1900s photo shows the impressive home of Grant W. and Catherine H. Hawkins. The 10-room house had two large halls and a porch featuring large white columns that wrapped around it. The house was razed, and currently the homes of Gladys Lyons Hawkins and Rebecca Hawkins Burwell occupy the lot on what is now St. Nicholas Street. (Courtesy of Gladys Lyons Hawkins.)

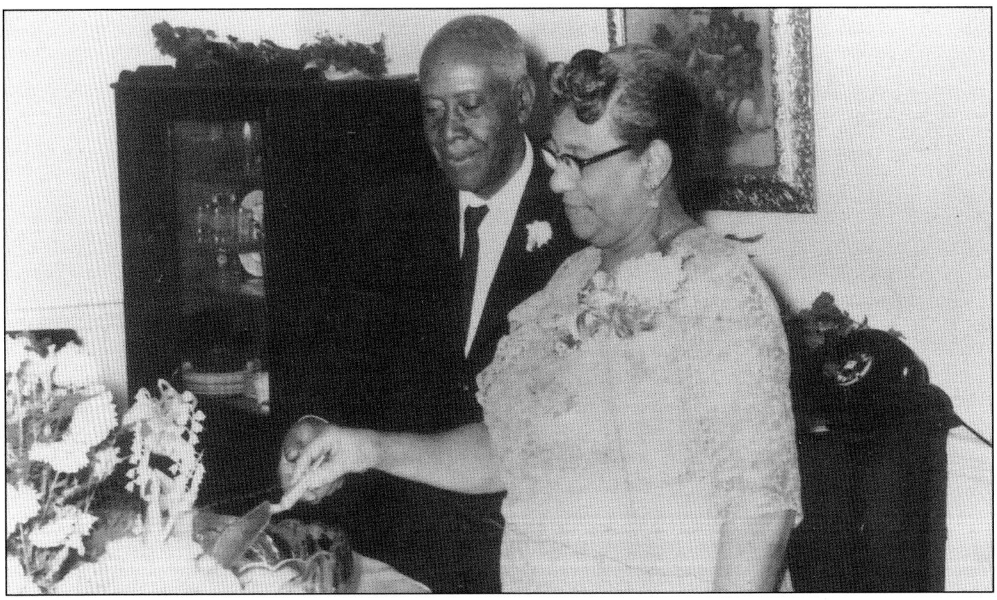

This is a wedding anniversary photo of John D. Vaughan (1886–1972) and Gertrude Cooke Vaughan, both residents of Winder Street in Henderson. John was a gifted blacksmith and a deacon for over 50 years at the Shiloh Baptist Church. Gertrude was a noted midwife for over 30 years in Vance and Warren Counties. They were the parents of John, Richard, and George Vaughan and are both interred in the Vaughan family plot in Blacknall Cemetery. (Courtesy of Tessie B. Vaughan and Gertrude V. Dickerson.)

This is a 1929 photo of the children of James Thomas and Harriet Hattie Hawkins Lyons, residents of 1607 Nicholas Street. From left to right are Robert, Gladys, and James Lyons. This photo was taken after church services at the Shiloh Baptist Church. (Courtesy of Gladys Lyons Hawkins.)

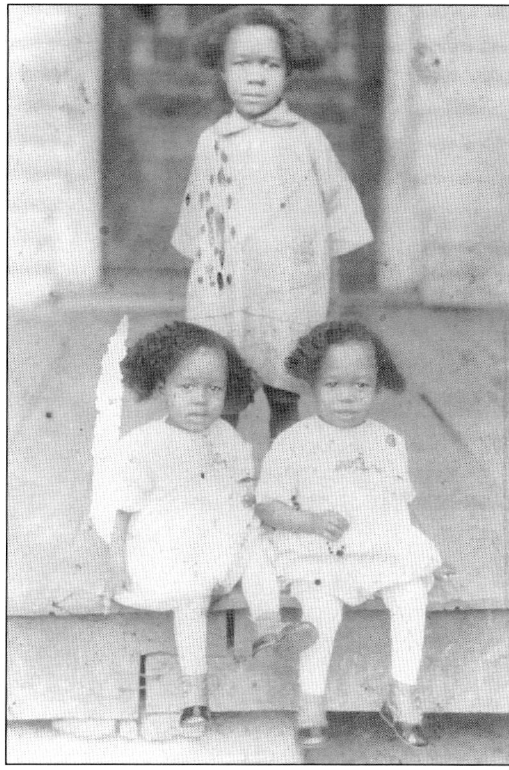

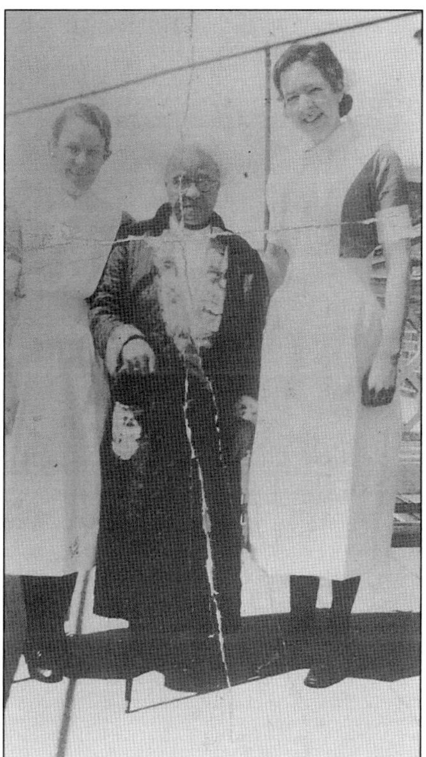

Caroline Carrie Frances Hawkins Willis (1865–1938) is pictured here in the 1930s. She was born in Mobile, the daughter of Mingo and Rebecca Hawkins, and was reared by Jane A. Hawkins, Rebecca's white half-sister in Raleigh, NC. Carrie Hawkins attended primary school at Shaw University in Raleigh. She later settled in Henderson and became the mother of Charlotte Hawkins Brown and Omega Hawkins. Dr. Charlotte Hawkins Brown became the founder of the Palmer Memorial Institute in Sedalia, NC, which was the nation's first private school created for blacks. Omega Hawkins was a postal employee and was the father of Charlotte, Maria, and Carolyn Hawkins. Maria Hawkins, who toured with the Duke Ellington Band, later married the noted entertainer Nat King Cole. (Courtesy of Andre D. Vann.)

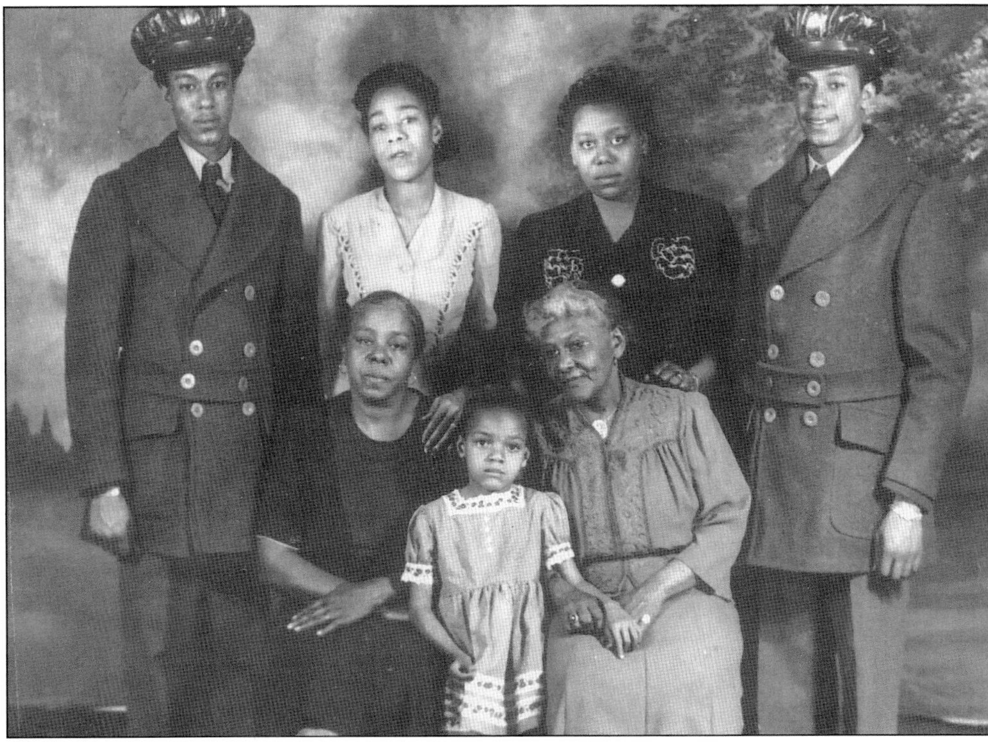

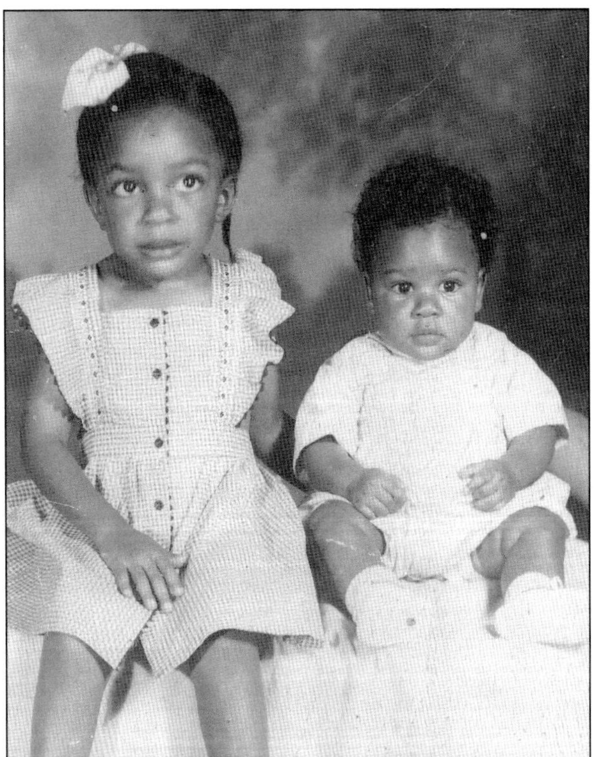

Members of the Lyons and Burwell family are seated for a family portrait during World War II. From left to right are (front row) Harriet Hawkins Lyons (1893–1980), little Iona Lyons, and Rebecca Hawkins Lyons (1888–1983); (back row) James Lyons, Gladys Lyons Hawkins, Ernestine Lyons, and Robert Lyons. (Courtesy of Gladys Lyons Hawkins.)

Siblings Patty Yarborough Foster and George Brady Yarborough Jr. are pictured in 1945. They are the children of George Brady and Lucy Dunston Yarborough. (Courtesy of Patty Y. Foster.)

This 1951 photo was taken of Phillip Andrew Hawkins (1899–1951) at the Colored Fair in Vance County. The son of Thomas and Cora Hawkins, he was a member of the Shiloh Baptist Church of Henderson. He was an employee of the India Cotton Mill in Mobile, and a member of the Henderson Choral Club. (Courtesy of Andre D. Vann.)

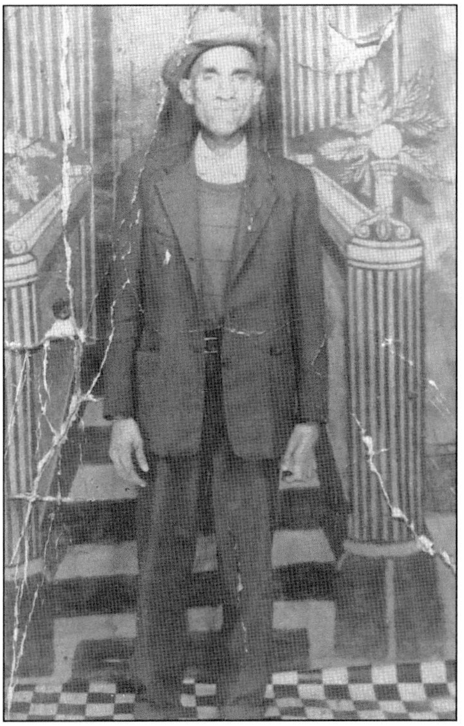

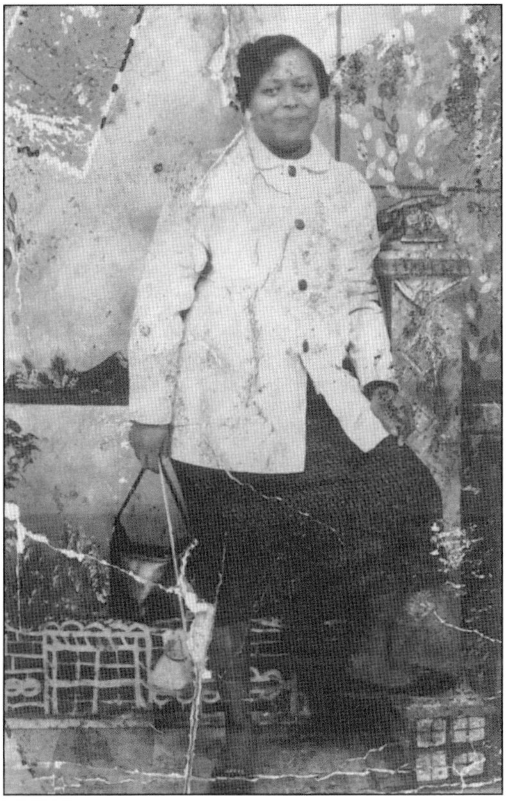

This is a 1950s photo of Martha Hawkins Vann (1933–1994), who was the daughter of Phillip A. and Annie Belle Hicks Hawkins. She was educated in the Vance County Public Schools and attended the Henderson Normal and Industrial Institute (HI) of Vance County. For a number of years, she was employed in the laboratory at the J.P. Taylor Tobacco Company and was also part-owner of Vann's Grocery and Fish Market at 340 Skenes Avenue. She was married to Edward C. Vann (1930–1998) and was the mother of Jacqueline, Paul L., Gloria J., John F., Joan F., Michael A., Cynthia M., Andre D., Tonya A., and Eugene Vann. A member of the Shiloh Baptist Church, she is interred in the Elmwood Cemetery. (Courtesy of Andre D. Vann.)

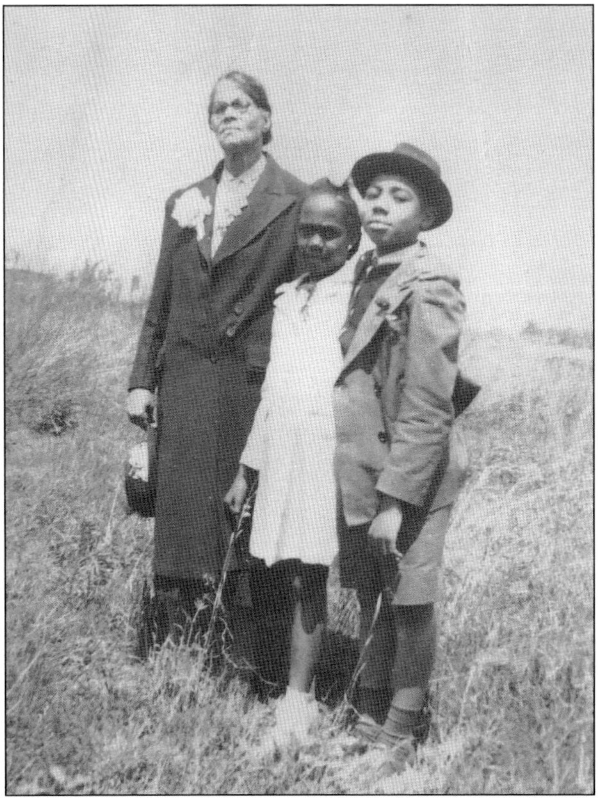

This photo, taken in the Mobile community in South Henderson, shows the late Cora Crutchfield Hawkins (1880–1941) and grandchildren Virginia Hawkins Jones and John Dewey Hawkins II. Cora Crutchfield Hawkins was the wife of Thomas Hawkins (1877–1937), a brick mason and horse trainer. They were the parents of Bennie, Magnolia, John Dewey, Carrie, Asker, Frederick, Phillip, and David Hawkins. They were all members of the Shiloh Baptist Church. (Courtesy of Andre D. Vann.)

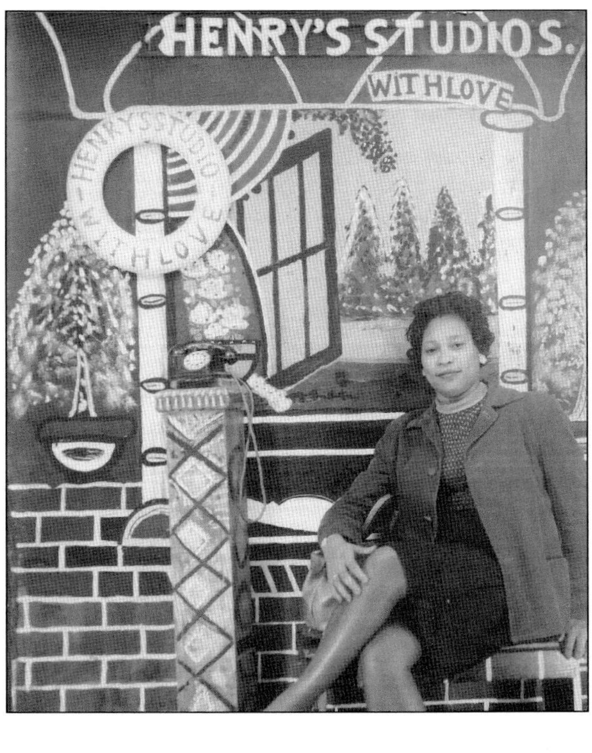

This is a 1950s photo of Ruth Hawkins Harris (1937–1990) taken at the Colored Fair in Vance County. She was married to Ralph Harris and was the mother of Sandra L. Darensburg. (Courtesy of Andre D. Vann.)

Edd Vann (1872–1953), the son of Louis and Amanda Eaton Vann of Vance County, posed for a photo in the 1940s. He was a farmer, a Mason, and a member of Mount Moriah African Methodist Episcopal Zion (AMEZ) Church. He was married to several women, namely, Hattie, Lucendia Marable, and Leona Parham Vann. He was the father of Oris, Samuel, Lemon, James, Charlie Vann, and Kizzie Vann Miller; Catherine Vann Williams; and Rosea Vann. He is interred in the Mt. Moriah Church Cemetery. (Courtesy of Andre D. Vann.)

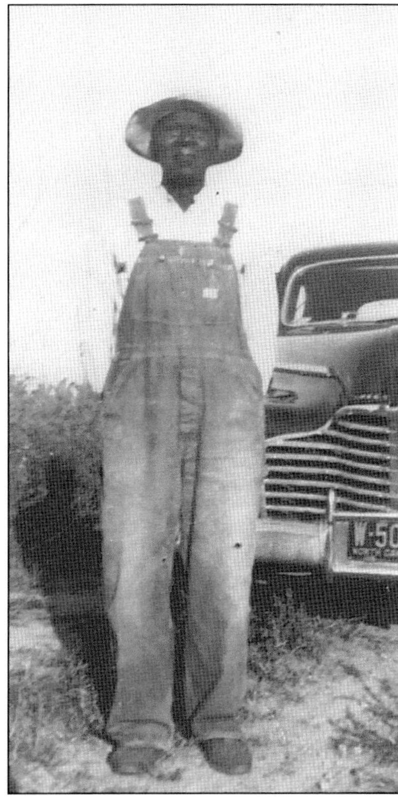

John Clark and Sarah Hawkins Jordan are shown here in the late 1890s. John Clark purchased his freedom and bought a farm in 1860 that would eventually include over 110 acres in Warren County. He was a trained cabinet maker, successful farmer, and builder of homes. In 1867 he became a founder and charter member of the Manson Baptist Church. Sarah Hawkins Clark Jordan was born in 1827 in Middleburg, NC. She was a trained as a maternity nurse and midwife under Drs. Joseph and Peter Hawkins and practiced in black and white homes of Vance and Warren Counties. She died at the age of 105. (Courtesy of the Henderson *Daily Dispatch* and Andre D. Vann.)

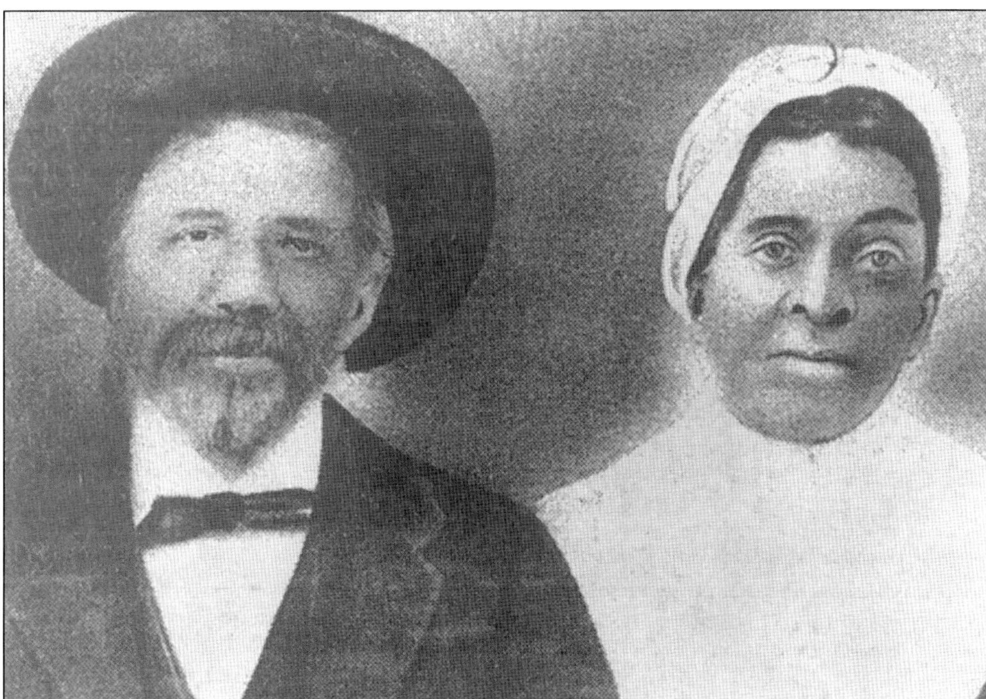

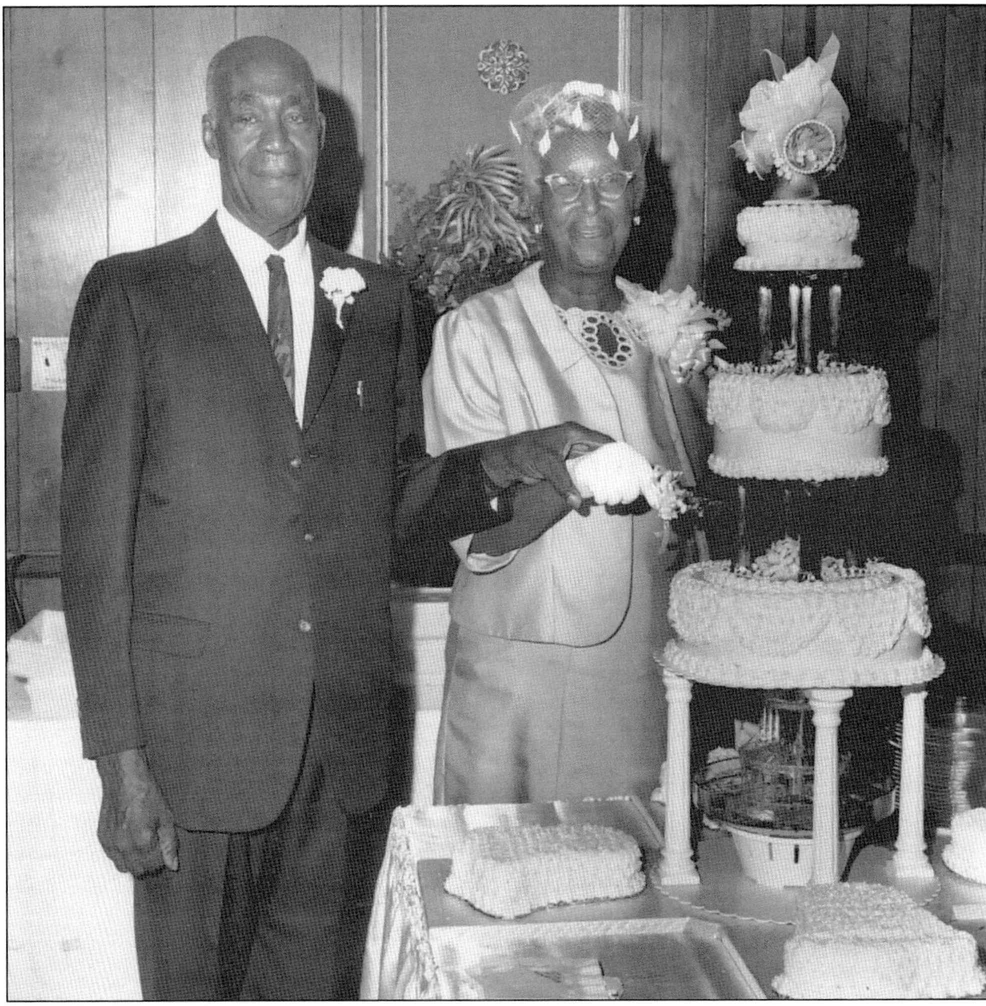

This is a 1970 photo of Rev. Lewis Boyd (1892–1990) and Maria Vesta Taylor Russell (1896–1986) as they celebrate their golden wedding anniversary. They were married in 1920 and were the parents of Richard B. and Edward G. Russell, Kizzie Brown, Olivia Blanding, Sophia Ramey, Cherry Williams, Mary Morton, Harriet Dixon, Elnora O'Hara, and Sallie Letterlough. Residents of 1529 Nicholas Street, they lived in the Mobile Community. L.B. "Bap" Russell lived in the Nutbush Township Community, and was educated in the local schools of Vance County. He graduated in 1916 from Elizabeth City State Normal School and taught in the public schools of Vance and Beaufort Counties for a number of years. He entered the ministry in 1928 and served as a pastor in North Carolina, South Carolina, and Virginia. A charter member of the Vance and Associates Ministerial Alliance, he also served as secretary for a number of years. He was a member of the Democratic Party and was the first black person on the Board of Elections, where he served for two terms. Maria V. Russell was born in Townsville, NC, was a 1917 graduate of HNI, and attended Knoxville College, in Knoxville, TN. She taught in Riceville, TN, Belhaven, NC, and Vance County for several years. She was an early member of the Townsville Presbyterian Church and in later years she was affiliated with Cooke's Chapel AMEZ. Church. She was a Sunday school teacher and church pianist. They are both interred in the Mt. Pleasant Baptist Church Cemetery. (Courtesy of the Henderson *Daily Dispatch*.)

This is a 1960s photo of Annie Henderson Green, who was born in Vance County to William B. Henderson Sr. W.B. Henderson was elected to the 11th Senatorial District of Warren and Vance Counties in 1896 and served in the Senate until 1900. Annie Henderson Green was married to William Green and was the mother of Sydney Green, Alice Smith, Katie Green, Hattie Holmes, Eva Donaldson, William Green, Jennie Fletcher, Annie Ponds, Dr. James P. Green, and Dr. Margaret Labat. A faithful member of Spring Street Baptist Church, she served as senior mother of the Church. She also served as president of the Graded School PTA when it was located on Pettigrew Street, and was a respected member of the Progressive Extension Homemakers Club. She was a charter member of the King's Daughters Club, and served as its first president. An advocate for the ballot, she voted in every election as long as health permitted and made sure that her family and neighbors were registered and voted. (Courtesy of Andre D. Vann.)

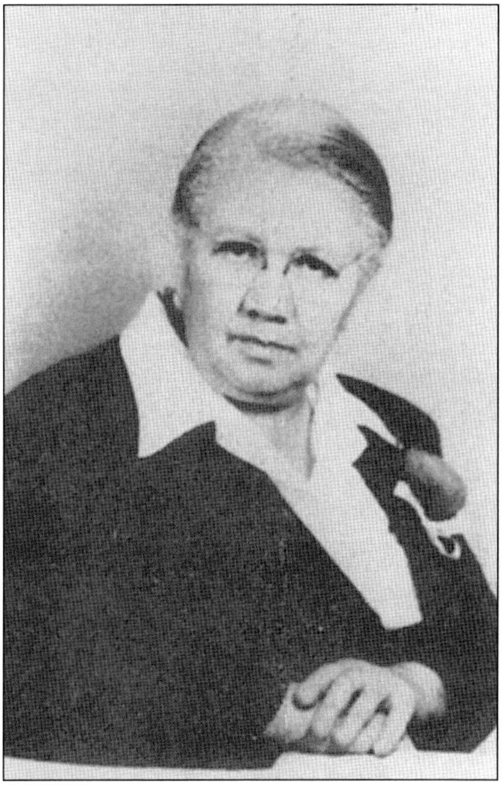

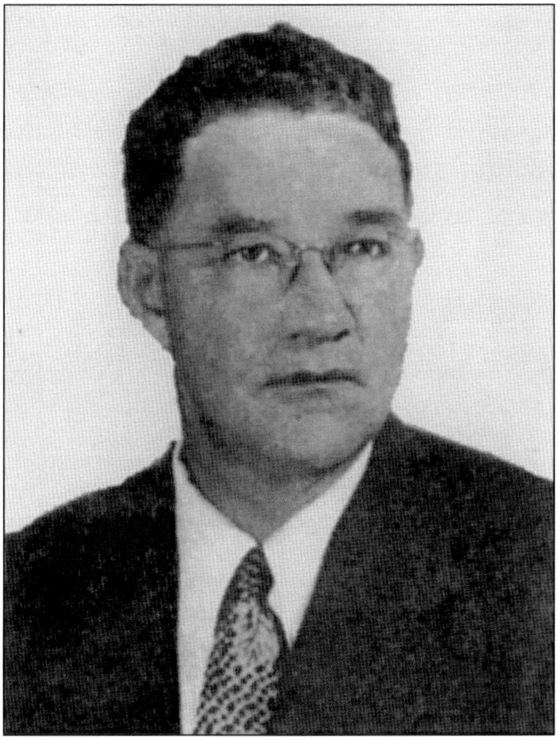

William B. Henderson Jr. (1894–1981) was born in Vance County to William B. Henderson Sr., and was a veteran of World War I. A highly respected member of the community, he was a great supporter of school activities and a noted farmer. He was married to Laura Paschall, and was the father of ten children. Later he married Jennie V. Henderson and was a stepfather to four daughters. He was a member of the Mount Pleasant Baptist Church in Manson, NC, where he served as a deacon for many years. Henderson is interred in the church cemetery. (Courtesy of Carolyn Green Boone.)

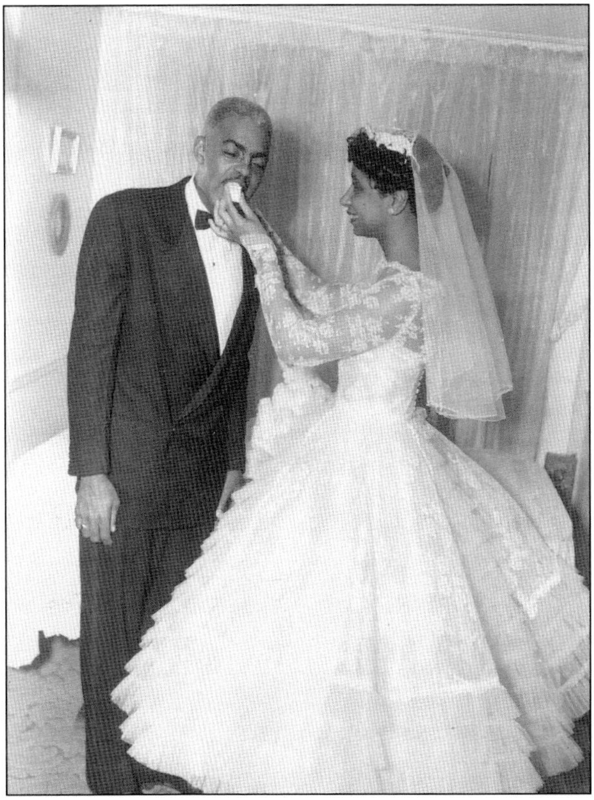

This photo shows longtime Henderson residents Dr. James Preston and Carolyn Smith Green on their wedding day in New Bern. From 1960 to the present the couple has participated in various educational, civic, and religious affairs in Henderson and Vance County. They are the parents of James P. Green Jr., Isaac H. Green, and Carolyn Green Boone. (Courtesy of Carolyn Green Boone.)

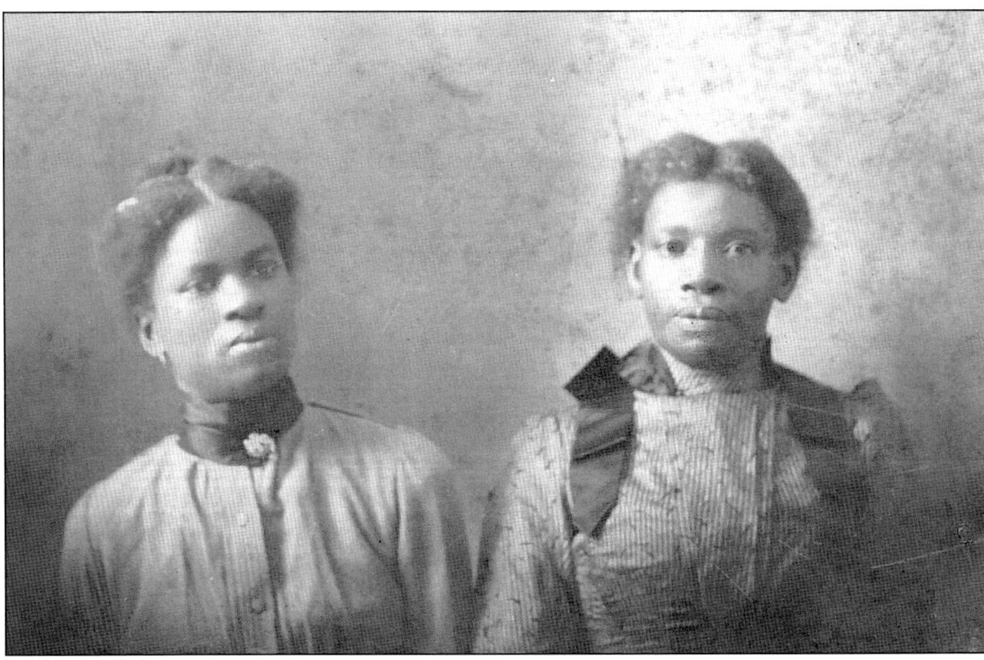

This *c.*1900 photo shows Lula "Hunsie" Brodie Burton Young (1877–1954), on the left, with her mother. (Courtesy of Johnnie M. Sanders.)

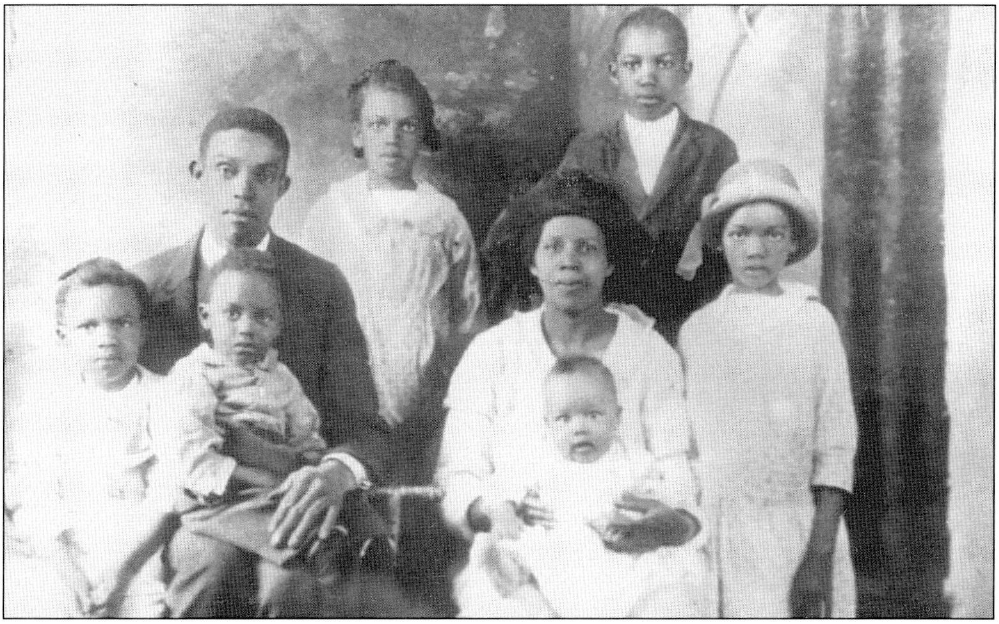

This is a *c.* 1928 family portrait of the Walter and Carrie Fields Christmas family with their children. From left to right are the following: (front row) Beatrice C. Burwell, Walter Jr., Carrie F. Christmas (with son Simon Peter), and Gertrude C. Stitt Bullock; (back row) Walter Christmas, Vergie C. Gladden, and Milton E. Christmas. Gertrude Stitt Bullock, a Vance County educator for a number of years, is the only surviving child of the Christmas family. They were members of the Flat Creek Baptist Church in Williamsboro, NC. (Courtesy of Gertrude Stitt-Bullock.)

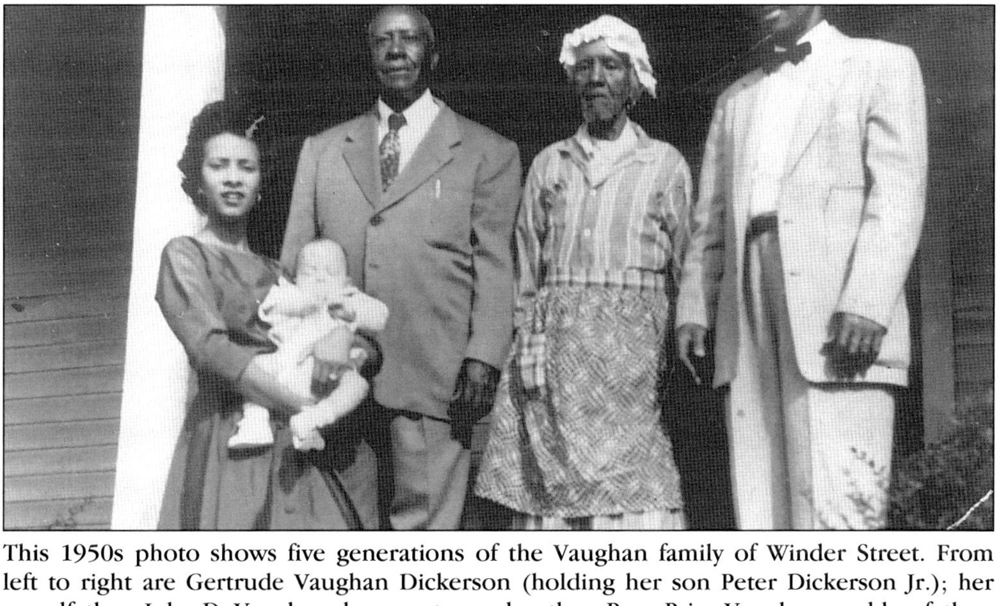

This 1950s photo shows five generations of the Vaughan family of Winder Street. From left to right are Gertrude Vaughan Dickerson (holding her son Peter Dickerson Jr.); her grandfather, John D. Vaughan; her great-grandmother, Rosa Price Vaughan; and her father, Richard I. Vaughan Sr. (partially obscured). (Courtesy of Gertrude Vaughan Dickerson and Tessie Bobbit Vaughan.)

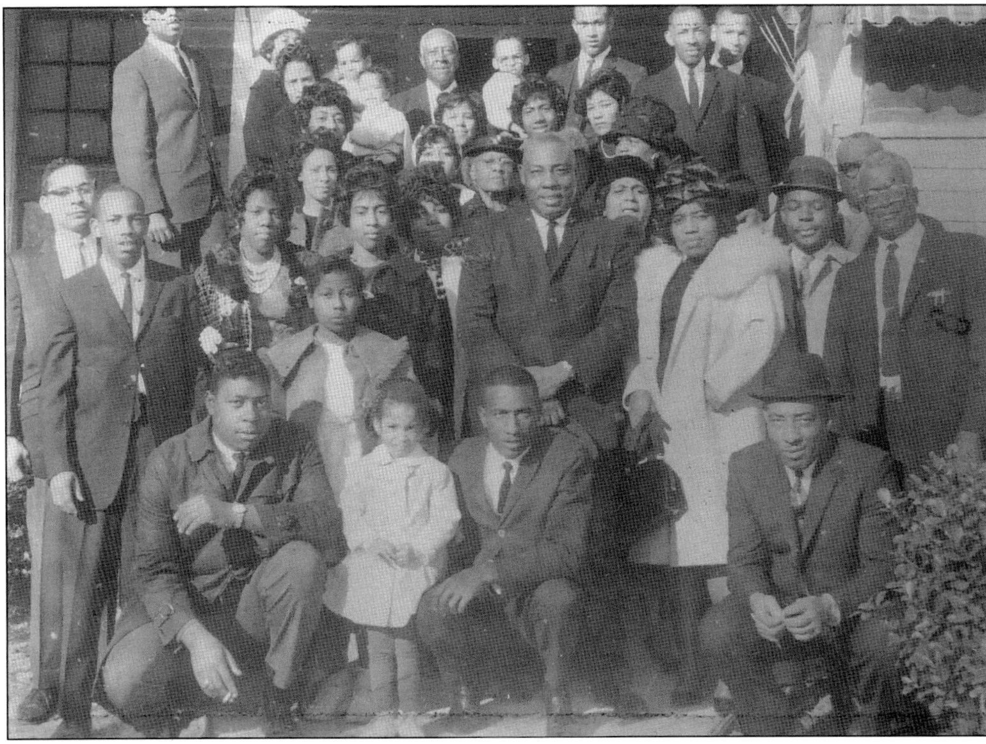

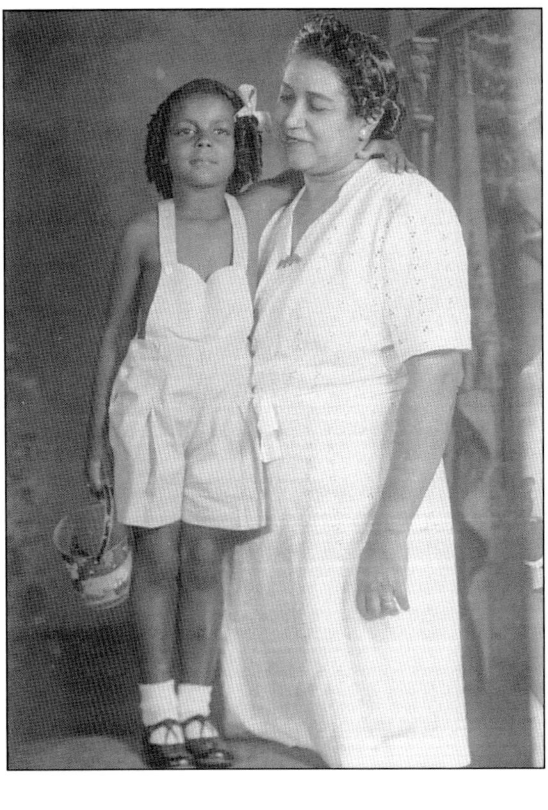

Pictured in the 1950s are four generations of the John Dolphes (1885–1972) and Gertrude Cooke Vaughan (1899–1963) family, posing for a family photograph after church services at the Shiloh Baptist Church. In the second row at the extreme left is Richard I. Vaughan Jr., an educator and owner of Tenax Enterprises and Loree's Apparel on Garnett Street. (Courtesy of Tessie B. Vaughan and Gertrude V. Dickerson.)

This 1940s photo shows Vance County educator Laura Gilliam Jordan with her niece in a postcard that was sent to family members and friends. (Courtesy of Andre D. Vann.)

This is an early 1930s photo of insurance executive Sherman G. Parham, who came to Henderson after graduation from Hampton Institute (now Hampton University). He married Lottie Allen Parham, an educator in the Vance County School System.

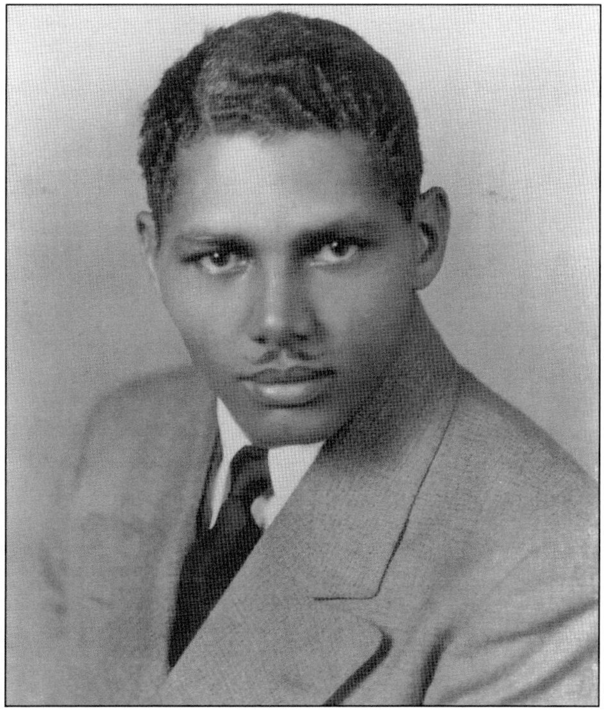

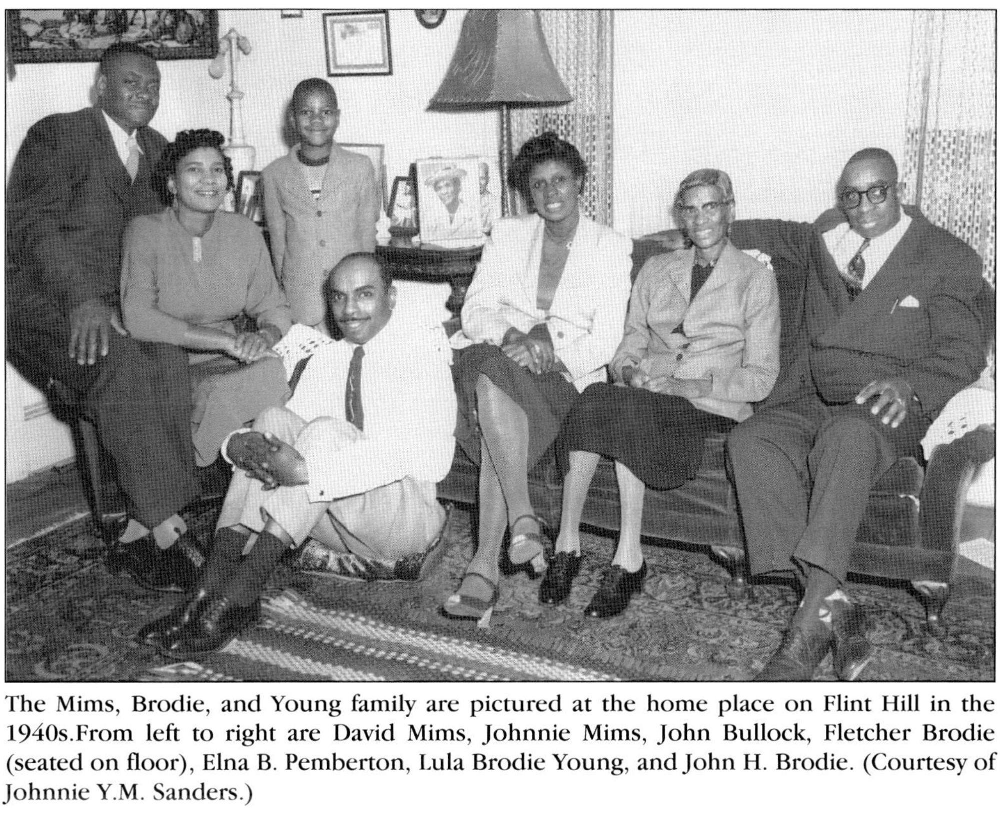

The Mims, Brodie, and Young family are pictured at the home place on Flint Hill in the 1940s.From left to right are David Mims, Johnnie Mims, John Bullock, Fletcher Brodie (seated on floor), Elna B. Pemberton, Lula Brodie Young, and John H. Brodie. (Courtesy of Johnnie Y.M. Sanders.)

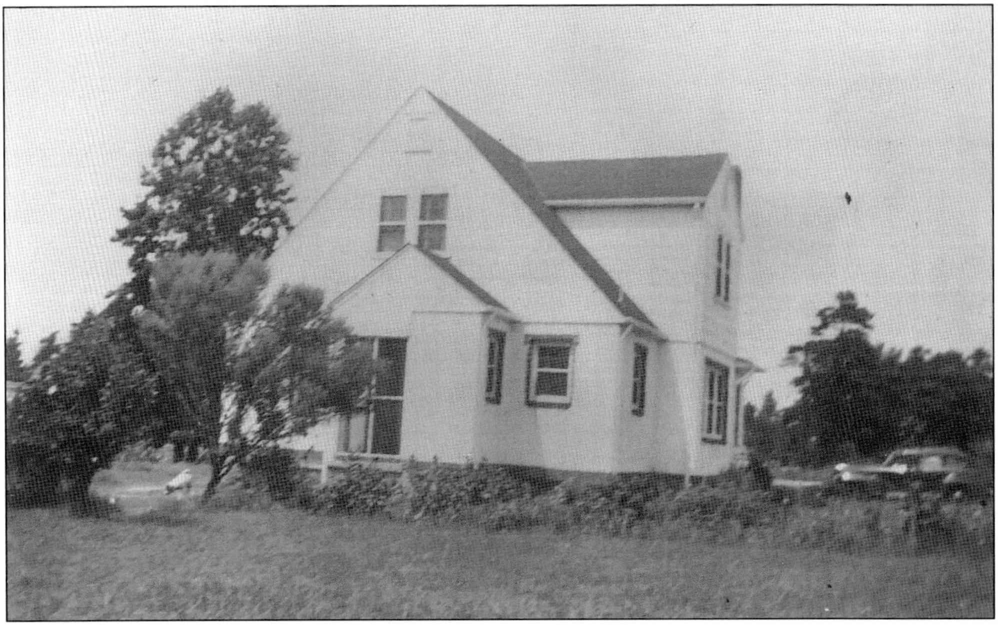

The home of Sherman and Lottie Parham, shown here in 1939, was built at 917 Parkway Drive by Sidney Hayes, a noted builder and contractor. It now has a brick covering and is still in the Parham family. (Courtesy of Sherman G. Parham.)

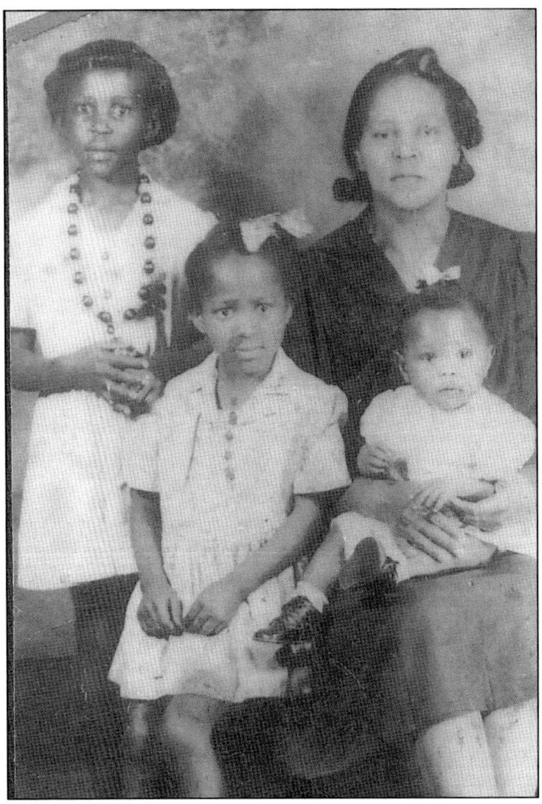

Alease Whitfield (1905–1950), a native of Franklin County and the wife of Freeman Whitfield, is seen with three of her seven children in a 1944 family snapshot. From left to right are Juanita, Madeline, and Alease (holding Ophelia). (Courtesy of Ophelia Jones and Juanita Hicks.)

A 1960s photo shows Freeman Whitfield (1895–1977), a native of Trenton, NC, and the son of Haywood and Hettie Whitfield. Freeman came to Vance County in 1910 and became active in numerous civic and business affairs in the city of Henderson. He was a sergeant in the United States Army and fought during World War I; after the war, he became a realtor, barber, building contractor, and owner of a moving business. He later became the owner and operator of the Red Front Grocery Store located in Southend Square from the early 1930s to the early 1960s. He was united in marriage to Alease Whitfield and was the father of Vera Evans, Ophelia Jones, Tampara Whitfield, Juanita Hicks, Madeline Whitfield, and Jimmie and Thurman Whitfield. The entire family held membership at the Welcome Chapel Baptist Church of Henderson. He is interred in the church cemetery. (Courtesy of Ophelia Jones and Juanita Hicks.)

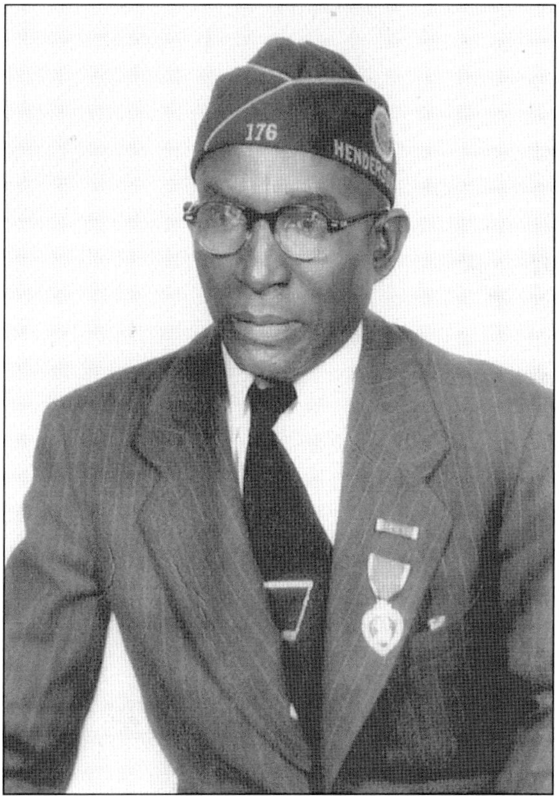

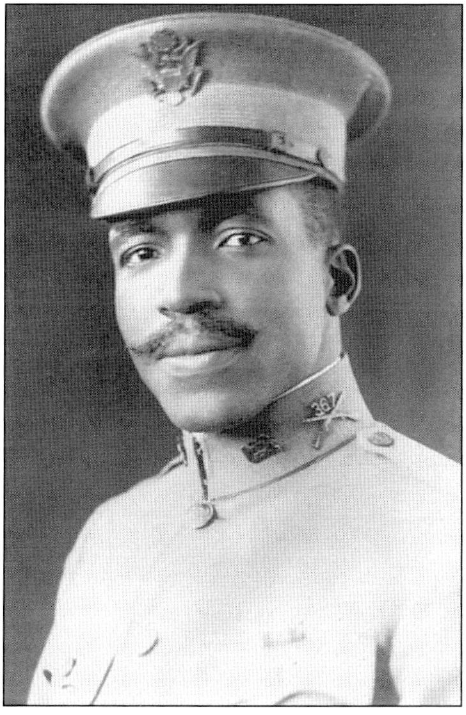

This is a 1917 military photo of Lt. Thomas J. Bullock, who was born in Henderson and was the son of Thomas and Nannie Bullock. Educated at HNII and Lincoln University, he saw action in the Spanish-American War as a boy in Cuba. After the war he entered the regular army and was assigned to the 25th Infantry Regiment. He was eventually sent to the Philippines, where his regiment was mustered out of service after the Philippine insurrection. Next he entered Lincoln University and graduated in 1911. He later worked as a school teacher, and enlisted in the 15th Regiment National Guard for the State of New York while employed with the US Post Office. Bullock was chosen to participate in the officer training course at Des Moines, IA. He served during World War I in the 367 Infantry Regiment, Company D, and was killed in action on September 2, 1918, in France. (Courtesy of NC Division of Archives and History.)

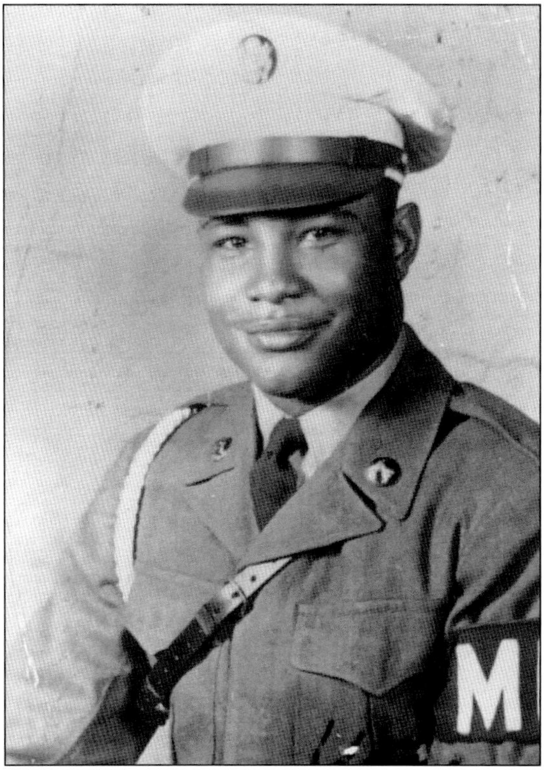

Asker Boyd Hawkins Jr. (1933–1958) was a native of Henderson and was the son of Asker B. and Anna F. Hawkins. He received his bachelor of science degree from Shaw University and was completing his masters degree in education at North Carolina College when he lost his life in an accident on his way to school in Durham. He was also a military police officer and was teaching at Elm City, NC. He is interred in the Hawkins family plot of Blacknall Cemetery . (Courtesy of Janie Hawkins Hicks.)

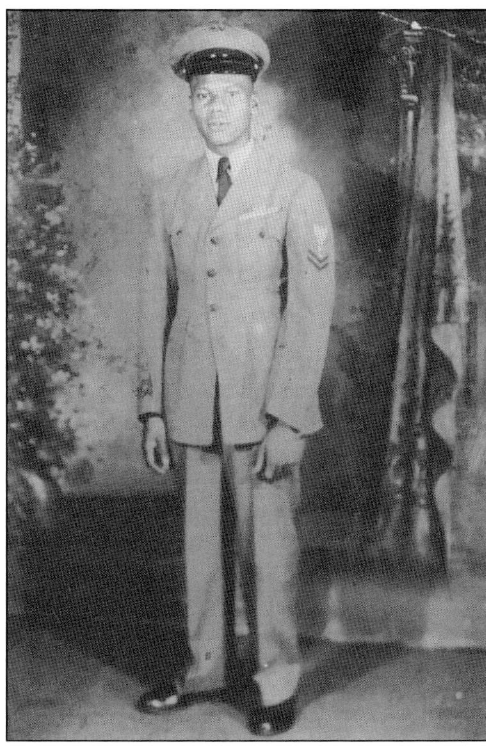

Thomas Doughlas Hawkins (1924–1981), seen here in the 1940s, was the son of Phillip and Marie Hawkins. He received his early education in Henderson, having attended the Old Central Graded School. He was a career service man and retired after 20 years of service with the Navy. He built a comfortable cottage on "Flint Hill" for his mother, Marie Hawkins, and for relatives who lived in the North. He was a member of the Shiloh Baptist Church and was the brother of Louise H. Vass, Janie H. Hicks, Cora H. Jackson, Martha H. Vann, Ruth H. Harris, John P. Hawkins, and Andrew Hawkins. He is interred in Elmwood Cemetery. (Courtesy of Janie Hawkins Hicks.)

Two

Black Businesses

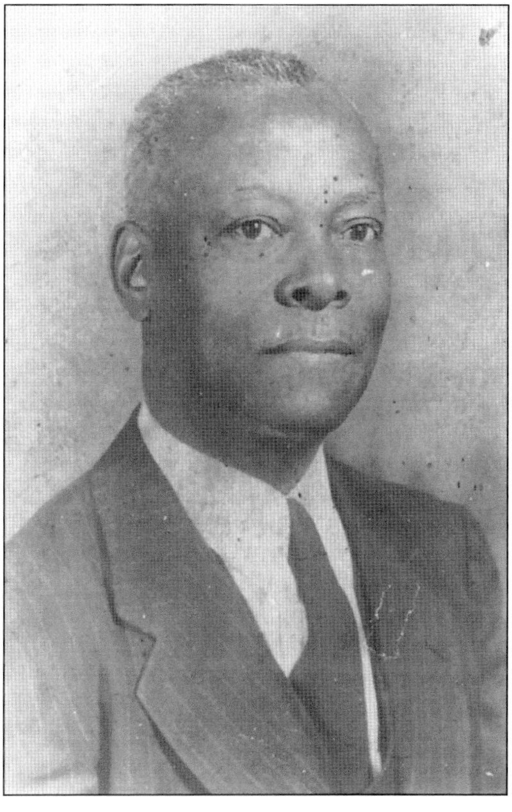

Herman A. Morrison, seen here in the 1930s, was Vance County's first African-American mortician. In 1919, he ventured to Henderson after leaving the Army. His establishment, known as Morrison's Funeral Home, was located at 429 Winder Street. He had a black-and-white hearse with metal draped curtains. He was not only known as an embalmer, but also as a vocalist. Morrison could be heard at numerous weddings and churches, and also directed the commencement march for seniors at Henderson Institute. He trained many other black morticians who would eventually open up shop in Vance County. (Courtesy of Andre D. Vann.)

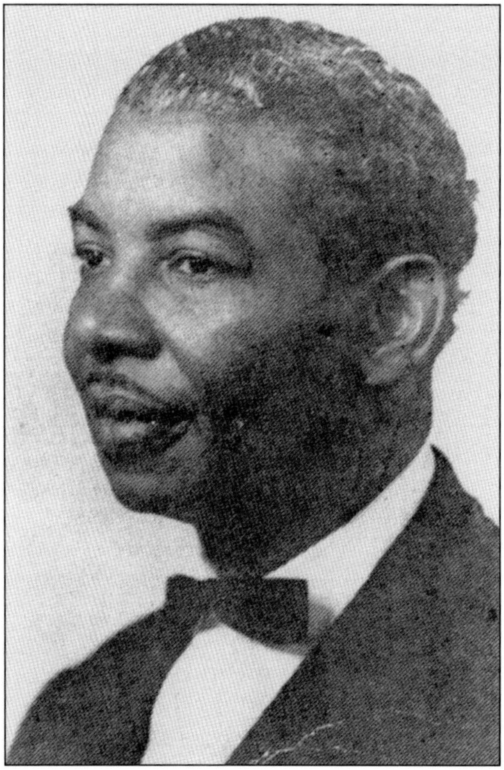

Walter Gillis "Sank" Garnes (1914–1980) was born in Henderson, the son of George and Jennie Brahme Garnes. A licensed funeral director and embalmer, he was the founder of Garnes Funeral Home. The motto of the business was and is "Reasonable and Reliable Funeral Service." The business was operated at 806 East Andrews Avenue and also served as his home, as he had an apartment upstairs. A trustee emeritus of Shiloh Baptist Church, Garnes was also instrumental in conceiving and developing the Beacon Light-Goodwill Baxter Apartments. He was married to Viola Garnes and was the father of twin sons, Lloyd and Floyd Garnes, who were born in 1942. He is interred in Blacknall Cemetery. Garnes Funeral Home is still in operation and is now under the direction of Lewis and Lorraine Feggins, and the second floor still serves as a primary residence for the owners. (Courtesy of Andre D. Vann.)

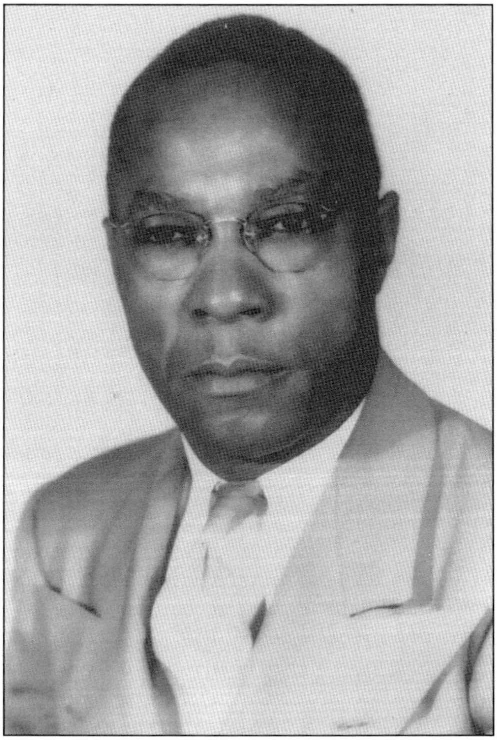

Charles Wesley Williamson (1904–1989) was born in Durham, NC, and attended Kittrell College. He received a bachelors of arts degree in political science from Kittrell in 1929 and continued his education at the Howard University School of Law, graduating in 1932. Upon graduation, Williamson returned to Durham to practice with R. McCants Andrews, his former Sunday school teacher, who died one month after Williamson's arrival. He then looked to Henderson to settle, and married Mamie Simon in 1933. He opened practice in late 1933 at 212 Montgomery Street, and had two children, Charles W. Jr. and Robbie. He became Henderson's first practicing black lawyer and civil rights advocate. In recognition of his contributions to Vance County, his portrait was hung in the Vance County Courthouse in 1982. Also, the local black bar association renamed itself the Charles W. Williamson Bar Association. He is interred in Elmwood Cemetery. (Courtesy of Randolph Baskerville.)

This is a 1940s photo of Ernestine Louise Lyons (1920–1984), daughter of James and Harriet Lyons of the Mobile community, working with one of her patients at the animal hospital. She had the distinction of being the first woman taxi driver in the Henderson area. Ernestine also worked with Dr. Yarl and Dr. Carmen as a veterinarian's assistant. Employed at the Carolina Bagging Company, she later became a professional dry cleaner. She was a member of the Shiloh Baptist Church of Henderson and is interred in the Grant Hawkins Sr. family plot of Blacknall Cemetery. (Courtesy of Gladys Lyons Hawkins.)

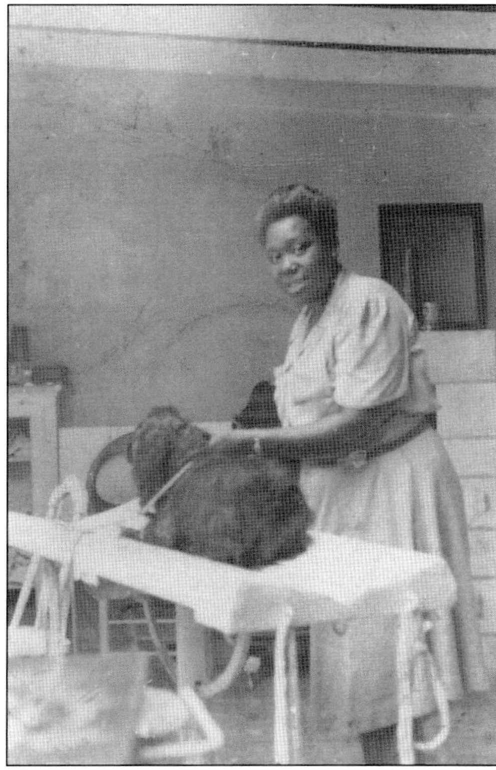

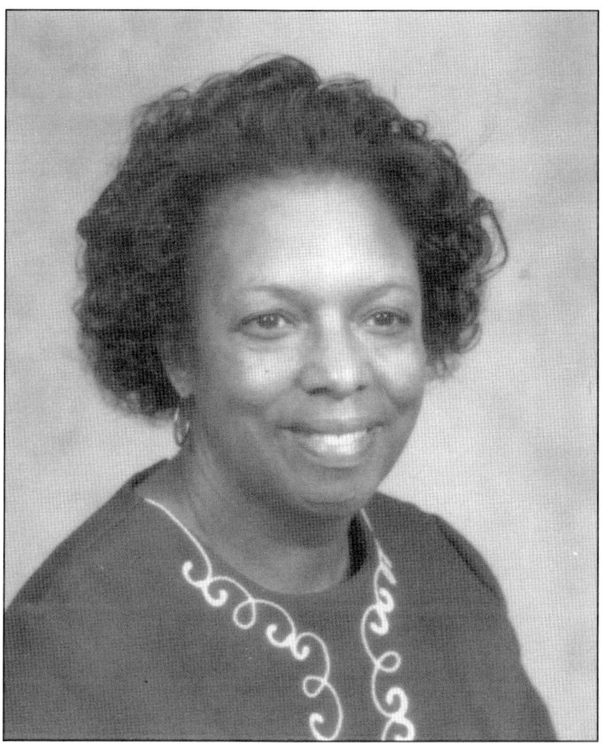

Lucile Hester Claiborne Brodie was born and reared in Henderson. Her parents, George Washington Claiborne Sr., an early insurance agent for the North Carolina Mutual Life Insurance Company, and Kittie L. Hester Claiborne, were residents of the West End. Brodie graduated from Henderson Institute and attended Winston Salem Teachers College. She was employed for over 40 years as the secretary, bookkeeper, and office manager at the Shepard Funeral Home. She was also a notary public and a member of the Shiloh Baptist Church for over 60 years. (Courtesy of Lucile H.C. Brodie.)

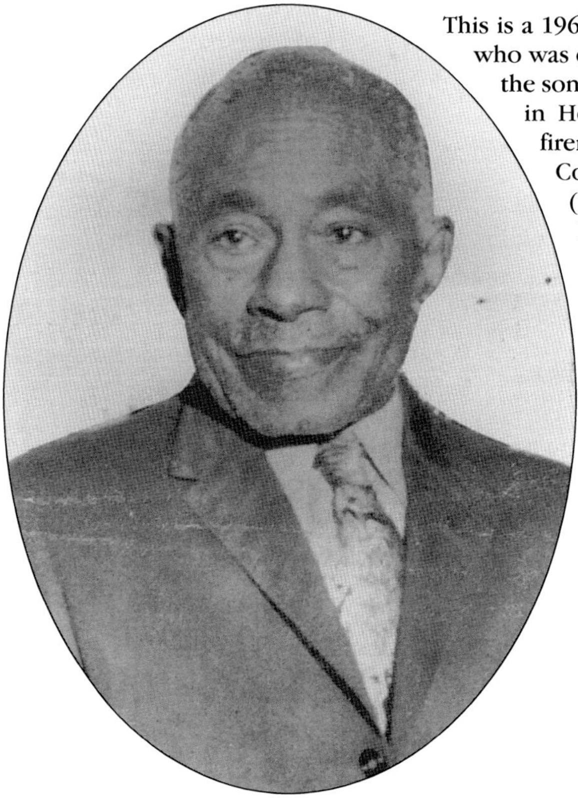

This is a 1960s photo of Neal Simon (1888–1966), who was originally from Anson County and was the son of Charles and Mattie Simon. He lived in Henderson for many years and was a fireman for the Seaboard Airline Railroad Company. Married to Desdy Simon (1892–1974), he was the father of Rosa B. Hill, Mamie Williamson, and Melvina Bulluck. He was affiliated with the Shiloh Baptist Church of Henderson, where he served as a member of the deacon board. (Courtesy of Andre D. Vann.)

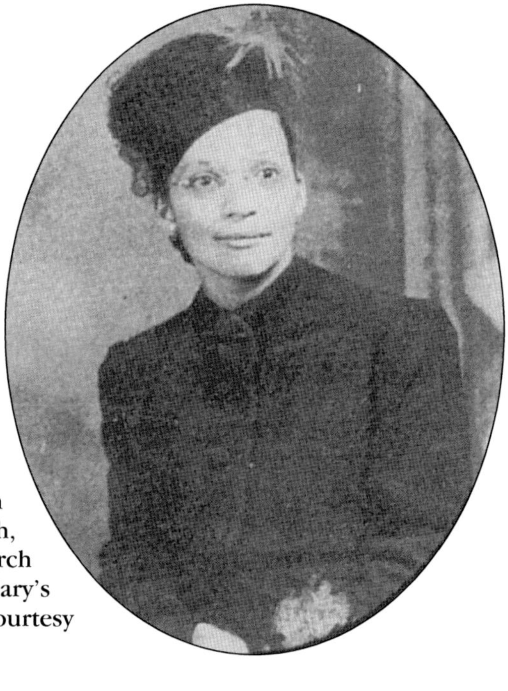

Mary Ward Tharrington (1908–1997), pictured here in the 1950s, was originally from Franklin County, NC. She was a graduate of Henderson Normal Institute, and later graduated from the McDowell Institute of Industrial Sewing in New York, NY. She was an expert seamstress, and at one time operated a small tailoring shop in Henderson. She was married to Rev. George Tharrington, and was the mother of Fannie, George Jr., and Lynwood. At an early age she joined St. Mary's AMEZ Church, and later joined Kesler Temple AMEZ Church of Henderson. She is interred in the St. Mary's AMEZ Church Cemetery, in Kittrell, NC. (Courtesy of Andre D. Vann.)

This is a 1970s photo of William Henry "Bill" Oliver (1912–1985), the son of Henry and Essie Oliver. He attended the local schools in Vance County and was employed for a number of years as a chauffeur and houseman for Mrs. Emma Rose. He was married to Mary L. Daniel Oliver and was the father of William H. Oliver Jr. A member of Shiloh Baptist Church, he served on the trustee board. He is interred in the Elmwood Cemetery. (Courtesy of Andre D. Vann.)

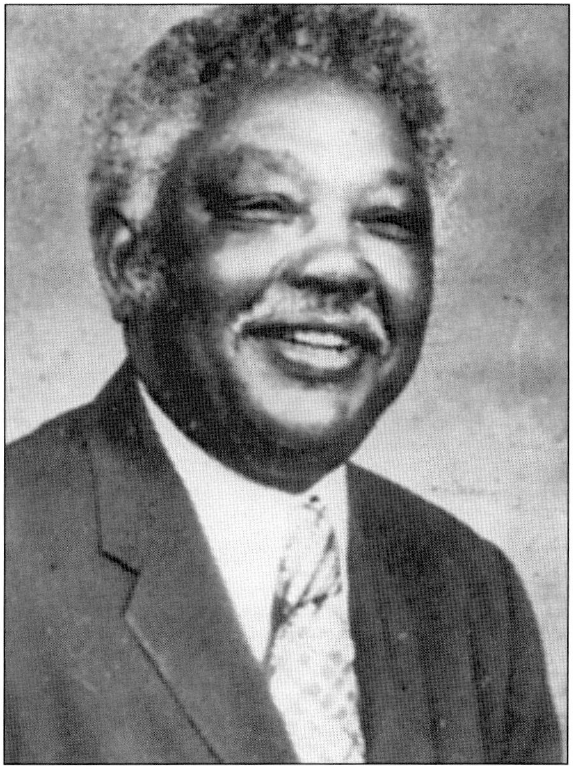

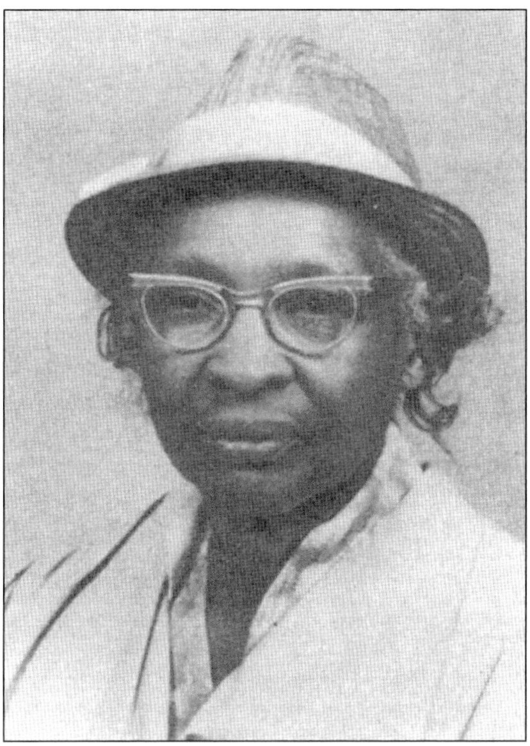

Annie Balthrope Glover (1907–1989), pictured here in the 1980s, lived at 427 Popular Street. The daughter of Hugh and Beulah Balthrope of Vance County, she worked for a number of years as a domestic for the family of attorney A.A. Zollicoffer Jr. At an early age she joined the Shiloh Baptist Church, and in 1936 she married James Glover. She is interred in the Big Ruin Creek Baptist Church Cemetery. (Courtesy of Andre D. Vann.)

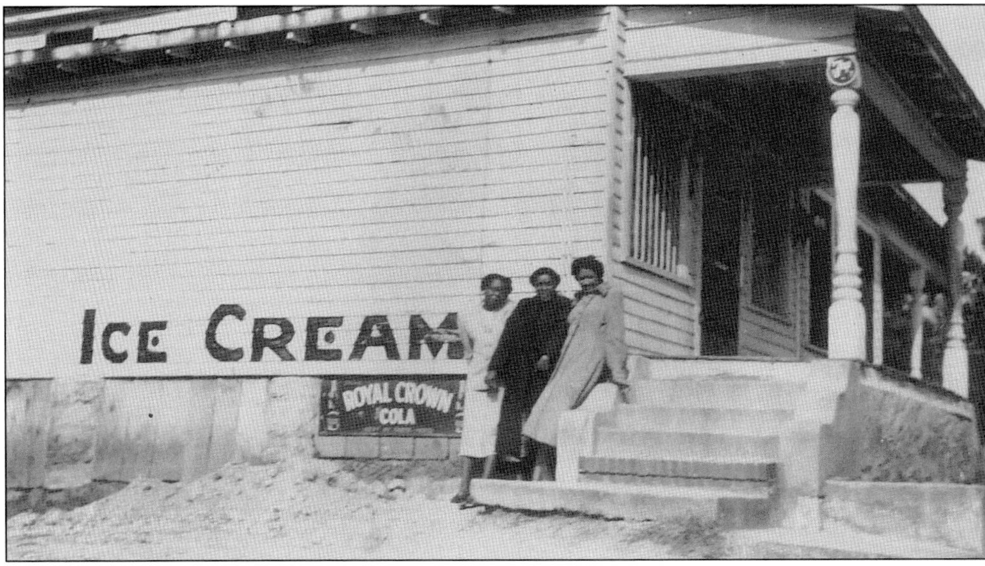

Willie Belle Lee (1912–1998), pictured third from the left in this 1940s photo, is seen with two beauticians outside of her business. In the early 1940s she moved with her family to Henderson from Norfolk, VA. She was a licensed beautician, and for more than 50 years owned and operated Lee's Beauty Nook at 331 Winder Street. The establishment served not only as a beauty salon, but also as a hotel to black travelers. She was well known to many generations as she fixed local girls' hair for the first day of school and other special occasions. Although she had no children of her own, she cared for several nieces and nephews. As a young adult, she joined Shiloh Baptist Church, where she was an active and faithful member for more than 50 years. Willie Belle Lee is interred in the Lee family plot of Blacknall Cemetery. (Courtesy of Hurley Taylor.)

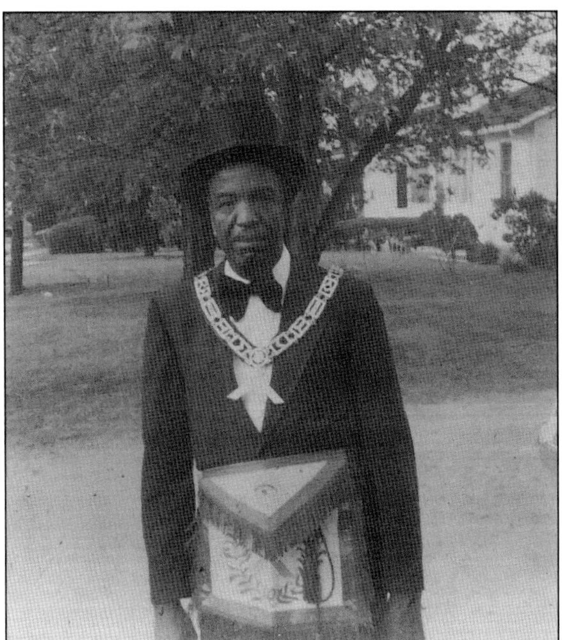

Charlie R. Marable (1919–) has been a barber in Vance County for over 50 years, and is the owner of the Deluxe Barbershop at 114 Montgomery Street. He is also a noted fraternal leader and member of the Masons, where he currently serves in various leadership posts with the Beacon Light Masonic Lodge #249 in Henderson. Marable serves as a deacon and trustee at the Spring Street Baptist Church. (Courtesy of Charlie R. Marable.)

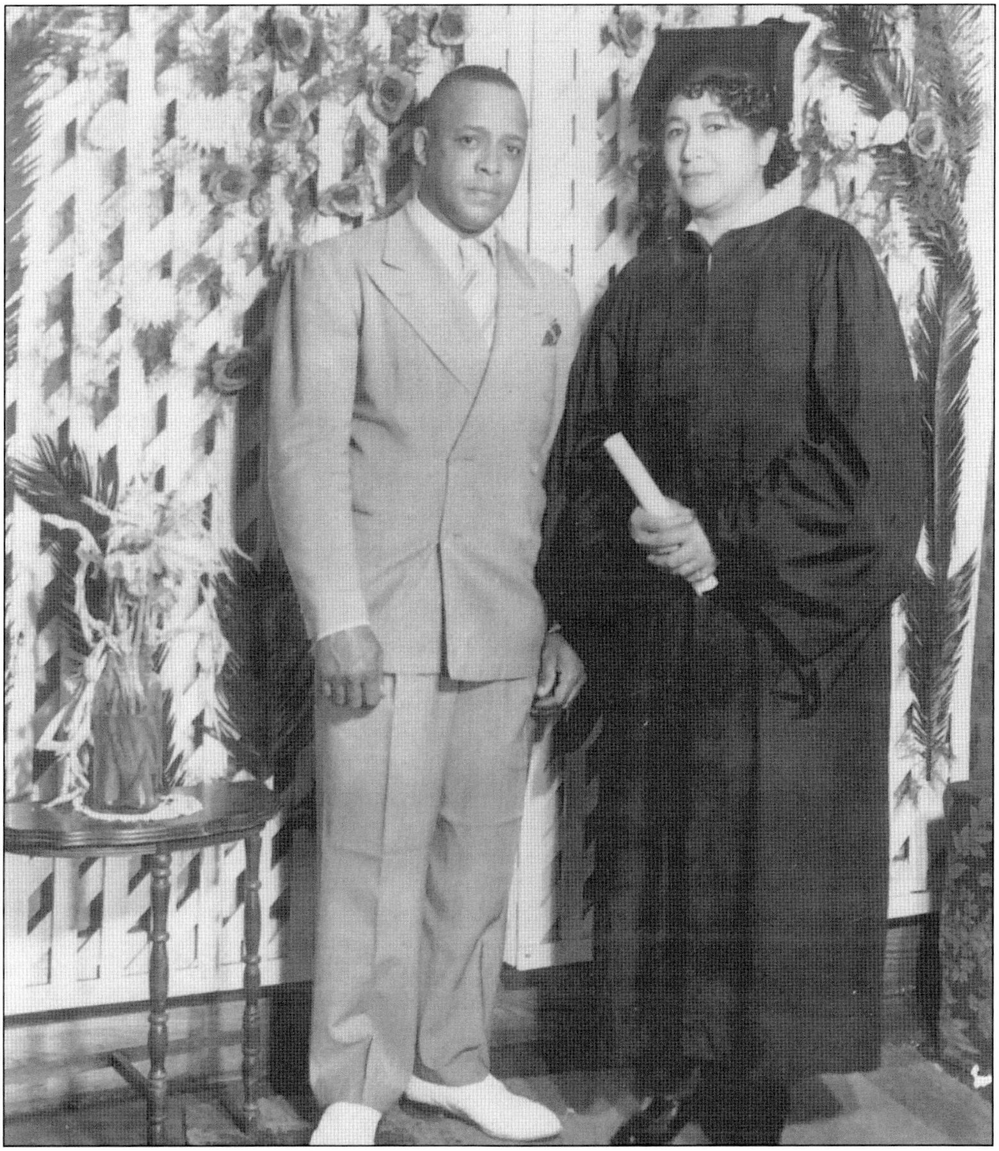

Edwin Aldophuis Jordan (1899–1961) and Laura Gilliam Jordan (?–1998), residents of 1122 Andrews Avenue Extension, are pictured here in the 1940s. This photo was taken after Laura received her graduate degree from North Carolina College for Negroes in Durham. Edwin Jordan was born in Atlanta, GA, the son of Dr. D.J. and Carrie Thomas Jordan. He came to North Carolina at an early age, when his father served as president of Kittrell College. He received his education in the schools of Greensboro, NC A&T College, Johnson C. Smith University, and Eckels Institute. He came to Henderson and for more than 30 years was a prominent mortician and businessman. He was the founder and owner of Jordan Funeral Home, which was located on Chestnut Street. Laura G. Jordan taught for over 50 years in the Vance County public schools. One son, Walter Jordan, was born to this couple and they also raised two nieces, Mable Blount and Marie Allen. They were members of the Shiloh Baptist Church and served on various boards. Edwin Jordan is interred in the Beechwood Cemetery beside the remains of his parents. (Courtesy of Andre D. Vann.)

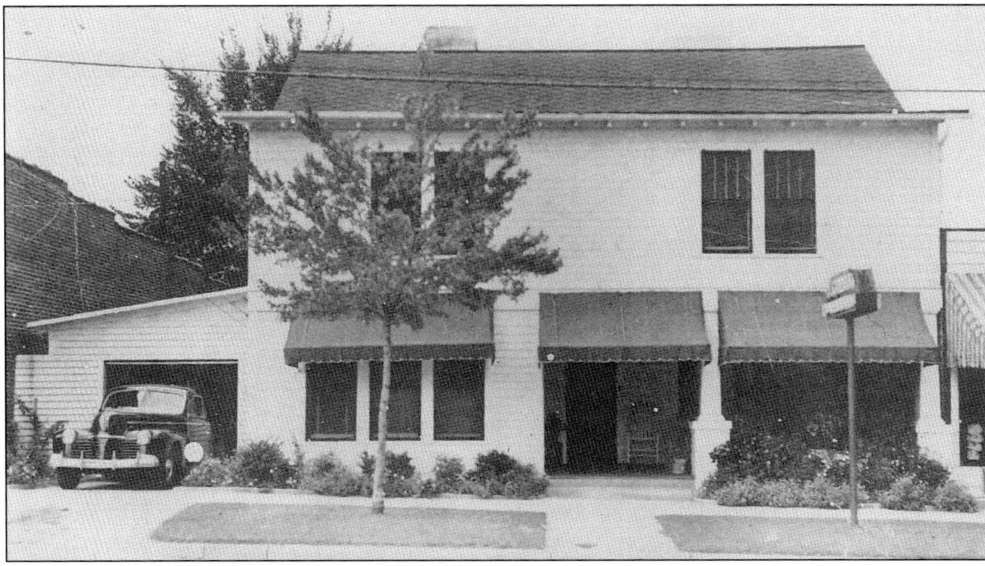

The Jordan Funeral Home was owned and operated by Edwin Jordan at 104 South Chestnut Street on the corner of Montgomery and Chestnut Streets. The Chestnut Street Café, also owned by the Jordan family, is partially visible at the far right. The establishment was later purchased by Allen Williams, and the name was changed to Williams Funeral Home. It is now under the direction of Ronald Vaughan. The second floor still serves as the primary residence of the owners. (Courtesy of Andre D. Vann.)

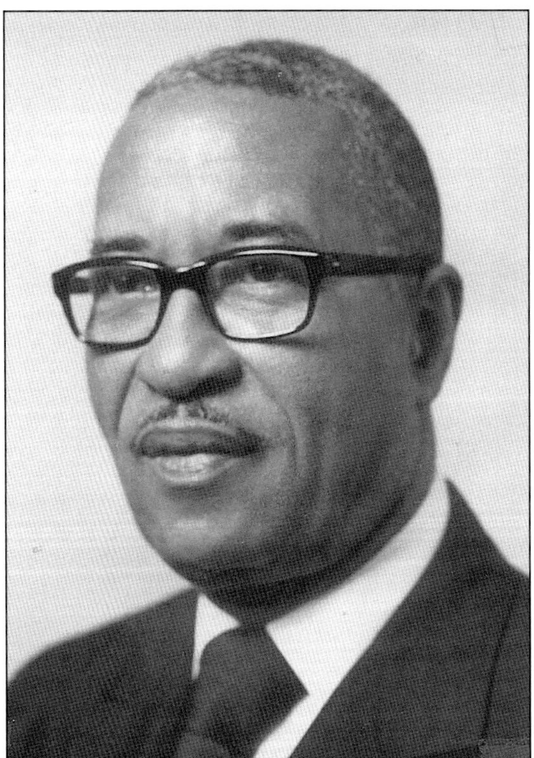

Allen Williams (1916–2000), a native of Warren County, was a graduate of John R. Hawkins High School and Gupton-Jones College of Embalming. A World War II veteran, he was employed by Shepard Funeral Home early in his career. In 1943, he became a partner in Garnes-Williams Funeral Home, and in 1959, he founded Williams Funeral Home. He retired in 1974, but in 1999, after many years of absence from the profession, began to advise and assist in the development of Wright Funeral Home of Henderson. The first black member on the Vance Granville Community College Board of Trustees, he was married to Hattie Ingram Williams and was a faithful member of the Coley Springs Missionary Baptist Church. He is interred in the Coley Springs church cemetery. (Courtesy of Hattie I. Williams.)

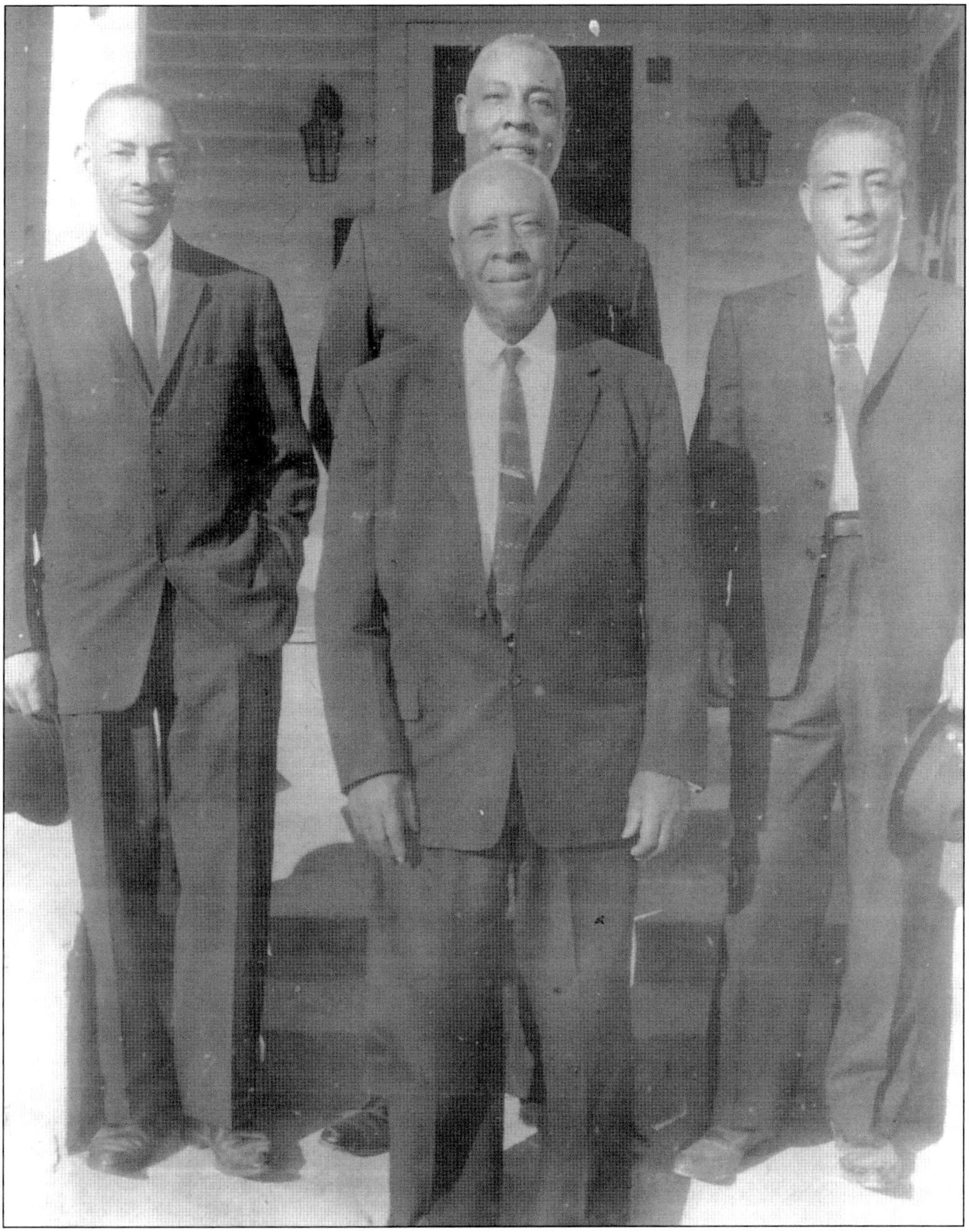

This is a 1950s photo of John D. Vaughan (1885–1972), a resident of 615 East Winder Street. Seen in the center, he is surrounded by his three sons, from left to right, Richard I. Vaughan (1913–1990), John Haywood Vaughan, and George W. Vaughan (1917–1987). All were noted craftsmen and builders in Vance County. John D. Vaughan born in Vance County, the son of John D. and Rosanna Clark Vaughan, and was long remembered as a master blacksmith and noted member of the deacon board at Shiloh Baptist Church for over 60 years. He was married to Gertrude Cooke Vaughan, a midwife for over 30 years in Henderson and the surrounding counties. (Courtesy of Tessie Bobbit Vaughan and Gertrude Vaughan Dickerson.)

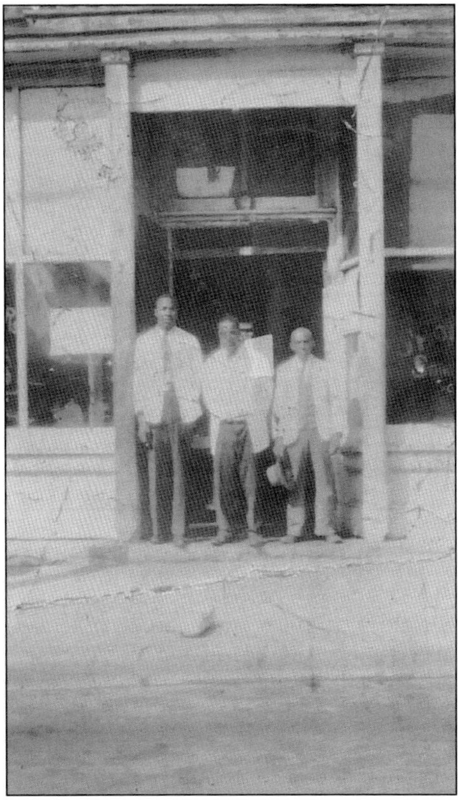

This is a 1930s photo of three of Vance County's earliest barbers outside of Haywood Cooke's Barbershop on Garnett Street, in downtown Henderson. Pictured from left to right are Claude Clement, J. Edwards, and Haywood Cooke. Cooke was the son of Isaac and Fannie Hawkins Cooke, and in 1880 he married Kayte Harris of Henderson. Known as the "Godfather of Colored Barbers," he helped many black barbers get their start in his shop. He also was a home and landowner, and a devout member of the Kesler Temple AMEZ church for over 50 years. The Cooke's children were Audie Hicks, Emma Cooke, Gertrude Vaughan, Elizabeth Sutton, Willie Cooke, Kayte Smart, Gladys Massenburg, and Stephen and Peter Cooke. All were teachers, preachers, and missionaries. (Courtesy of Ethel C.R. Smith.)

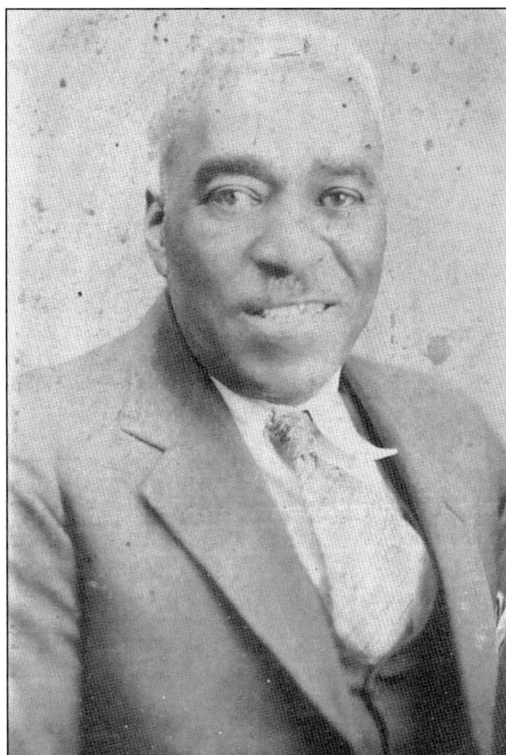

Thomas Hawkins (1873–1937), the son of Mingo and Rebecca Hawkins, is long remembered as a noted craftsman and brick mason in Vance County. He worked on numerous buildings in the city and was also a noted horse trainer. Upon his death the *Daily Dispatch* wrote "Negro Brick Mason Passes on Tuesday – Thomas Hawkins, well known Negro brick mason, died at his home in South Henderson Tuesday, after an illness of three weeks." He was married to Cora Hawkins Crutchfield and was the father of Magnolia Kirk, Carrie H. Marable, Bennie, Asker, Phillip, John Dewey, Frederick, and David Hawkins. He was a member of the Shiloh Baptist Church of Henderson and was a Mason. He is interred in the Hawkins family plot of Blacknall Cemetery. (Courtesy of Andre D. Vann.)

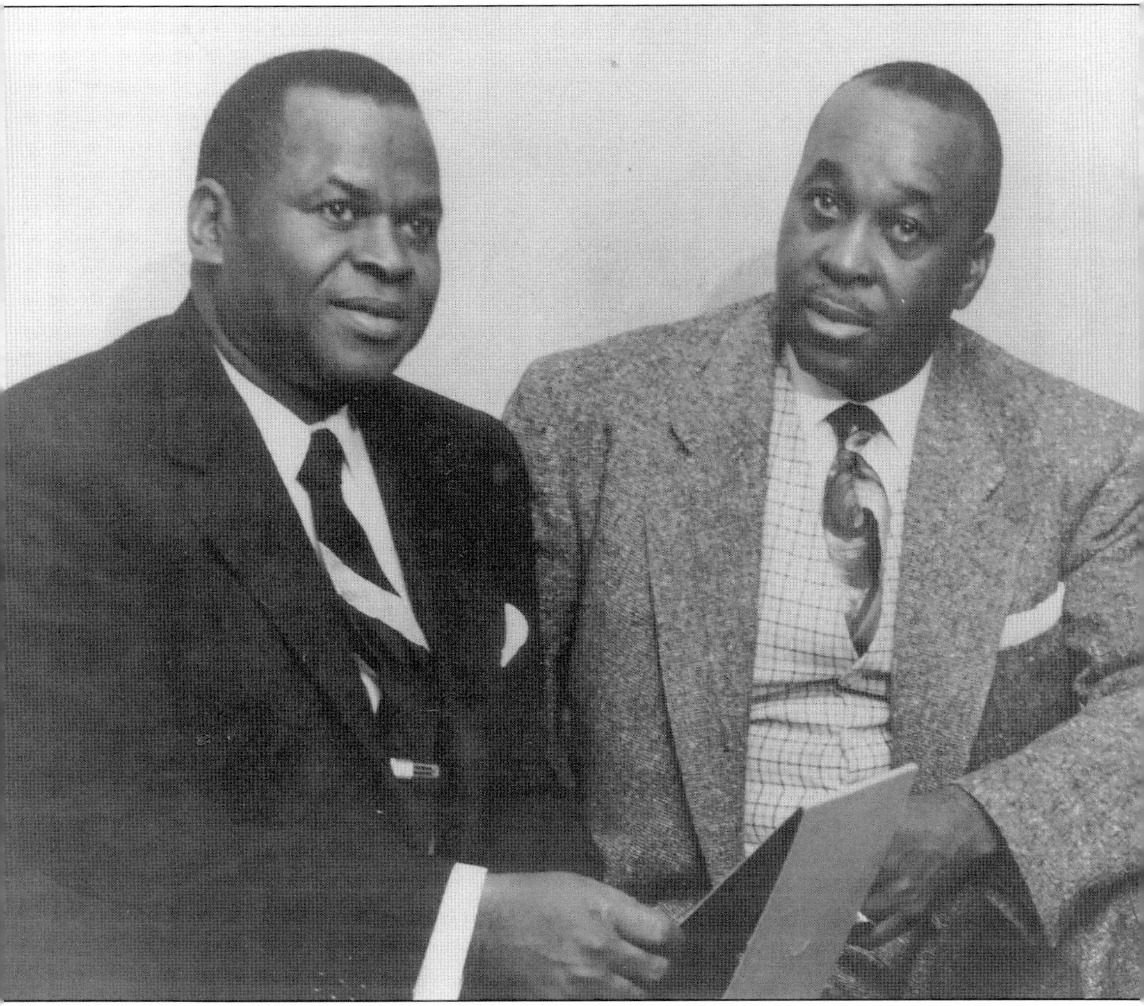

Rev. Dr. Marshall Shepard (left) and Robert Leslie Shepard (1897–1969) were the children of Robert and Pattie Gilliam Shepard, of Oxford, NC. Robert L. Shepard was the owner and operator of the Shepard Funeral Service of Oxford and Henderson and the Home Benefit Mutual Burial Association since 1922. The Shepard Funeral Home in Henderson was located in the West End Community at 403 Pettigrew Street. It served families in Vance, Granville, Franklin, Warren, and other surrounding areas. He was married to Elizabeth Davis Shepard (1903–1990), a registered nurse, and they were the parents of Richard L. and William D. Shepard. He was a faithful member of the First Baptist Church of Oxford. In 1943, Shepard bought the R.J. Gill House, which was built in 1875 for his funeral home business. The two-story frame building sheathed with aluminum siding has porches that have been altered. Shepard and his son Richard Charles had a brisk business. The business in the latter years was directed by Richard Shepard and Mary Davis-Royster, and was eventually sold to Douglas McMillan Jr. Robert Shepard is interred in the H.P. Cheatham Memorial Park. (Courtesy of Mary Davis-Royster.)

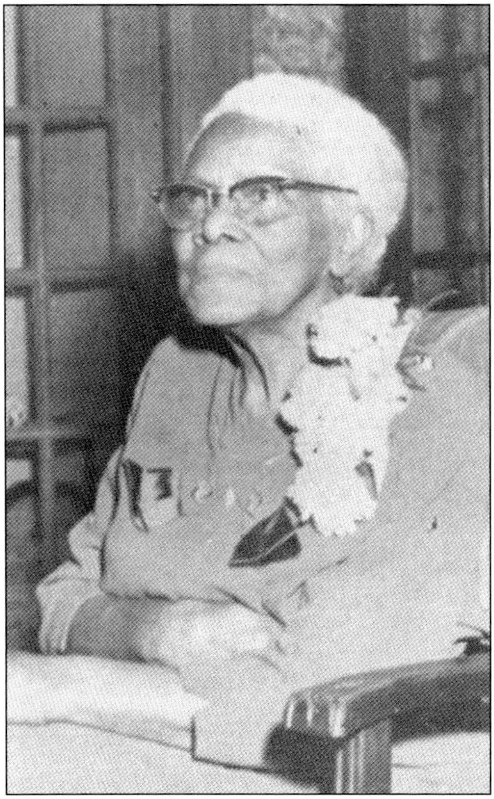

India Graham Bing Davis (1875–1970) was born in Middleburg, and is remembered as a noted midwife and practical nurse. As a professional midwife she served both blacks and whites. It is recalled that Dr. Dorsey, who owned a drugstore on Garnett Street, employed India Davis to care for his children and was so impressed that he recommended her to every pregnant patient that came into his drugstore. As a result she built a lucrative profession and a sound reputation in the community. She was married to Richard Davis (1865–1929), who worked at the rock quarry in Wise, NC, and at the Greystone Granite Quarry in Greystone, NC. They were the parents of James, Nannie, Melvin, William, George, Hartwell, Leslie, Bettye, and Thurston. The Davis family purchased a large farm and home on Route Six, and supplemented their income by working at the Greystone Rock Quarry. India Davis and other members of the family are interred in the Brookston Baptist Church cemetery. (Courtesy of Andre D. Vann.)

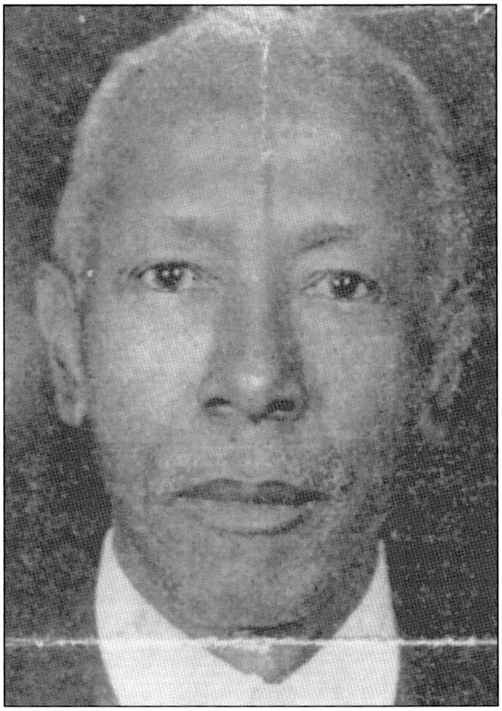

Dr. John Earl Baxter (1878–1947) was the first black licensed doctor to come to Henderson and played an active part in the establishment of the Jubilee Hospital. A native of Carteret County, he attended the Washburn Seminary and Talledega College in Alabama. In 1905, he graduated from the Leonard Medical College at Shaw University. Following graduation he interned at Long Island College Hospital in Brooklyn, NY. In 1908 he moved to Henderson, where he built an extensive general practice. He was married to Pauline Garland (1888–1920), a graduate of Kittrell College, and after she died he married Helen Kittrell. He was a member of the Shiloh Baptist Church for over 42 years. He also had large land holdings in Rocky Mount and Henderson. He is interred in Blacknall Cemetery. (Courtesy of Andre D. Vann.)

Dr. Samuel McDonald Beckford (1886–1959), a resident of 723 East Andrews Avenue, was born in Jamaica, and educated in the local schools of Jamaica, Howard University, and Boston University. He served as professor of anatomy and assistant in physiology at Shaw University, 1917–1918. In 1919, he opened his general practice of medicine in Henderson at 212 Montgomery Street. In 1922, he became surgeon and chief operator of the Jubilee Hospital. He had the distinction of being the first black licensed surgeon in Vance County. He was married to Georgianna Bowie in 1912, was later married to Cora Beckford, and was the father of Cora B. Davis. He was a member of the Masons and the Odd Fellows, and the United Presbyterian Church (later renamed Cotton Memorial). There is a street in Henderson named in his honor, as well as the Beckford Avenue Medical Center. He is interred in Blacknall Cemetery. (Courtesy of Andre D. Vann.)

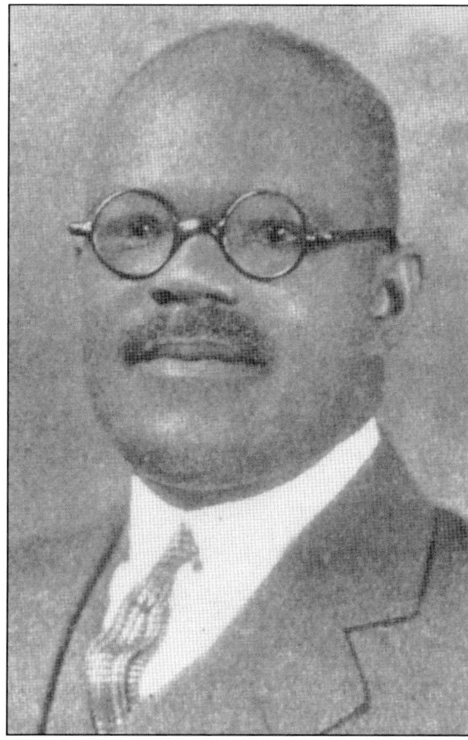

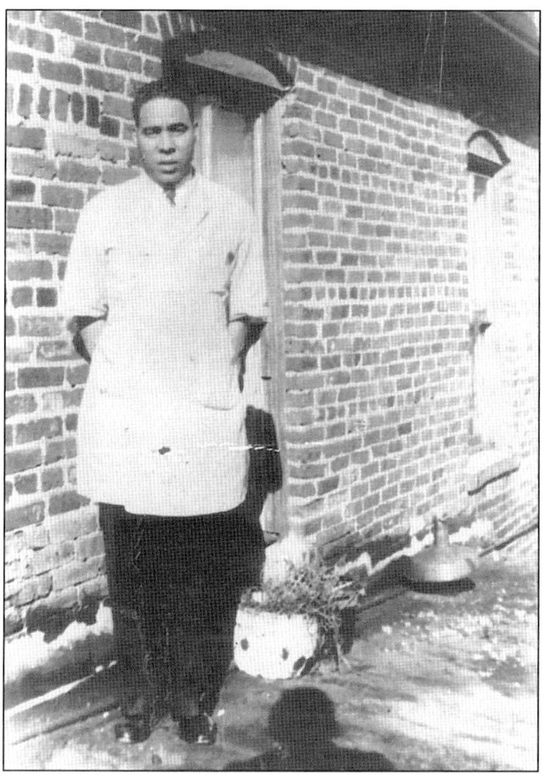

Dr. John Dewey Hawkins (1901–1988) was born the son of Thomas and Cora Crutchfield Hawkins. He married Bertha Lucille Long in 1929 and had one son, John Dewey Hawkins Jr. In 1931, he graduated from Howard University Dental College. He established a large practice in Henderson and served all, without regard to race or position. Once the largest black tax payer in Vance County, he organized an outstanding Henderson Jubilee Choir, Henderson Choral Club, and a jazz band. He owned a semi-pro baseball team, the Henderson Grays, and a stadium. He built, at his own expense, the Big Tree Amusement Park. He served on the trustee board of Palmer Memorial Institute and Shiloh Baptist Church. He left Vance County in 1950s and later settled in Bridgeport, CT, with his family. (Courtesy of Andre D. Vann.)

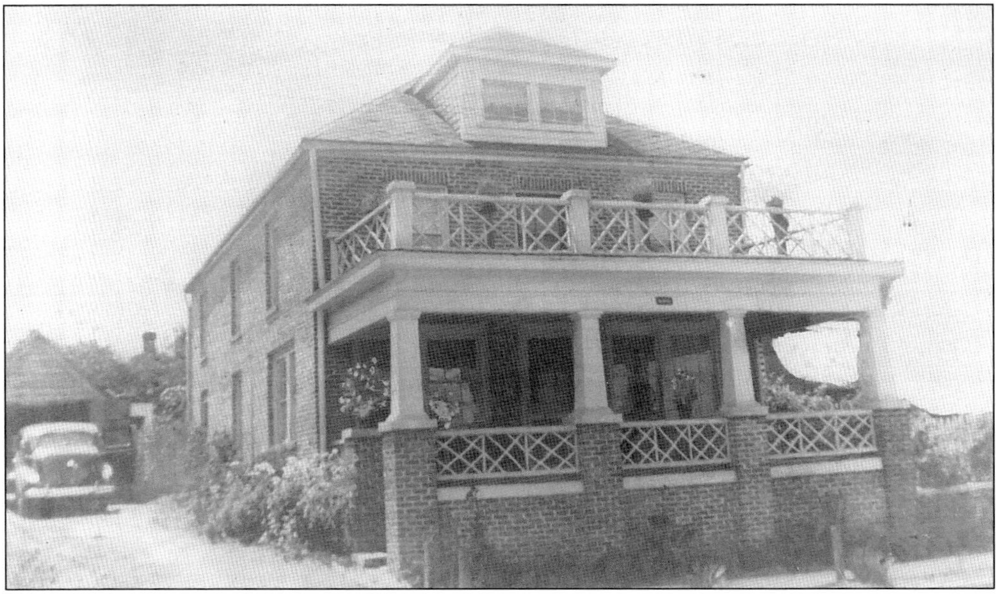

This is a 1930s photo of the first home of Dr. John Dewey and Lucille Hawkins, located at 323 West Rock Spring Street. The home is still used as a primary residence and is located directly across from the Vance Elks Lodge. (Courtesy of Andre D. Vann.)

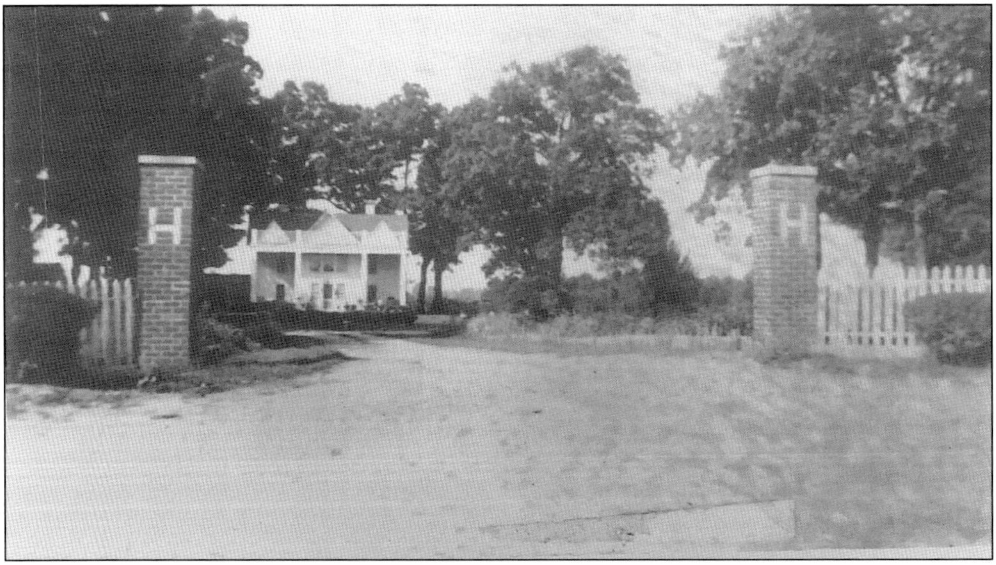

The second impressive home of Dr. John Dewey and Lucille Hawkins was located at the East Andrews Avenue Extension, and is seen here in the 1940s. This home was once used to host a reception for Dr. Dewey's cousin Maria Hawkins Cole, who was wed to entertainer Nat "King" Cole. The home is still in use as a primary residence. (Courtesy of Gladys Lyon Hawkins.)

This is a 1960s photo of Dr. Dallas Anthony Hawkins (1895–1968), a resident of 721 Vaughan Street and a native of Franklin County, NC. He attended Saint Paul College in Lawrenceville, VA, and Tuskegee Institute, AL. A veteran of World War I, his professional training was completed at Meharry Dental School in Knoxville, TN. He practiced dentistry for over 40 years at 212 West Montgomery Street in Henderson. He was married for a number of years to Iola Branch Hawkins, and was active in many church and professional organizations. He is interred in the National Cemetery in Raleigh. (Courtesy of Andre D. Vann.)

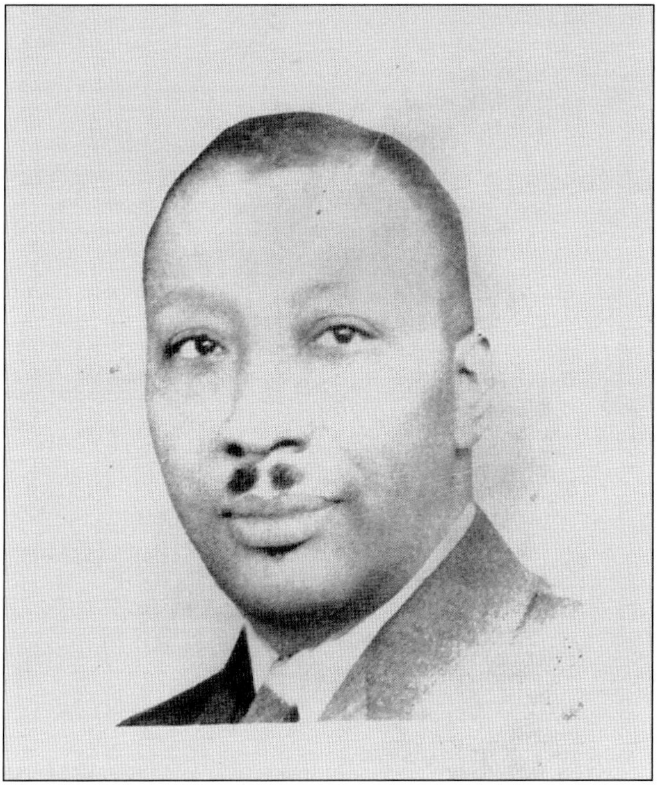

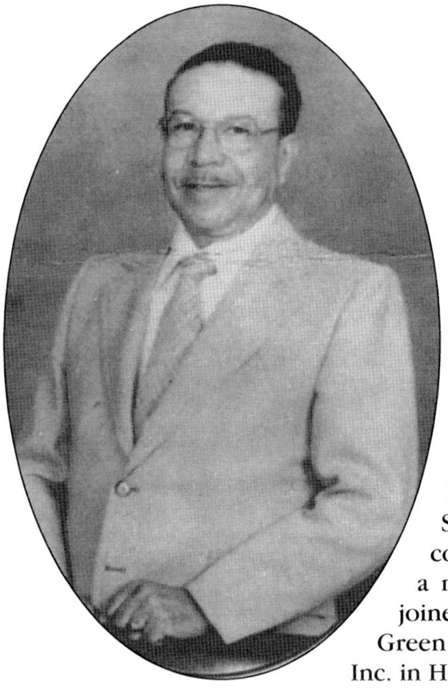

Dr. Joseph Herman Green (1922–1993), a resident of Omega Road, was a native of Warren County, NC. He received his bachelor's degree from Virginia State University and a degree in dentistry from Howard University. He was married to Annie Laura Green (1921–1988), who was a graduate of Shaw University in Raleigh, NC. She was a licensed cosmetologist and certified dental assistant. He was a member of the Manson Baptist Church and later joined the Shiloh Baptist Church of Henderson. Dr. Green and his wife are both entombed in Sunset Gardens, Inc. in Henderson. (Andre D. Vann.)

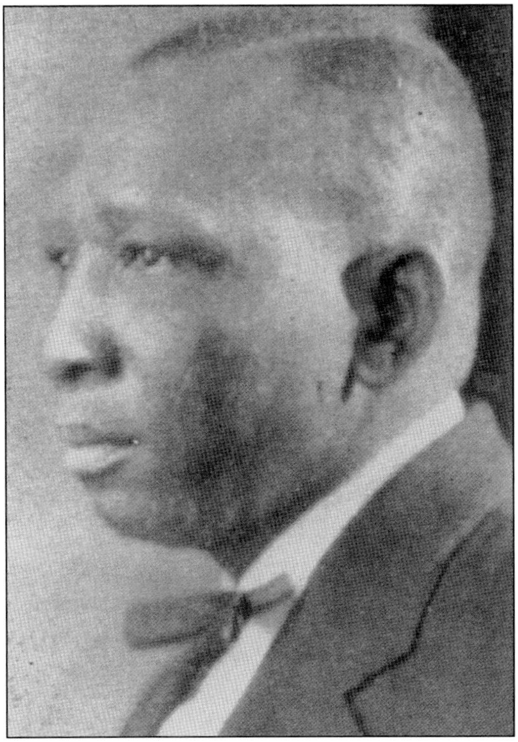

This is a 1950s photo of Dr. Junius D. Douglas (1873–1973), a native of Marlboro, SC. Following graduation from State College in Orangeburg, SC, he taught for two years before entering the school of pharmacy at Shaw University. Completing his pharmaceutical education in 1903, he began work in Durham, NC, in 1904. He operated stores in Durham, Rocky Mount, and Henderson, NC, and was Henderson's first black pharmacist. The Douglas Drug Store was located on Horner Street, where he was assisted by his son Dr. Junius D. Douglas Jr and Dr. Hill. He was married to Lucy Hines Douglas and was the father of Junius Jr., Melba, and Alonzo Douglas. (Courtesy of Andre D. Vann.)

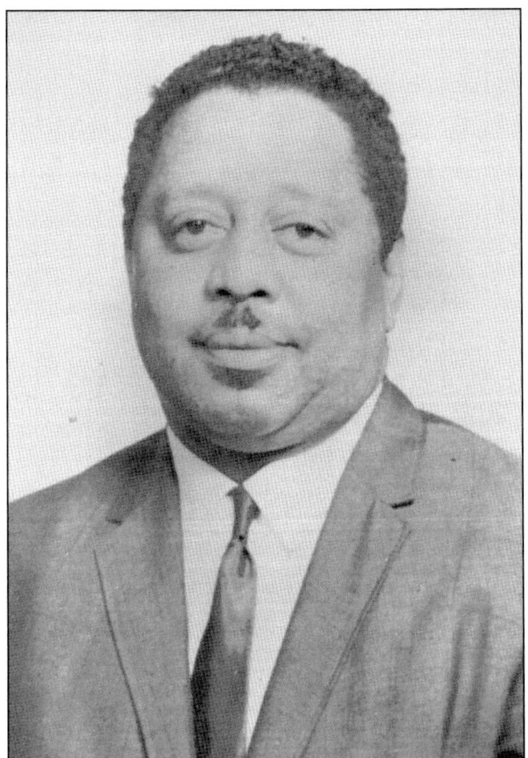

Dr. Andrew Lee Harris (1921–1984), a native of Vance County, was the son of Peter and Beulah Harris. He received a bachelor of science degree from North Carolina Central University, and the doctor of dental surgery degree from Howard University. He began practice in the city of Henderson, which was interrupted by a call to service in the US Navy. Returning to Henderson, he practiced dentistry in both Vance and Warren Counties for 30 years. He was married to Geneva Smith Harris, and was the father of Andrea L. and Andrew Lee Harris Jr. He was a faithful member of the Brookston Baptist Church and is interred in Elmwood Cemetery. (Courtesy of Andre D. Vann.)

Artelia Brodie Pritchett (1925–1998) was a native of Boydton, VA, and the daughter of James and Della Brodie. She was a 1943 graduate of De Shazor's Beauty College in Durham and the founder and owner of Artelia's Beauty Salon in Henderson. Pritchett went on to complete her bachelor of arts degree in education at Saint Augustine's College in Raleigh. In 1966, she became the first black social worker hired by the Vance County Department of Social Services. She was married to Robert Pritchett and was the mother of Ronald Pritchett. Robert Pritchett and his brother Eugene Pritchett ran a taxi cab company on the corner of Horner Street. She eventually inherited the company and became the owner of Pritchett's Taxicabs. After many years at New Bethel Baptist Church, she affiliated with Brookston Baptist Church, where she served faithfully until death. (Courtesy of Andre D. Vann.)

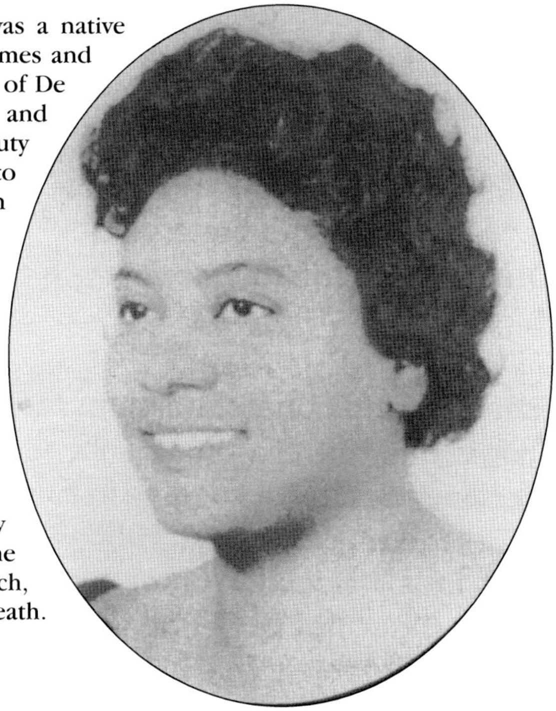

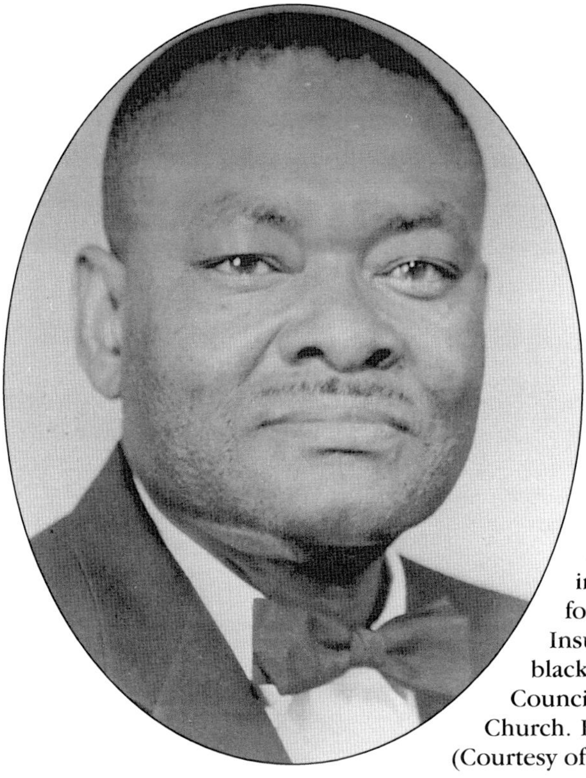

David Leroy Mims (1908–1979), a resident of 616 Arch Street in the Flint Hill community, was a native of Waco, TX. Following eight years of service during World War II with the US Army and Air Force, he married Johnnie Jakie Young and established residence in Henderson. He was employed for 22 years as an insurance agent and as debit manager for the North Carolina Mutual Life Insurance Company. Mims was the first black member of the Henderson City Council and a member of the Shiloh Baptist Church. He is interred in Elmwood Cemetery. (Courtesy of Johnnie Y. Mims Sanders.)

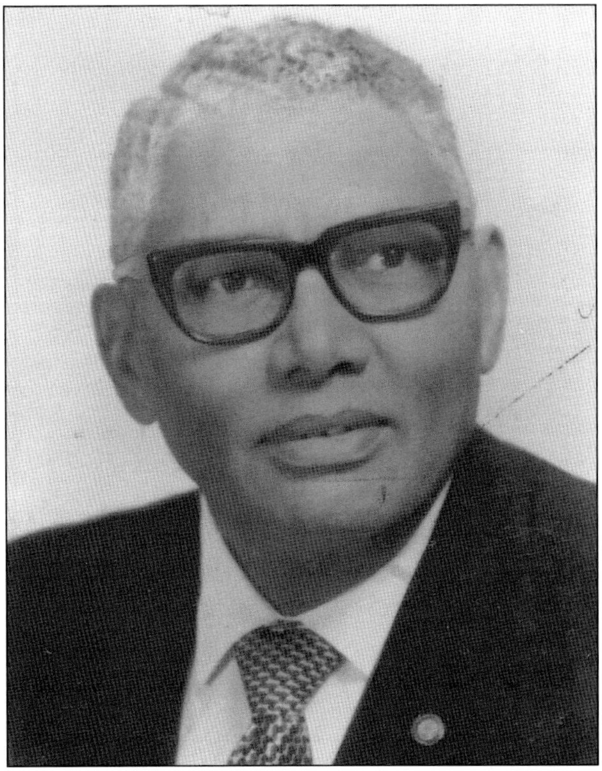

Sherman G. Parham (1908–), noted businessman and executive, came to Henderson during the 1930s after he married educator Lottie Allen. He is a graduate of Hampton Institute (now Hampton University) and worked several decades in the insurance industry, retiring as district manager of the NC Mutual Life Insurance Company. He also acquired a great deal of real estate throughout the county and owns numerous rental properties in the city. He belongs to many fraternal, civic, and religious organizations such as the Masons and Omega Psi Phi and is a member of the Cotton Memorial Presbyterian Church. (Courtesy of Sherman G. Parham.)

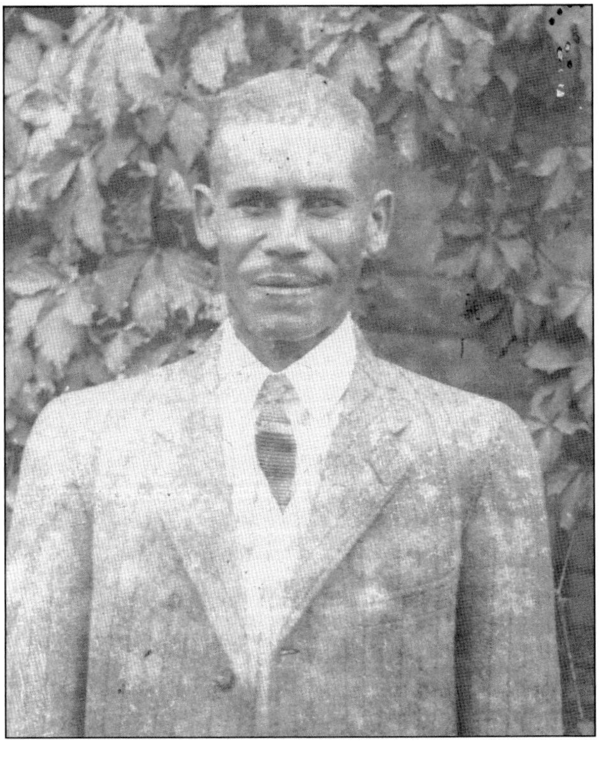

This is a 1940s photo of Edward Young who, along with his father John Young, was a noted well digger and mason in Vance County. He was known for his ability to locate springs of water underground and supplied black and white residents with fresh drinking water long before city municipalities came into effect. Edward married Lula Brodie and was the father of Jakie Young Mims Sanders of Flint Hill. He also was a member of the Masons. (Courtesy of Johnnie M. Sanders.)

Three

Education

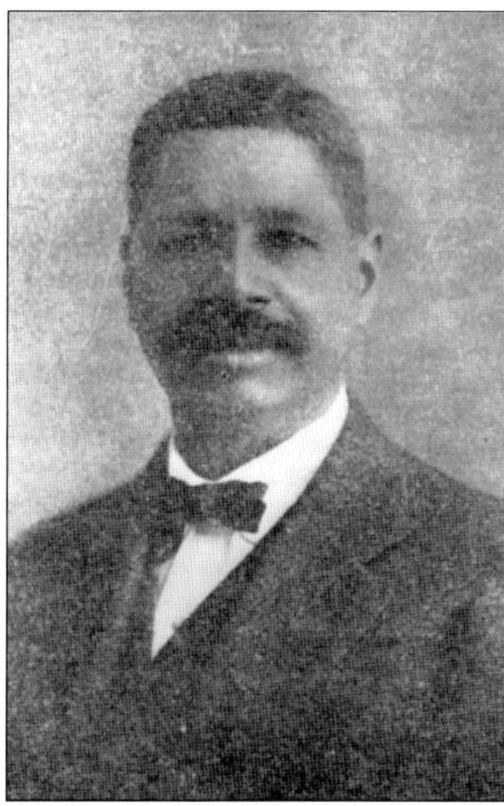

James Youman Eaton Sr. (1866–1928), a resident of 511 Orange Street in the West End community, was born in Louisburg, NC, the son of Thomas S. and Annie Burwell Eaton. He earned a law degree from Shaw University in 1884, and in 1896 was elected by the Vance County Board of Commissioners as county attorney. Although he practiced law for more than 25 years and handled a number of important cases, he is best remembered as an educator. In 1899, he became founder and principal of the first Central Colored Graded School. During his reign, the school's enrollment grew from less than 100 to over 700. Eaton was married to Mary A. Cooper Eaton, and they had five children—Coresce, Thomas R., James Jr., Annie Wilbur, and Mary Virginia. Eaton-Johnson Middle School at Henderson still bears his name. He was a member of the Flat Creek Baptist Church, and his entire family is interred in the Eaton plot of Blacknall Cemetery. (Courtesy of NC Division of Archives and History.)

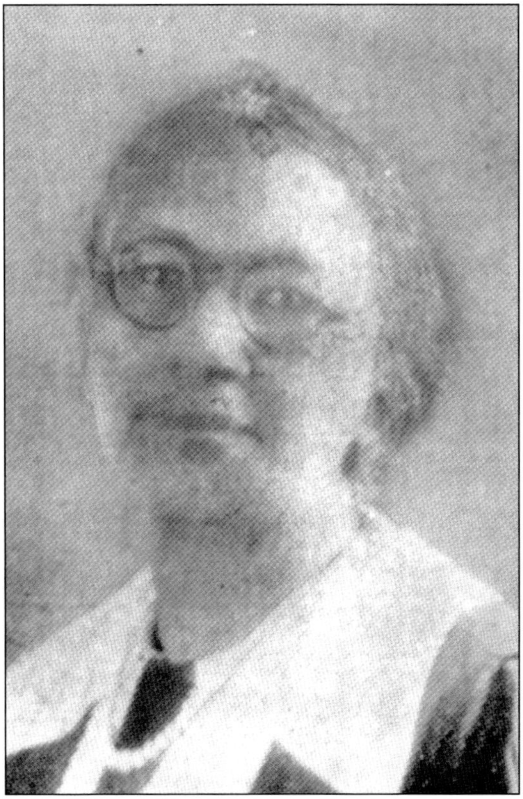

Sallie Ann "Tom" Walden Eaton (1875–1957), a resident of 304 Clark Street, was born in Winton, NC. She attended the Waters Institute in Winton, NC, Shaw University in Raleigh, NC, and Winston-Salem Teachers College. She served as an assistant to her husband, Thomas S. Eaton (1860–1934), who was register of deeds in Vance County from 1888 to 1898. Sallie Eaton taught in the city schools for 36 years, having taught in the county system before joining the city system. For around 50 years she was a Sunday school teacher at the Shiloh Baptist Church. She and her husband raised two nieces, Annie M. Omohundro Alston and Mildred Omohundro Gilmore, as their own. Eaton was also a businesswoman, who owned a valuable home and other property in Henderson. The town of Henderson named Eaton Street in honor of Sallie and her husband. They both are interred in Blacknall Cemetery in Henderson. (Courtesy of Andre D. Vann.)

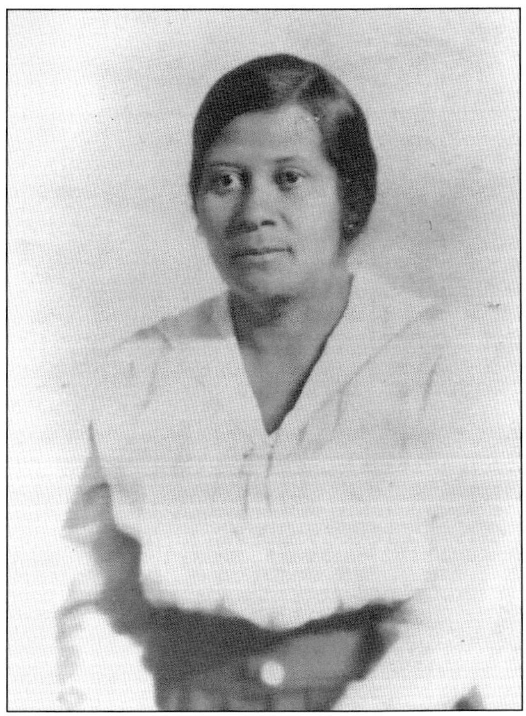

Adelaide Royster Bullock (1889–1980) was a daughter of Alexander and Malissia Royster of 314 Cherry Street. She was educated in the local public schools, and taught for over 40 years in the Vance County School System. She was a charter member of the Daisy Garden Club. (Courtesy of Bessie L. Bullock.)

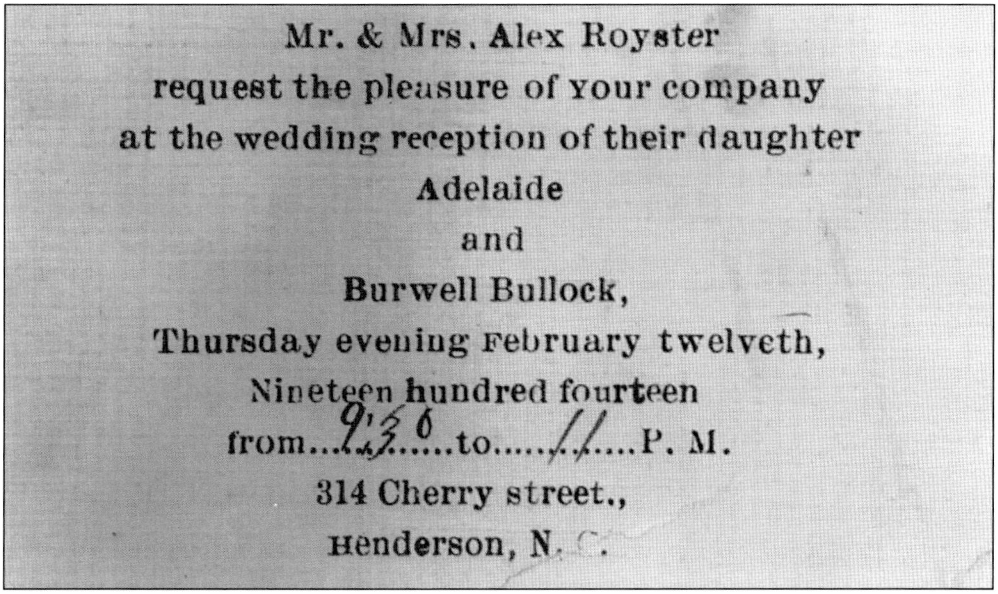
Mr. & Mrs. Alex Royster
request the pleasure of your company
at the wedding reception of their daughter
Adelaide
and
Burwell Bullock,
Thursday evening February twelveth,
Nineteen hundred fourteen
from...9:30...to.....11....P. M.
314 Cherry street.,
Henderson, N. C.

This is the 1914 wedding reception invitation announcing the marriage of Adelaide Royster to Burwell Bullock. He was a Spanish-American War veteran and grocery store owner. The couple were the parents of Melvin, Dorothy, Ralph, and Bessie Bullock. All four attended college on scholarships. The two daughters were valedictorians of their classes; the sons were salutatorians. Adelaide was known for taking her children with her as she visited students' homes in the evenings. (Courtesy of Bessie L. Bullock.)

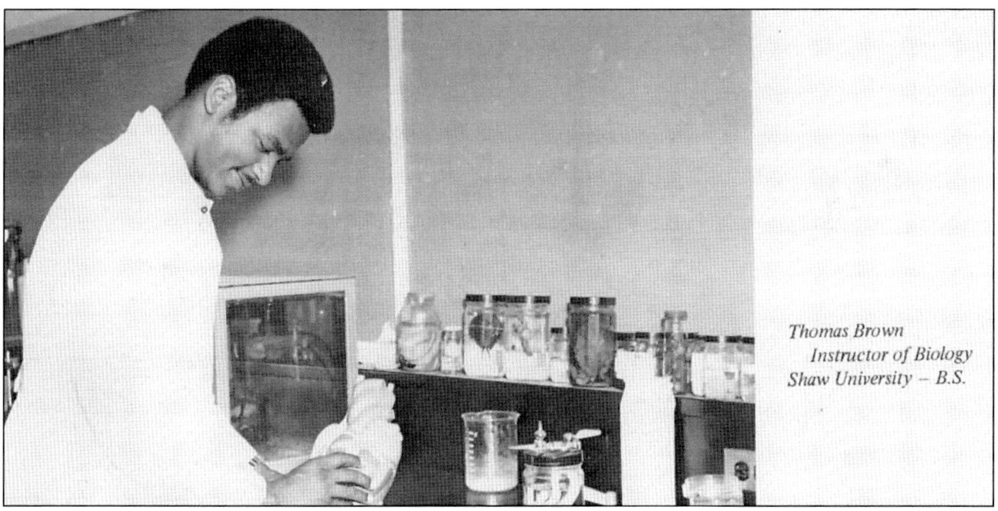

Thomas E. Brown is pictured in 1971. He is remembered affectionately in the *Bulldog*, the official school album of Kittrell College. The dedication reads, "One who has performed his offical duties with dispatch and perpetual good humor, who has given generously of himself in his counseling with students." Brown is a native of Vance County and was a biology instructor at Kittrell College from 1969 to 1975. A graduate of Shaw University, he has taught health and science in the Vance County School System for over 25 years. He is a member of Alph Phi Alpha Fraternity Inc. and the St. Paul United Church of Christ. (Courtesy of Thomas E. Brown.)

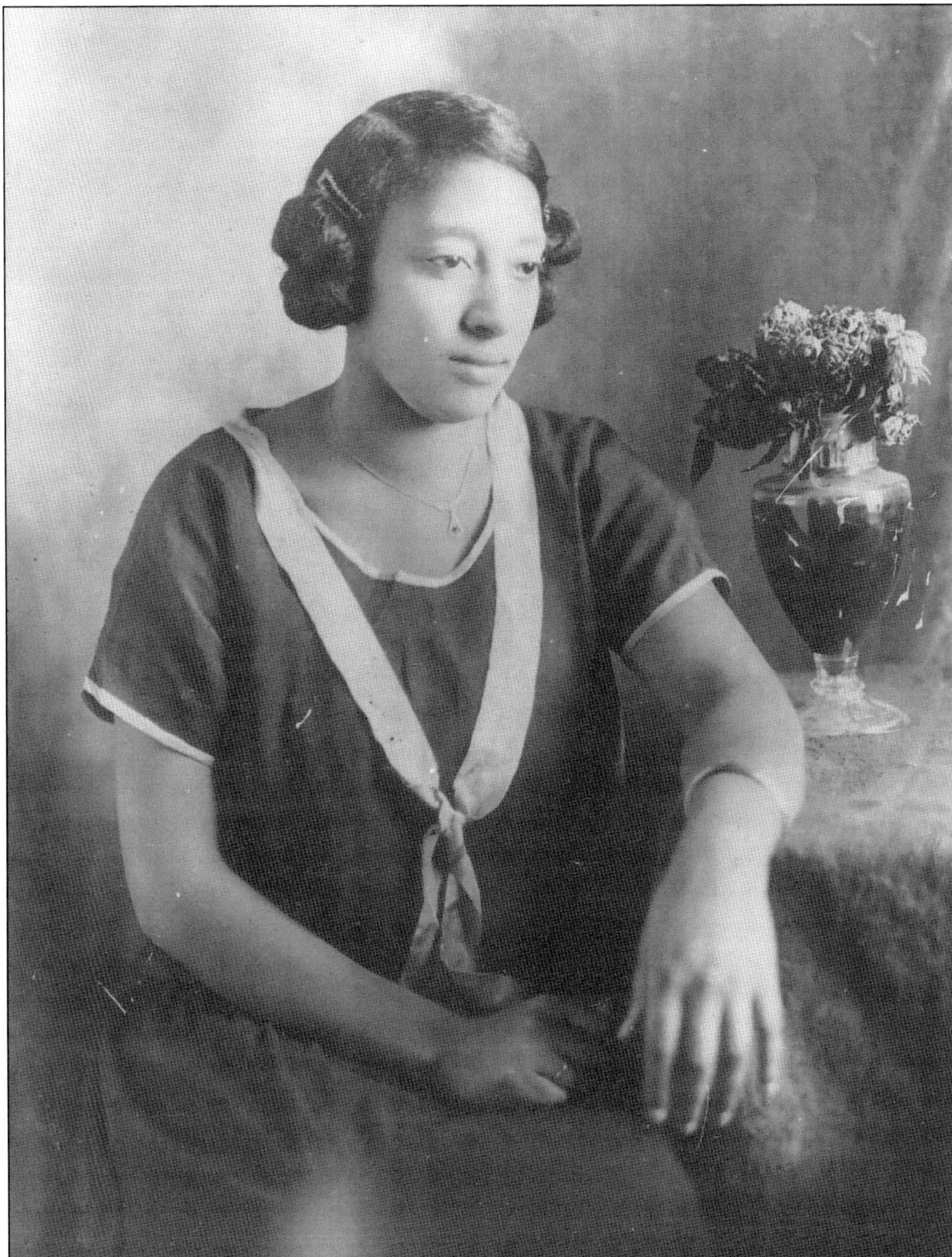

This is a 1940s photo of Eloise L. Brame (1905–1990), a resident of Route 8 in Henderson. She was a native of Vance County, and a graduate of Franklin Christian College and Shaw University. She taught in the Vance County School System for many years, and was the wife of Fred Brame and the mother of Ramona B. Ramseur. She was a member of Flat Creek Baptist Church, where she participated in the senior choir and the Missionary Circle. Brame was a church musician and a Sunday school teacher. She is interred in the Flat Creek Baptist Church cemetery. (Courtesy of Ramona Ramseur.)

Asker Boyd Hawkins (1905–1963), a resident of the Mobile Community, was a native of Henderson and the son of Thomas and Cora Crutchfield Hawkins. He received his A.B. degree from North Carolina College and his M.A. degree from New York University. He also received a fellowship to Worchester University in Massachusetts. While in Henderson he was certified by the New York School of Mechanical Dentistry in 1943 and operated an oral factory on Montgomery Street in a building owned by his brother, Dr. John D. Hawkins. He joined the Shiloh Baptist Church at an early age, served as church pianist for several years, and was married to Anna Fields. Their children were William Earl and Asker B. Hawkins Jr. He is interred in the Hawkins family plot in Blacknall Cemetery. (Courtesy of Andre D. Vann.)

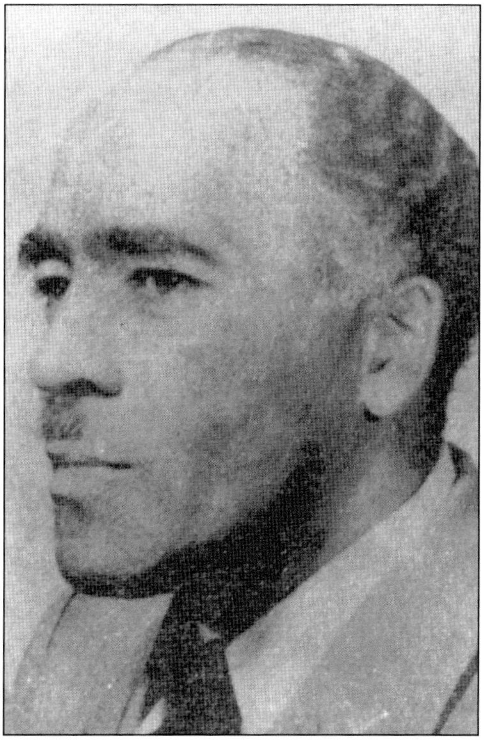

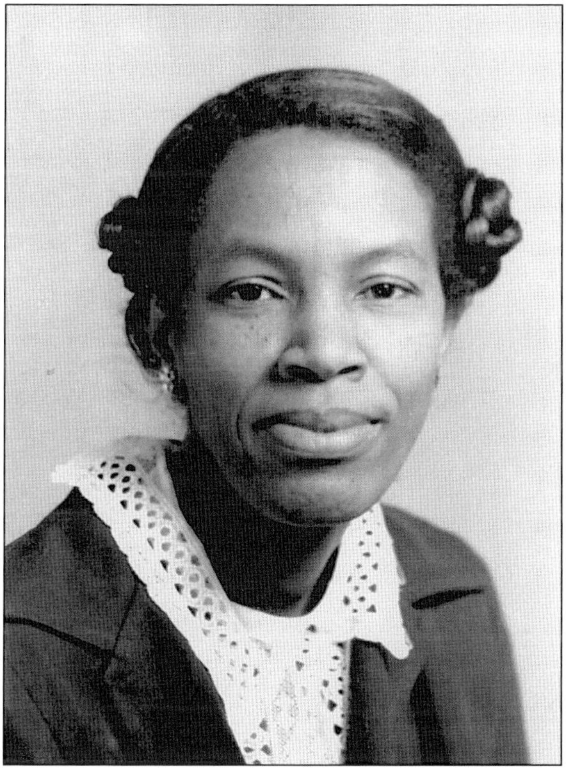

Mamie Simon Williamson (1907–1991), a native of Raleigh Road, was born and reared in Henderson, where she spent the major part of her life. She was the daughter of Neal and Desdy Crawford Simon, and attended HNI, Kittrell College, Hampton University, and Livingstone College. She did further study at NC Central University. She taught in the Vance County Public School System and was a life-long member of the Kesler Temple AMEZ Church. She also was a charter member of Phi Zeta Chapter of Zeta Phi Beta Sorority, and was a member of the Urban-Suburban Garden Club of Henderson. In 1933 she married attorney Charles W. Williamson (1904–1989) and was the mother of Dr. Charles W. Jr. and Robbie Williamson. She is interred in Elmwood Cemetery. (Courtesy of Andre D. Vann.)

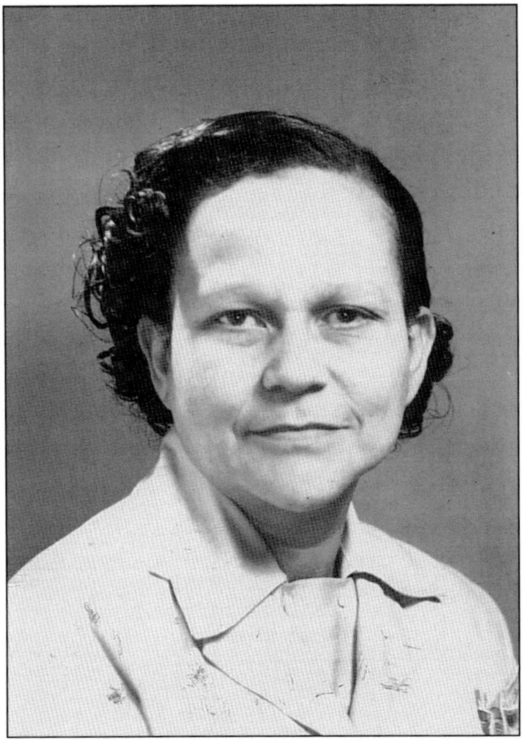

Queen E. Davis (1915–1997), a resident of 517 Winder Street, was a native of Vance County and the daughter of William Sherman and Amanda Moss Davis. She completed her early education at the Central Colored Graded School, then attended Kittrell College. She graduated in 1946 from Shaw University. Davis taught for 42 years in the Vance County School System, serving as a classroom teacher, and also as a special reading instructor until retirement in 1977. She was a member of Shiloh Baptist Church for over 70 years. She is interred in the Davis family plot in Blacknall Cemetery. (Courtesy of Andre D. Vann.)

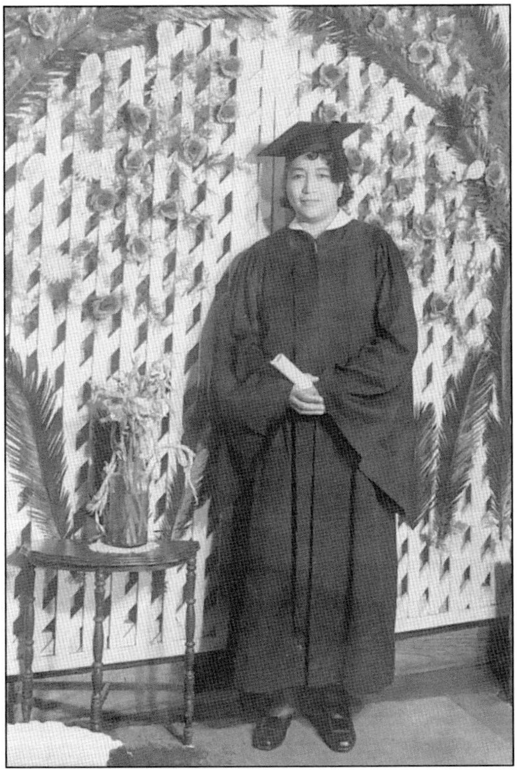

Laura Gilliam Jordan (1905–1998) was a teacher in the Vance County Public School System for over 50 years. She was a member of the Shiloh Baptist Church of Henderson, where she served in various capacities. She is interred in Sunset Memorial Gardens in Henderson. (Courtesy of Andre D. Vann.)

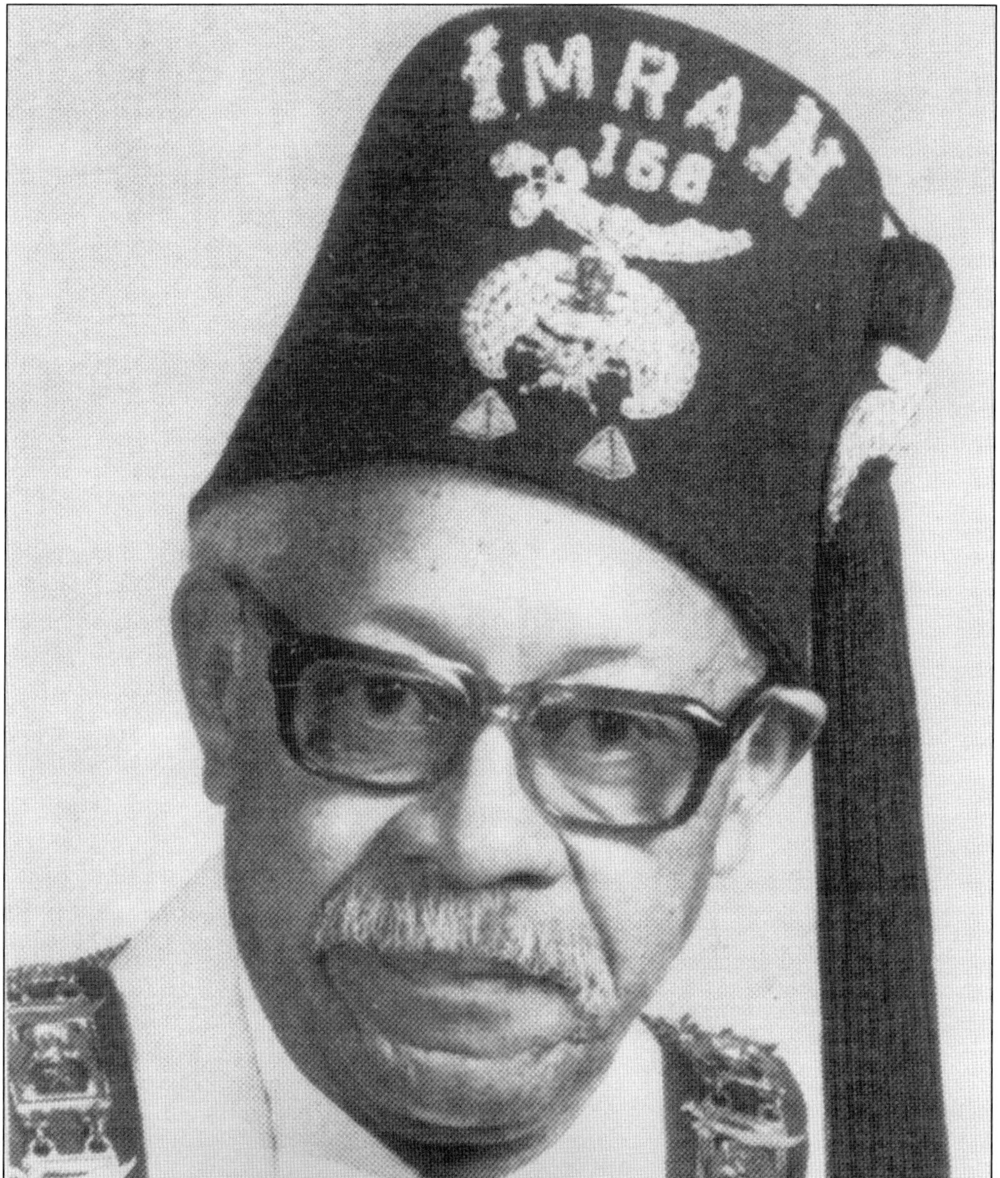

James Rufus Barnes (1914–1996), a resident of 426 Pearl Street and a native of Rocky Mount, NC, was educated in the Rocky Mount Public School System and attended Fayetteville State University, Winston-Salem State University, and NC Central University. He was both a teacher and principal in the Vance County School System. He joined the Shiloh Baptist Church of Henderson in 1940, served on the board of deacons, and also helped to design the current Shiloh Baptist Church structure on College Street. Barnes was a member of the Beacon Light Lodge #249, Henderson Consistory #195, Imran Temple #168, and the Vance County Chamber of Commerce. He was married to Nellie Wyatt Barnes, an educator in the school system. This union was blessed with one daughter, Annetta L. Barnes Dadey. He and his wife are both interred in Sunset Memorial Gardens in Henderson. (Courtesy of Andre D. Vann.)

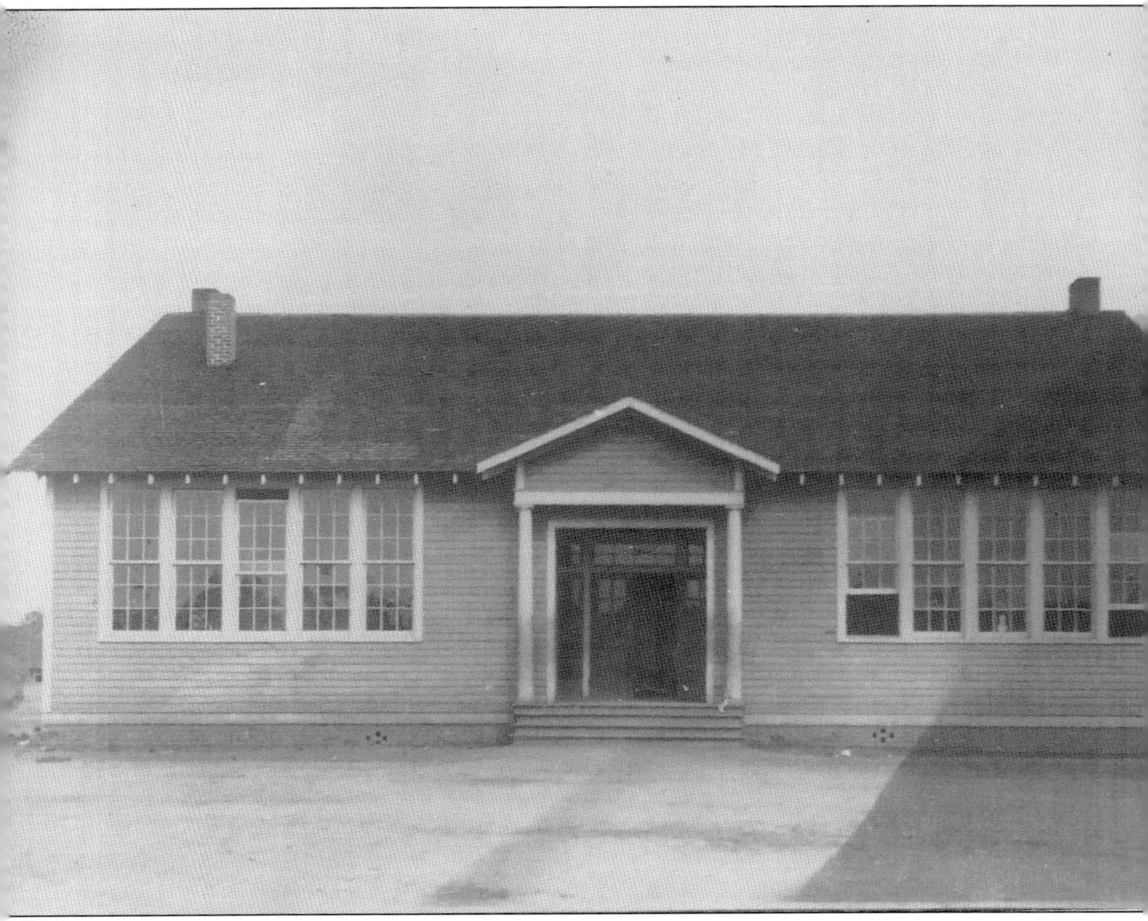

This is a 1930s photo of the Williamsboro Elementary School that was built with financial support provided by the Rosenwald Fund. The wooden structure contained two individual classrooms and a large multi-purpose room, which served as an auditorium and had two folding walls to divide it into two classrooms. The building was heated by big "potbelly" wood burning stoves. The school opened in 1926 and served pupils from the primary level through eight grades. Since there was no consistent schooling provided for black children, the age of the students ranged anywhere from 6 to 20 years old. Phillip Lewis was the first principal of the school and Randall Howell was the last principal before Williamsboro and Townsville schools merged into New Hope School in 1954. (Courtesy of Ramona B. Ramseur.)

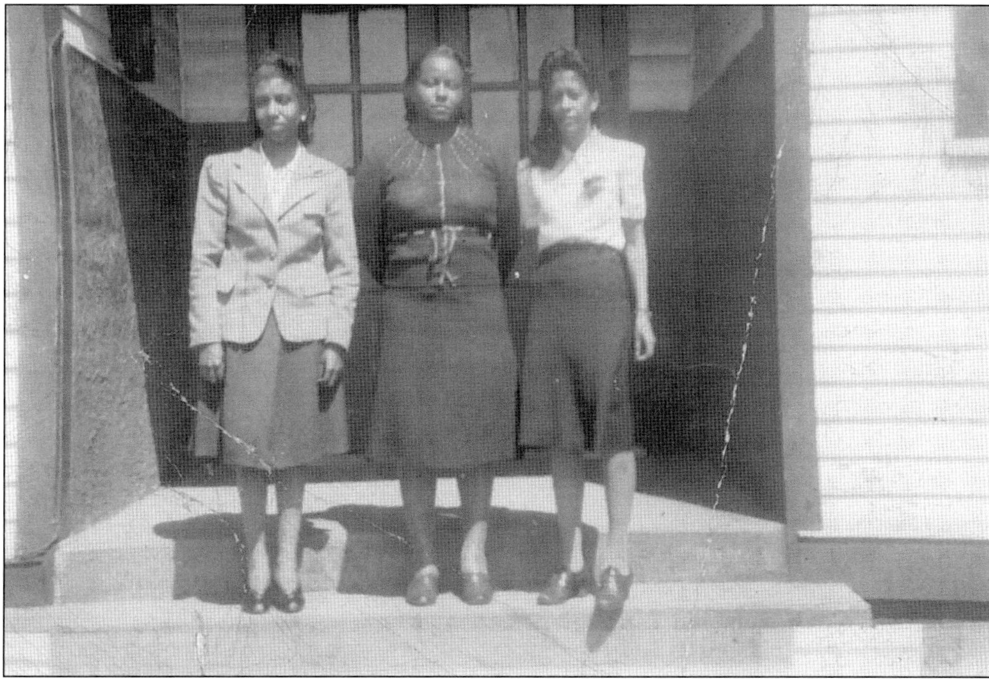

From left to right, third grade teacher Annie Garnes Walker, second grade teacher Annie Mae Gill Wyche, and first grade teacher Esther M. Bullock stand in the entrance of the Williamsboro Elementary School in the late 1930s. (Courtesy of Ethel C. R. Smith.)

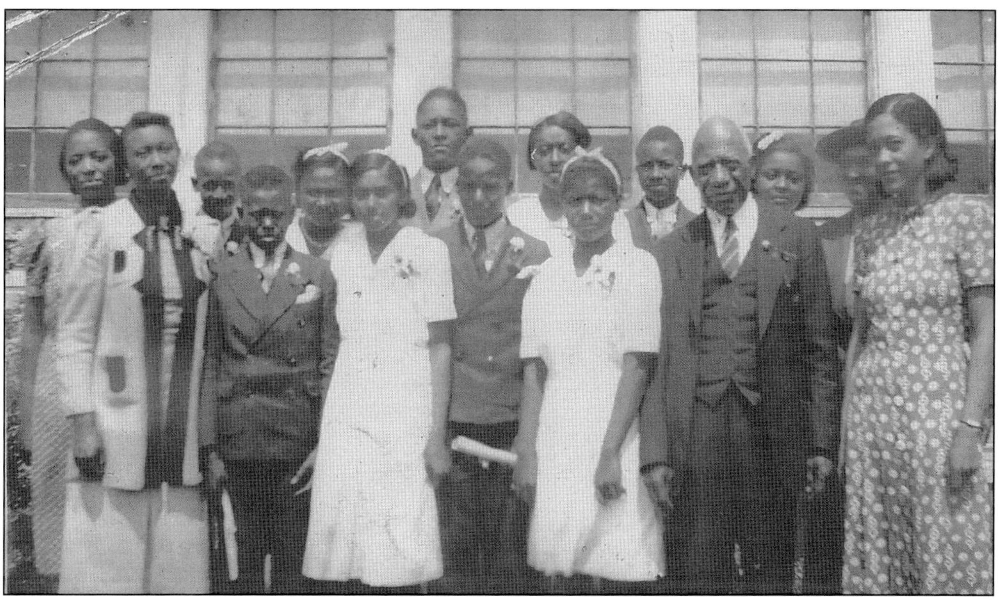

Graduating seniors are pictured with their teachers outside of the Williamsboro Elementary School in the 1940s. From left to right are teachers Mable Wyche and Ethel C.R. Smith, students in graduation attire, and Principal Phil Lewis, Lelia B. Yancey, and Esther M. Bullock. (Courtesy of Ethel C.R. Smith.)

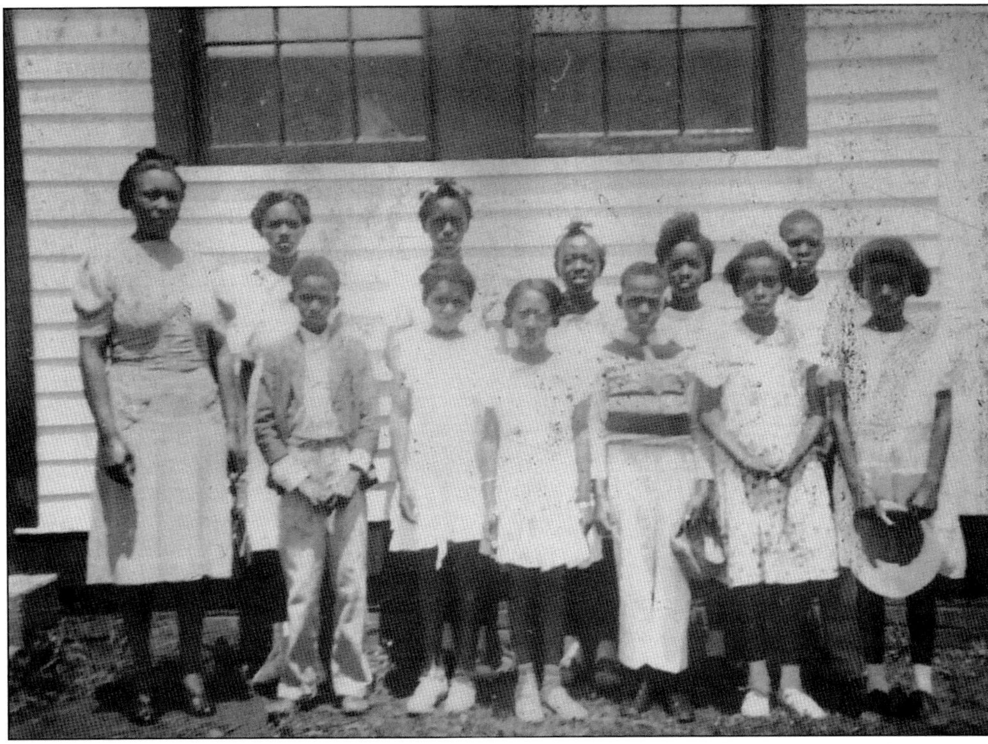

Ethel C.R. Smith is seen in this 1940s photo with students in her second and third grade classes. (Courtesy of Ethel C.R. Smith.)

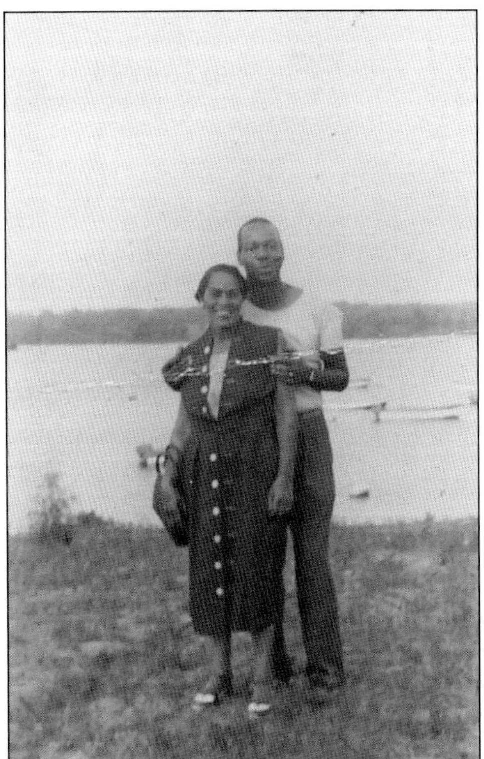

Vance County educators Carrie Lovette Hawkins Sowell Marable (1903–1984) and William T. Marable were residents of 1000 East Andrews Avenue. Carrie Marable, daughter of Thomas and Cora Crutchfield Hawkins, was born in Mobile, South Henderson. She earned her B.A. degree at Winston-Salem Teachers College in 1926, and received her masters degree from Columbia University in New York City. She taught in the Vance County School System for over 40 years. She first married a Dr. Sewell from Kentucky, and in 1947 she was united to William "Bill" Marable. She was a noted traveler in Vance County, having visited five of the seven continents and most of the Atlantic and Pacific Islands. She was an early member of the Shiloh Baptist Church of Henderson. She is interred in the Elmwood Cemetery beside her younger brother David Hawkins. (Courtesy of Andre D. Vann.)

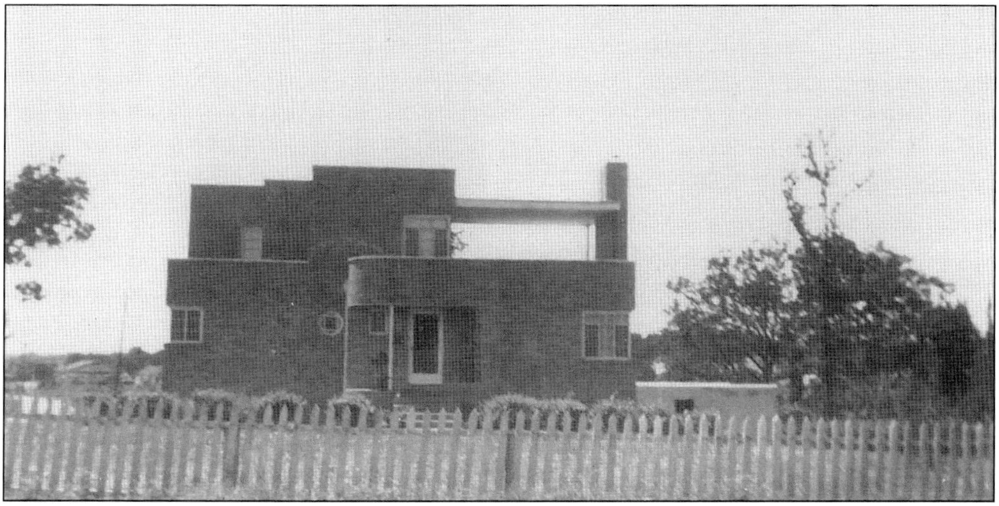

This is a 1950s photo of the home of Carrie Hawkins Marable and William T. Marable. A California-style house, it was the scene of numerous social gatherings. The house was recently sold to the Harold Thompson Sr. family. (Courtesy of Andre D. Vann.)

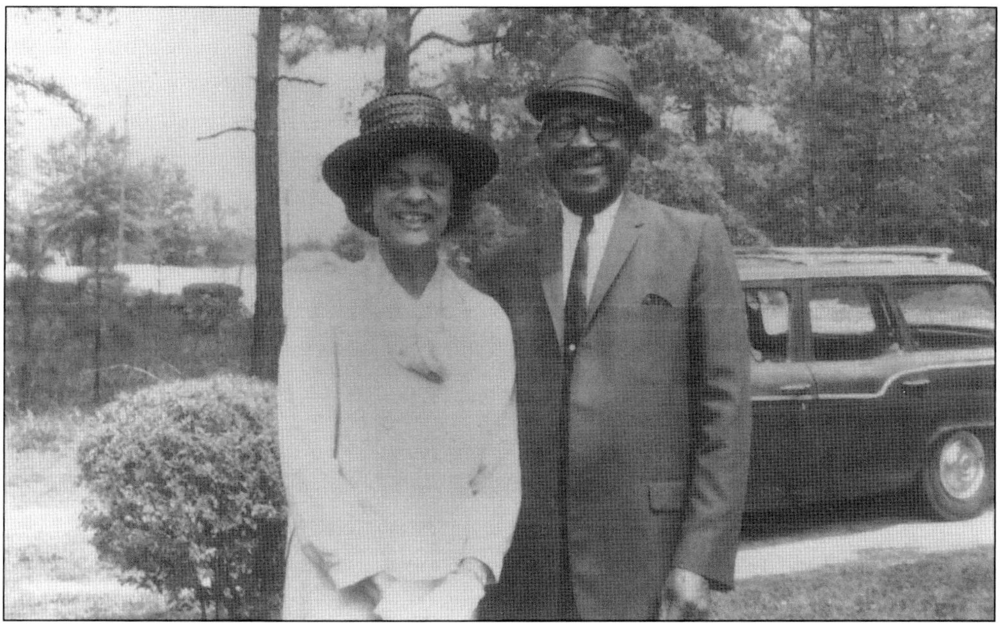

This is a 1967 photo of Vance County educators Ethel Lancaster Adams (1908–1998) and Raynah Adams Jr. (1906–1983) at their home on Norlina Road. Ethel Adams graduated from Thyne Institute High School in 1926, and attended Hampton Institute and Virginia State College. In 1935, she married R.A. Adams Jr. and they journeyed to Henderson, where they became the parents of Raynah III, Paul, and Eva. R.A. Adams Jr. was born on the campus of HNI, where his parents were both teachers, and graduated from Hampton Institute in 1927. He received graduate training at Boston University and North Carolina College at Durham. An underwriter for the NC Mutual Life Insurance Company, he also owned and operated the first black Esso Service Station in Henderson. The Adamses retired from teaching in June 1973. They are interred in the Adams Family Cemetery.(Courtesy of Raynah Adams, III.)

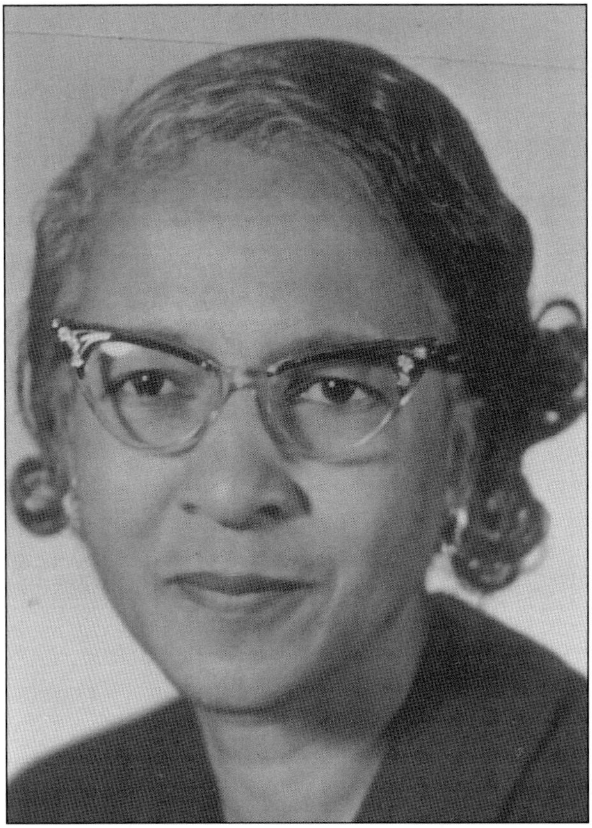

Lottie Allen Parham (1907–1982), was the daughter of George Allen and Mable Hicks Allen Jackson. She received her early education in the Henderson City School System. A graduate of Winston-Salem Teachers College, she did further study at Hampton Institute. Parham retired from the Henderson City School System after 45 years of service. She was a member of the Urban Suburban Garden Club, the Contractite Bridge Club, Daughter of Isis, Imran Court #55, and the Quettes. She was married to Sherman Parham, and they reared Robert and Dorothy Mable Lewis at their home on Parkway Drive. The Kesler Temple AMEZ Church was where she served as a member of the trustee board and the deaconess board, was a Sunday school teacher, and was the former church organist. She is interred in Blacknall Cemetery. (Courtesy of Sherman Parham.)

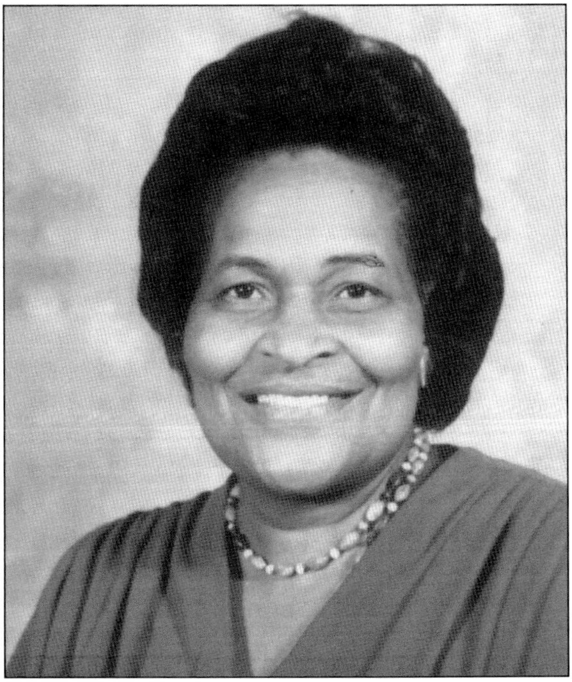

Valeria Jordan Alston, a native of Burgaw, NC, graduated from C.F. Pope High School, Shaw University, and North Carolina Central University. Alston received advanced training at the Dreyfus Institute at Princeton University. She has taught at Kittrell Junior College, Henderson Institute (1957–1968), and Northern Vance High School (1968–1993). In 1986 she was chosen teacher of the year for Vance County and received from President Reagan the presidential award for excellence in science teaching for North Carolina. She attends Holy Temple United Holy Church. Her husband is Rev. Roosevelt Alston, and they are the parents of Elaine Brewer, Dr. Sebastain Alston, and Valeria Johnson. (Courtesy of Valeria Alston.)

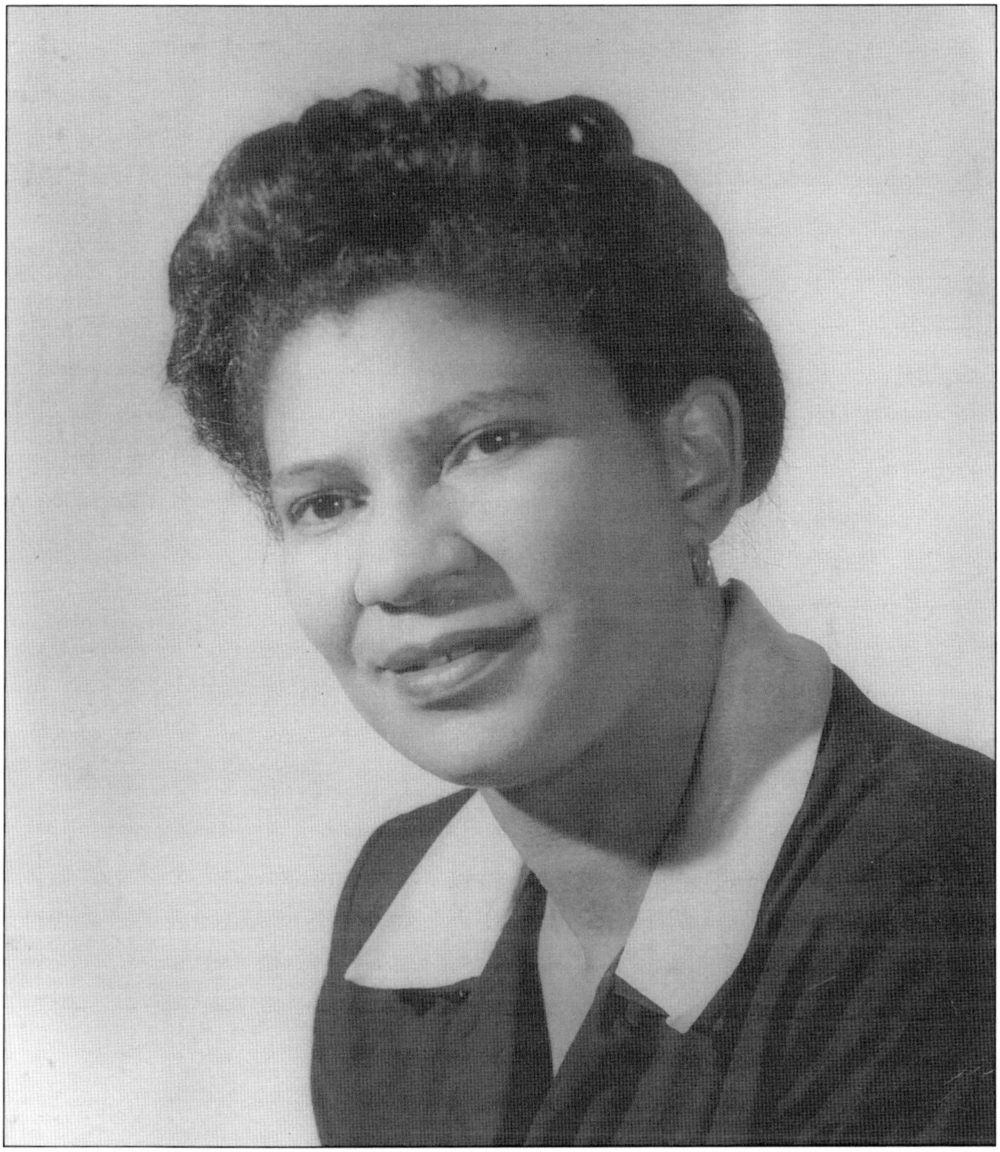

Johnnie Jacqueline "Jakie" Young Mims Sanders (1914–), daughter of Edward and Lula Burton Brodie Young, was born on Flint Hill where she still lives and is a noted educator and musician in Vance County. She attended the Central Colored Graded School and HNI. She is a 1942 graduate of North Carolina College for Negros, now NCCU. After college she returned to Vance County and worked for over 40 years as an educator and librarian in the public schools. She is an active member of the Shiloh Baptist Church, where she served as the church chorister for over 50 years and has sung at numerous weddings, funerals, and community events. Sanders was first married to David L. Mims and later married Fletcher Sanders, both of whom are deceased. She is involved in numerous civic, religious, and philanthropic endeavors in the community. (Courtesy of Andre D. Vann.)

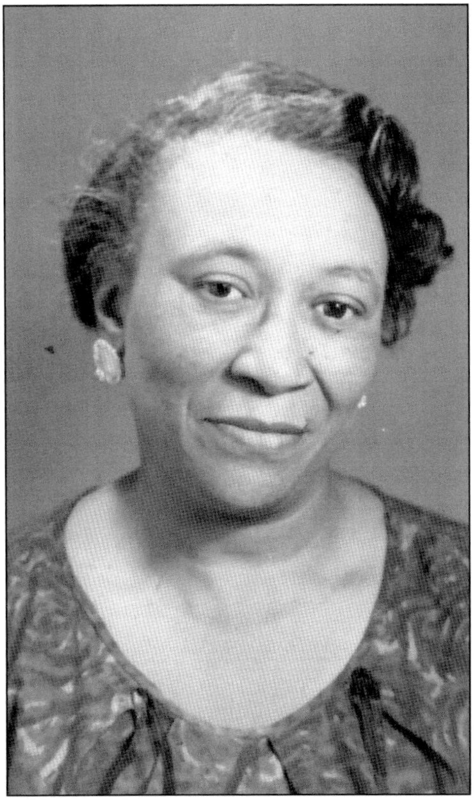

Ethel Vivian Clements Rhodes Smith (1911–) was born in Williamsboro, the daughter of Rev. Thomas B. Hicks and Hattie Sommerville Hicks. She was home schooled by her mother and entered the third grade in Newark, NJ. She graduated from HNI and received her teacher training at Fayetteville State Teachers College and Shaw University. Advanced training was received at North Carolina College and East Carolina University, where she was certified in reading. She served as an educator and principal in Cumberland County, and later transferred to the Vance County School System. She retired in 1972 after 42 years as an educator. She is an active member of the Shiloh Baptist Church, and a member of the Phi Zeta Chapter of Zeta Phi Beta Sorority, Inc. She was married first to Claude Clements, then to Wilford Rhodes, and then to Jesse Smith, all of whom are deceased. In 1998, she donated $40,000 to Shaw University in order to endow the Ethel C.R. Smith and Jesse J. Smith Scholarship Fund, in memory of her husband, who died in 1997. (Courtesy of Ethel C. R. Smith/Andre D. Vann.)

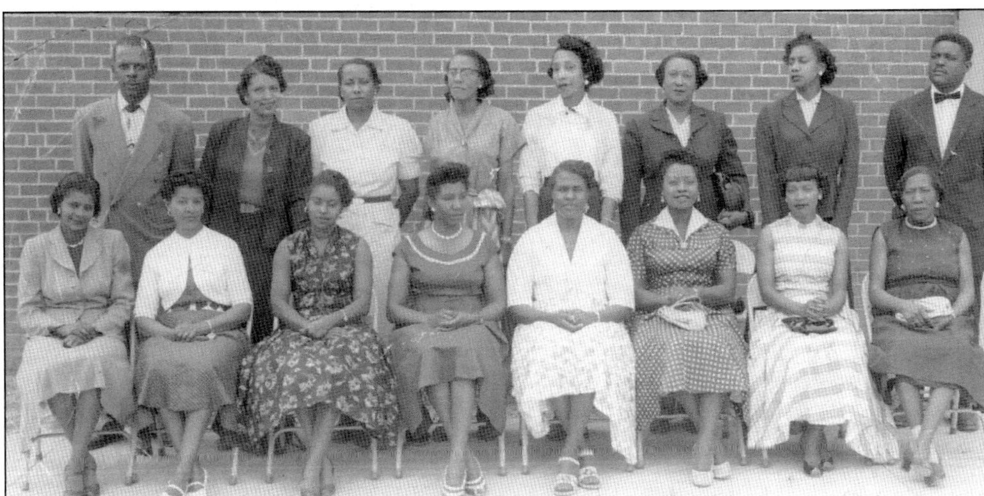

This is a 1960s photo of the faculty outside of the New Hope Elementary School, which served grades one through nine. Students then completed their high school training at HNI. From left to right are as follows: (seated) Nellie Barnes, Pearl Fitts, Virginia Butler, Annie Garnes Walker, Pinkie Venable, A. Poe, Mattie C. Taylor, and Elnora Burwell; (standing) Reynolds Howell (principal), Alice Green Smith, Annie Gill Wyche, Lizzie Brame Bullock, Lena B. Howell, Ethel C.R. Smith, Clara Hunt, and H.B. Wilkins. (Courtesy of Ethel C.R. Smith.)

Hattie B.I. Williams, a resident of Pinkston Street, was born and reared in Warren County and graduated from Fayetteville State Teachers College (now Fayetteville State University.) She taught for 42 years at Northside Elementary School in Norlina, NC. She was both an educator and administrator in the Warren County Public Schools, and an active volunteer at Maria Parham Hospital. Williams was married to Allen Williams, a noted mortician and businessman in Henderson. She is also an active member of the Shiloh Baptist Church. (Courtesy of Hattie B.I. Williams.)

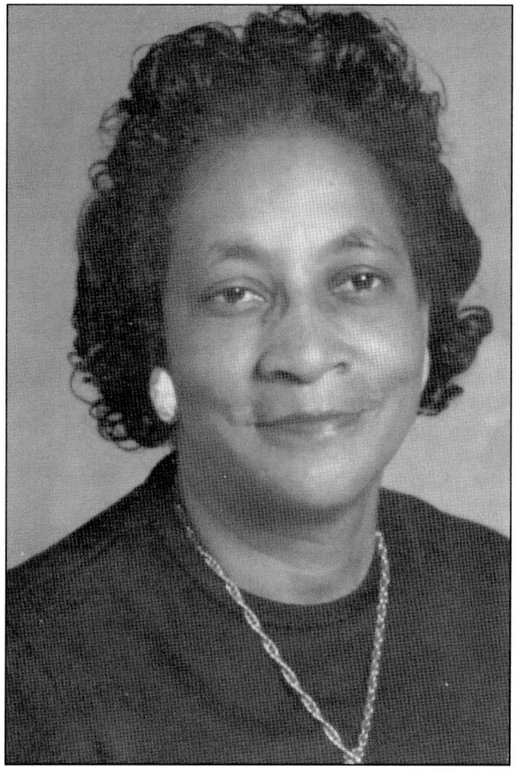

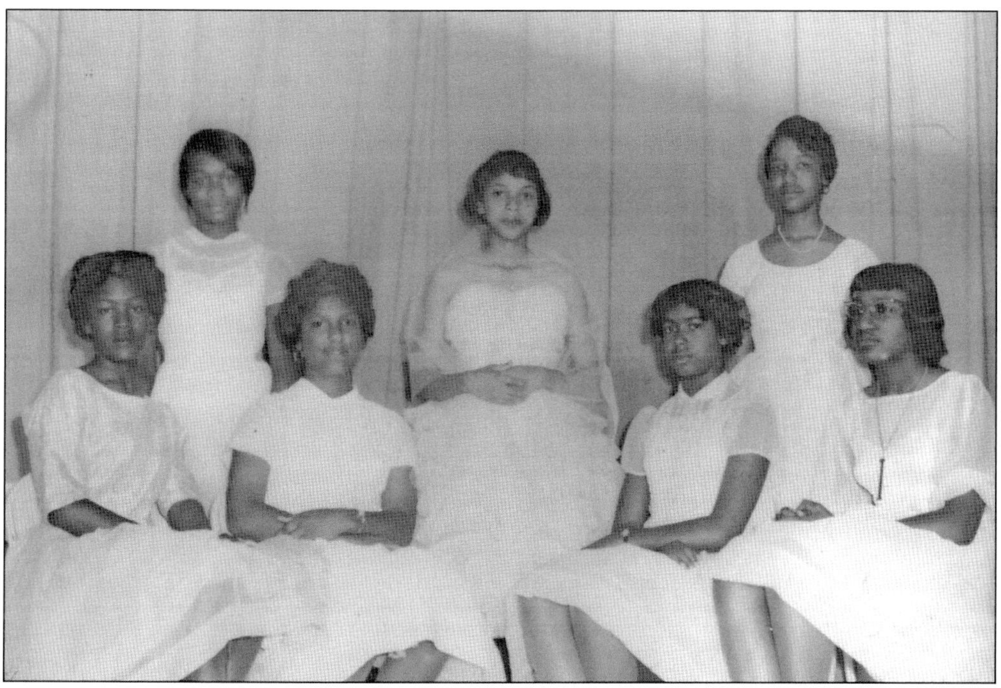

This is a 1950s photo of students at the Carver School in Vance County. (Courtesy of Henderson *Daily Dispatch*.)

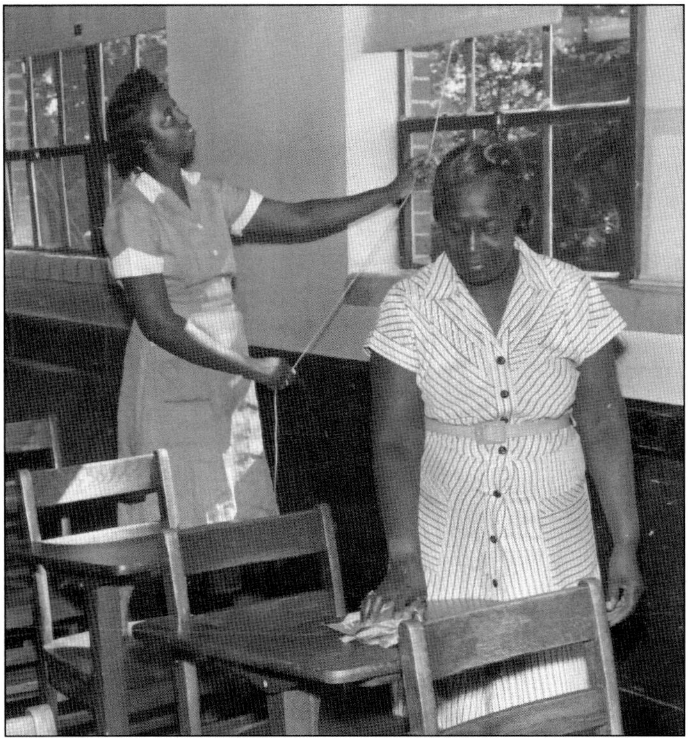

Employees prepare for the opening of Henderson High School in this 1950s photo. The irony was that black students in Vance County were not allowed to attend Henderson High at that time. (Courtesy of Henderson *Daily Dispatch*.)

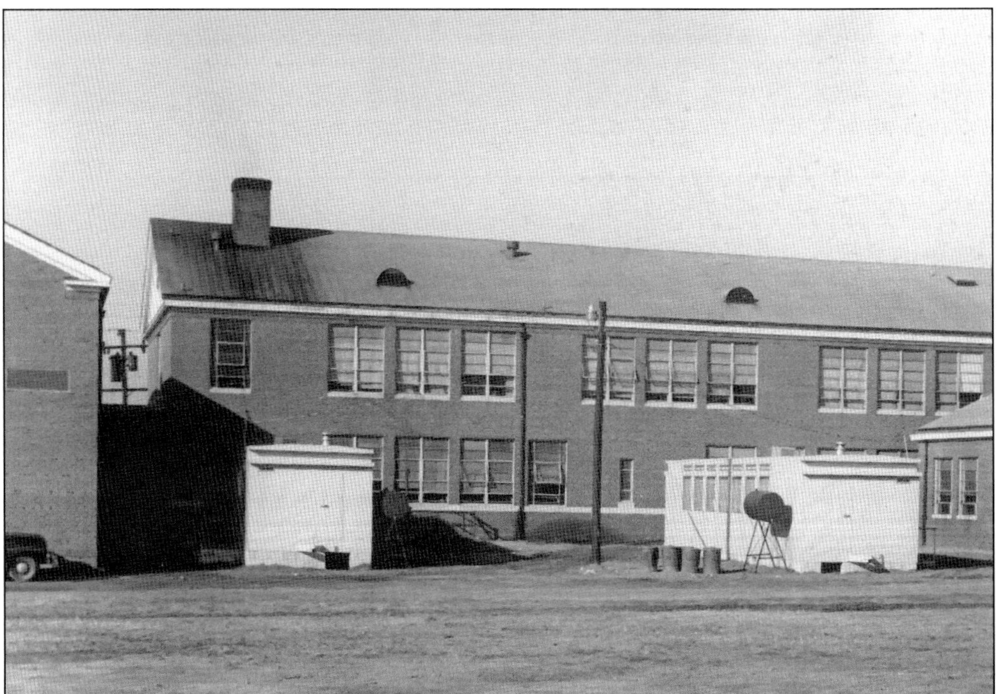

This is a 1960s photo of the mobile classrooms used at the Eaton-Johnson School. (Courtesy of Henderson *Daily Dispatch*.)

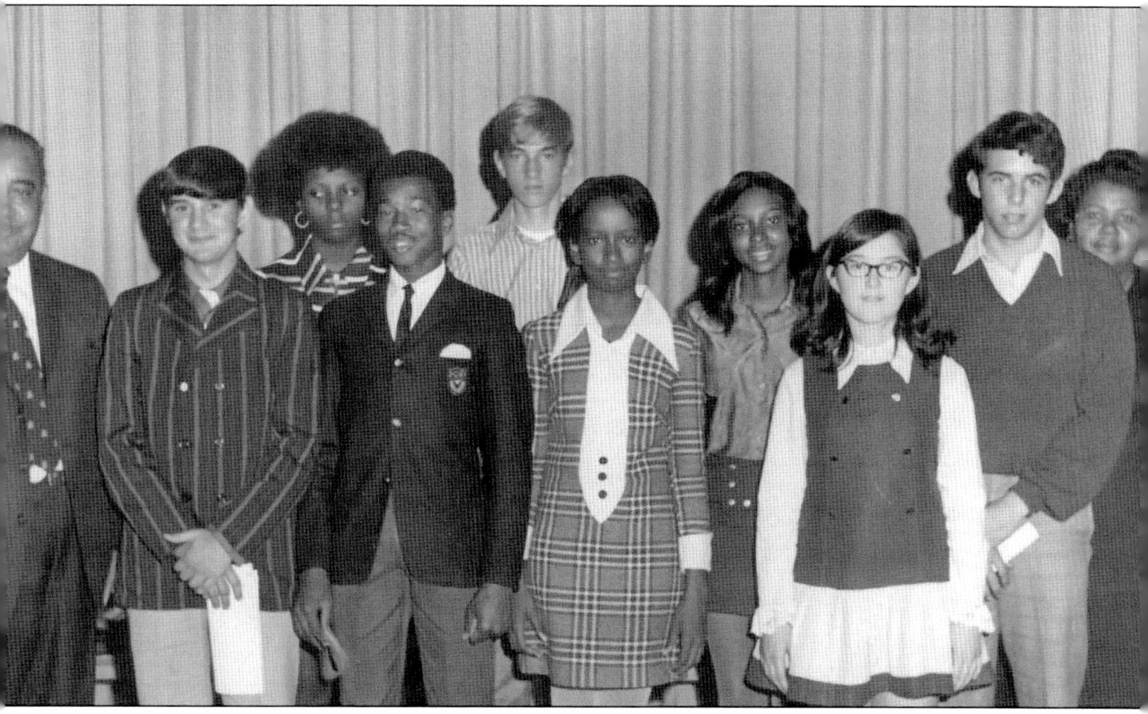

The integrated members of the Pinkston Street Student Council are shown in this 1970 photo. (Courtesy of Henderson *Daily Dispatch*.)

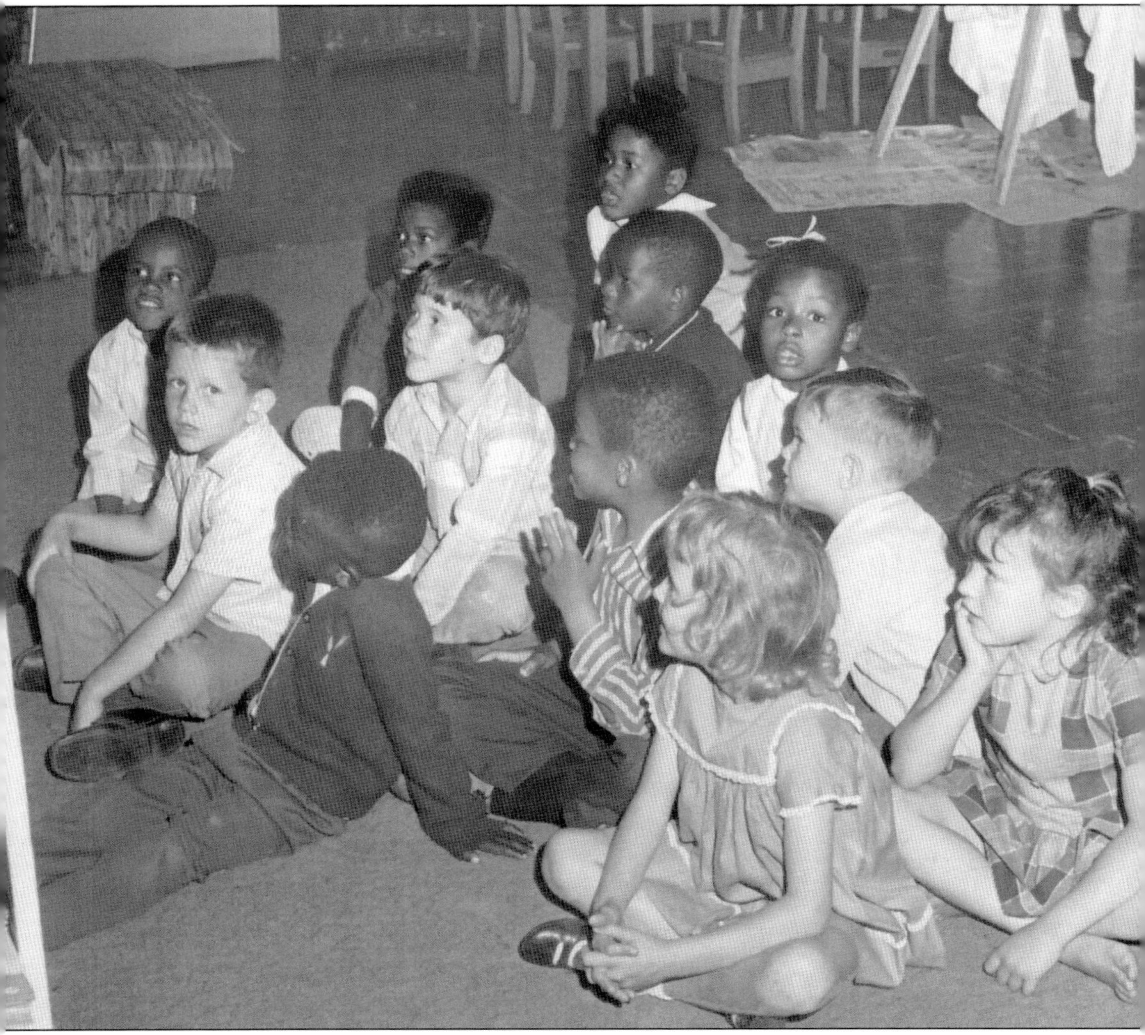

A 1970s photo shows eager students listening at story time at the Church of the Holy Innocents Episcopal Kindergarten. (Courtesy of Henderson *Daily Dispatch*.)

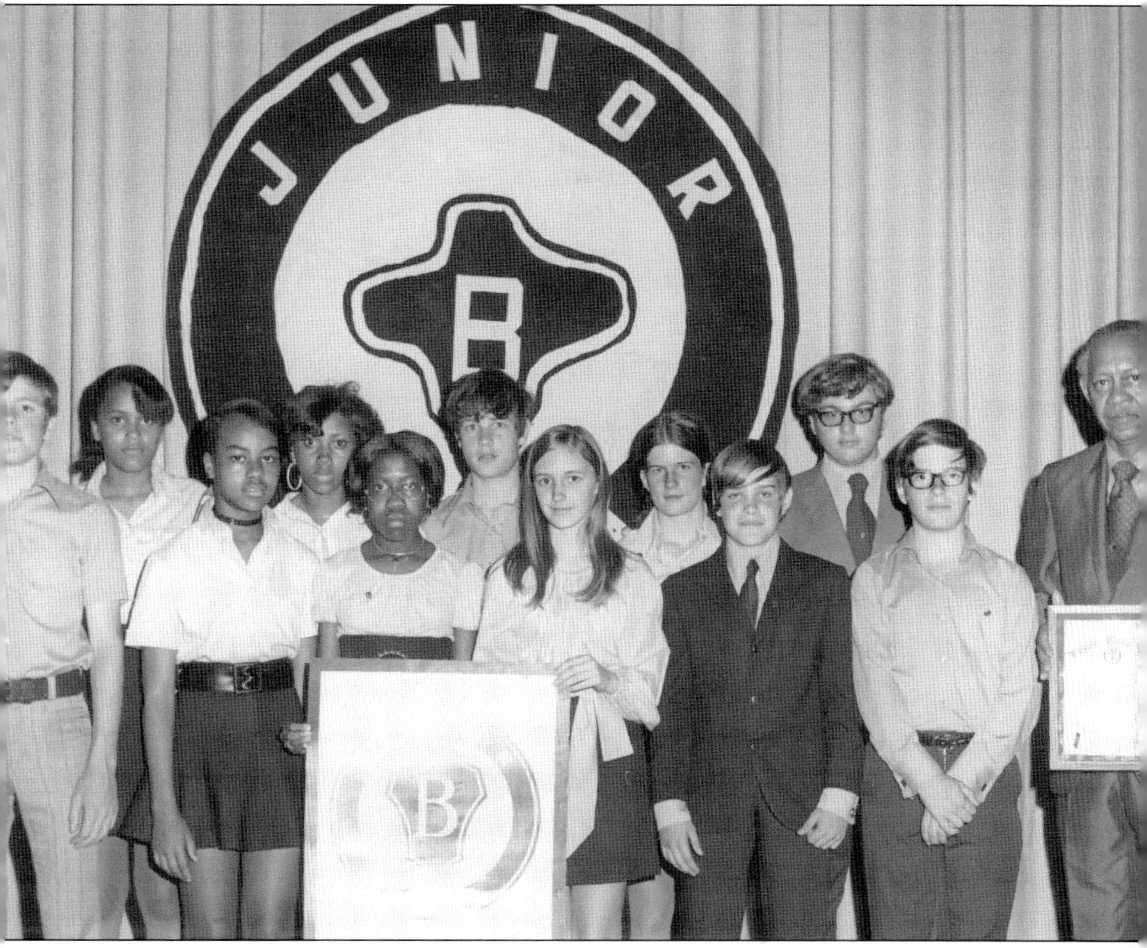

Principal James R. Barnes, seen to the extreme right, is holding the citation with the officers of the Junior Beta Club at Eaton-Johnson Junior High School in this 1970s photo. (Courtesy of Henderson *Daily Dispatch*.)

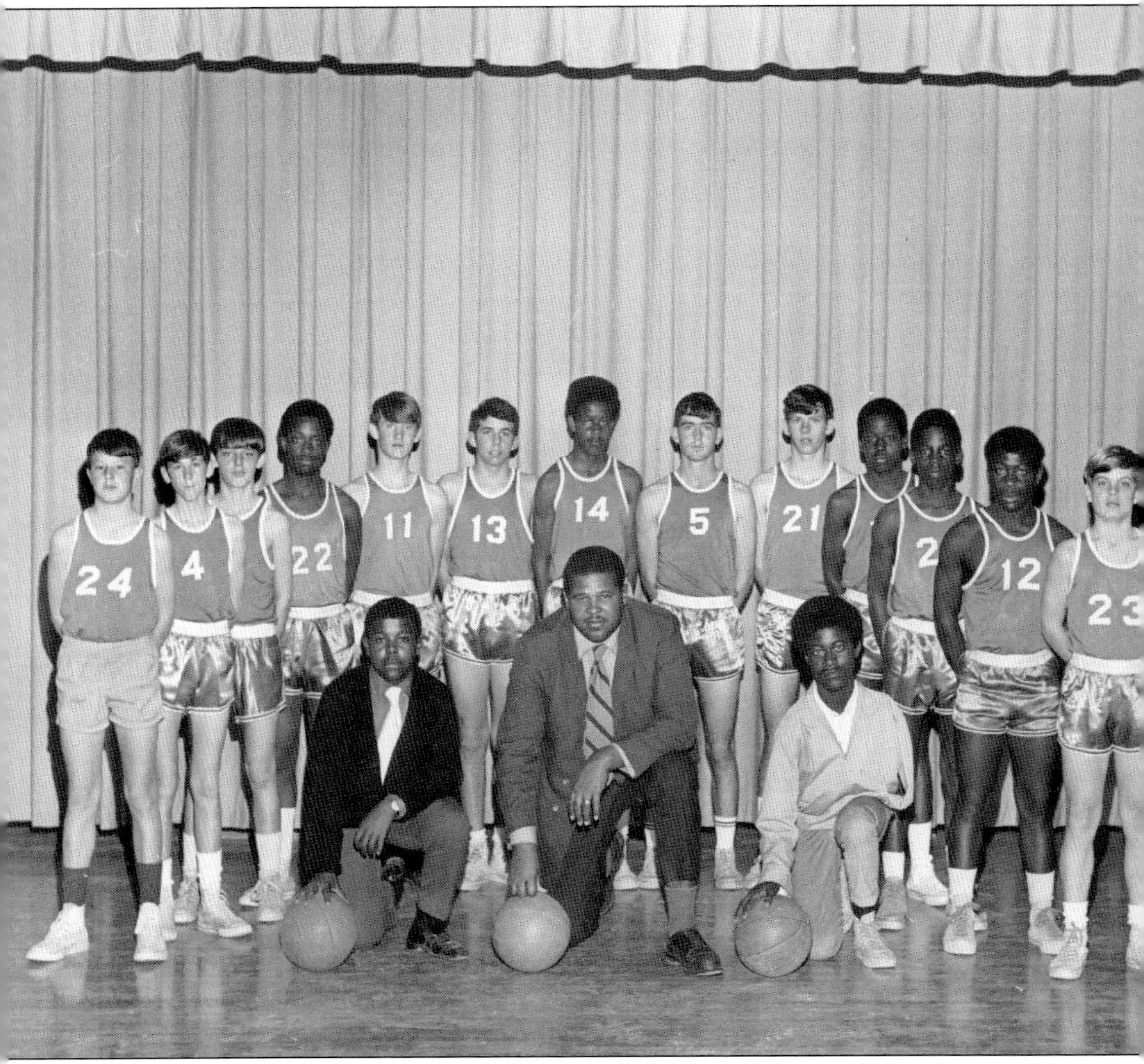

Coach Emeron Cash (center) is surrounded by his players in this 1968 photo taken at the Pinkston Street School. Cash is now a member of the Vance County School Board. This was the first integrated team in the history of the county. (Courtesy of Henderson *Daily Dispatch*.)

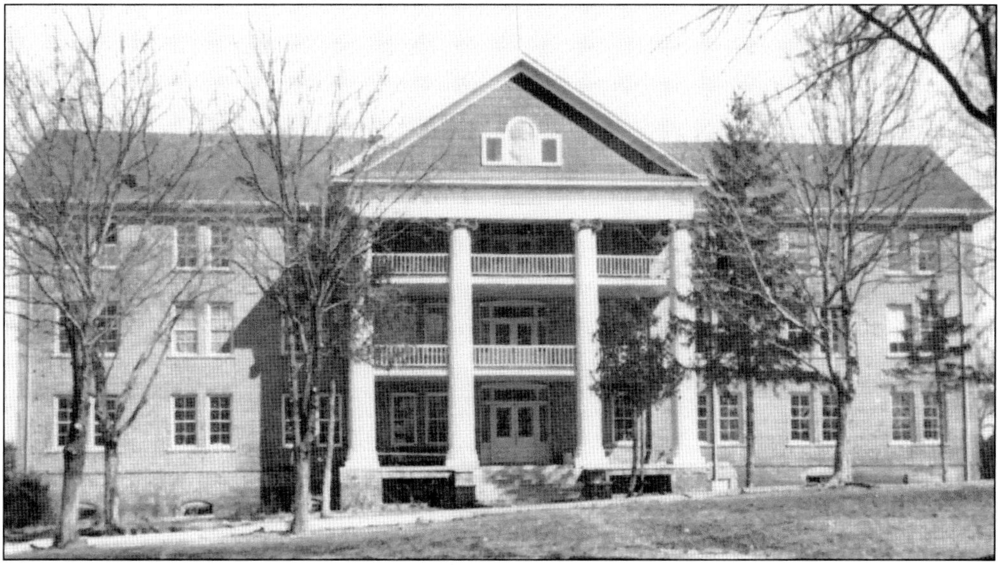

This is a 1940s photo of Duke Memorial Hall on the Kittrell College campus. Duke Hall, a large three-story structure, served as administrative offices, and the upper floors were used as a boys' dormitory. This building, along with numerous others, was donated by Benjamin Newton Duke. They were "previously used" buildings from the Duke University campus (then Trinity College) that were taken apart in Durham, delivered to the Kittrell campus, and reassembled there. Fires at the turn of the 20th century destroyed the buildings; the new campus buildings were made of brick and stone, and were much larger than the originals. (Courtesy of Andre D. Vann.)

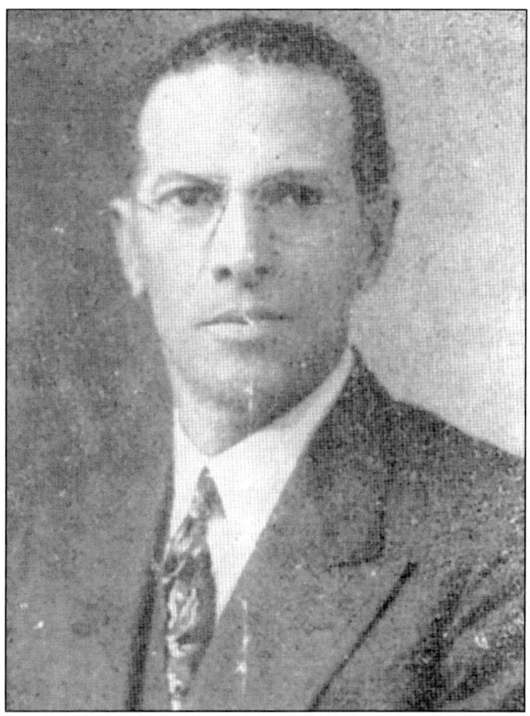

Dr. Charles E. Stewart served as president of Kittrell College. He received his academic training at Wilberforce University, Payne Theological Seminary and College, the Howard University School of Law, and the Chicago Musical College. He was noted as one of the most outstanding educators, pulpiteers, lecturers, and clergymen of the African Methodist Episcopal (AME) Church. (Courtesy of Andre D. Vann.)

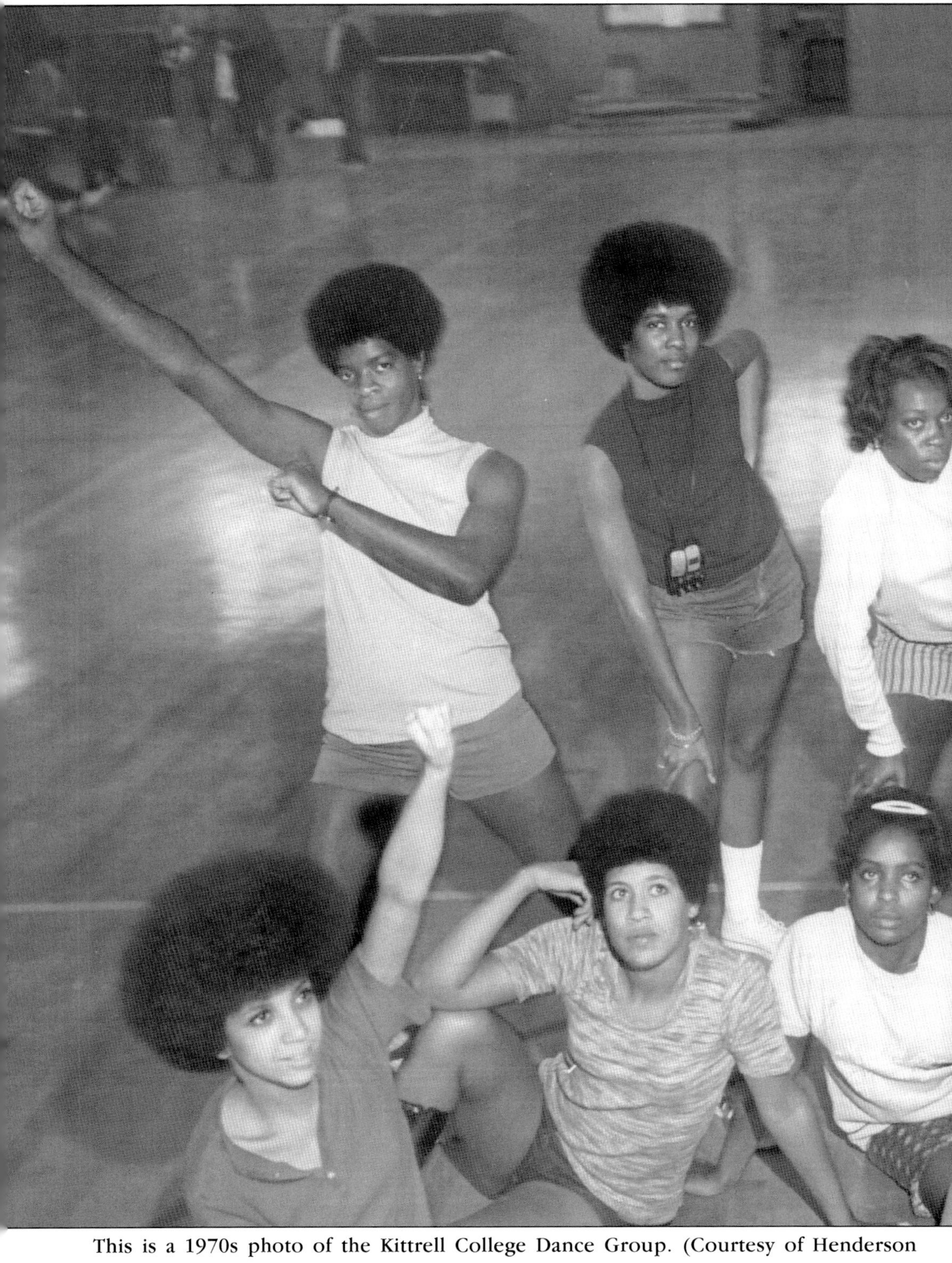

This is a 1970s photo of the Kittrell College Dance Group. (Courtesy of Henderson

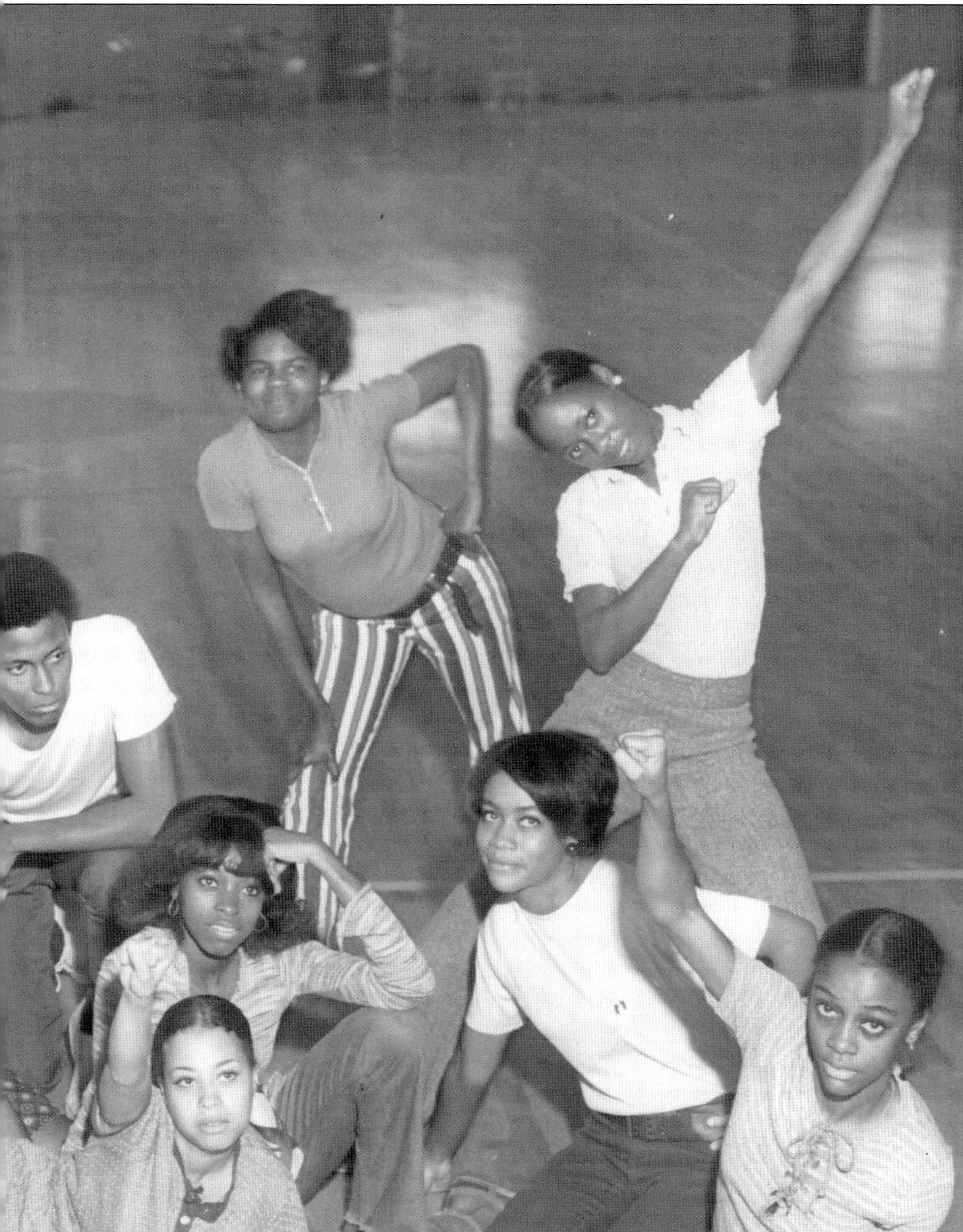

Daily Dispatch.)

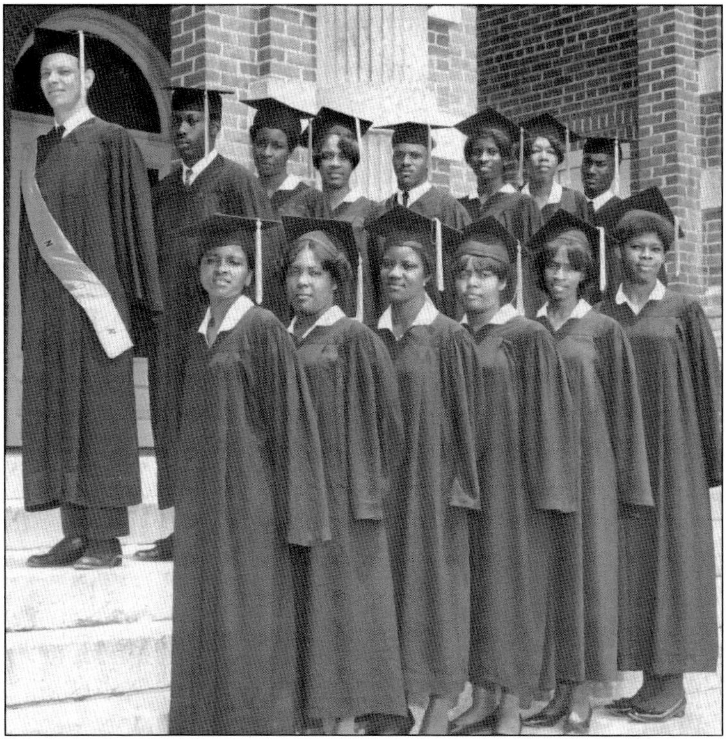

Graduates of Kittrell College assembled in front of Duke Memorial Hall in this 1969 photo. (Courtesy of Henderson *Daily Dispatch*.)

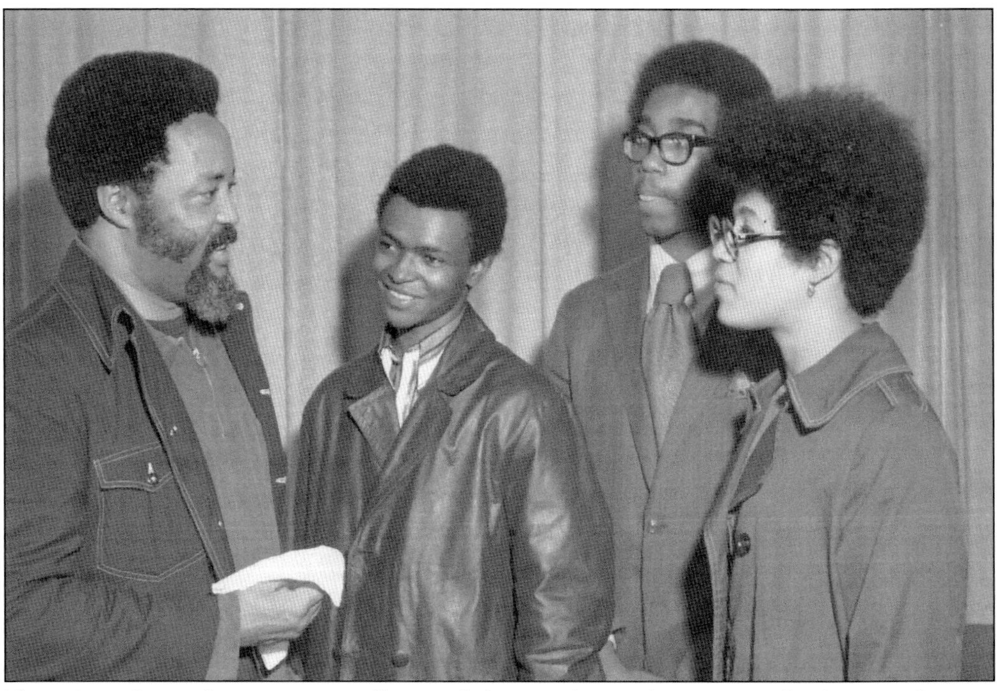

This 1972 photo shows Hosea Williams of the Southern Christian Leadership Conference chatting with students as he visits the Kittrell College campus. (Courtesy of Henderson *Daily Dispatch*.)

Four

Church and Religion

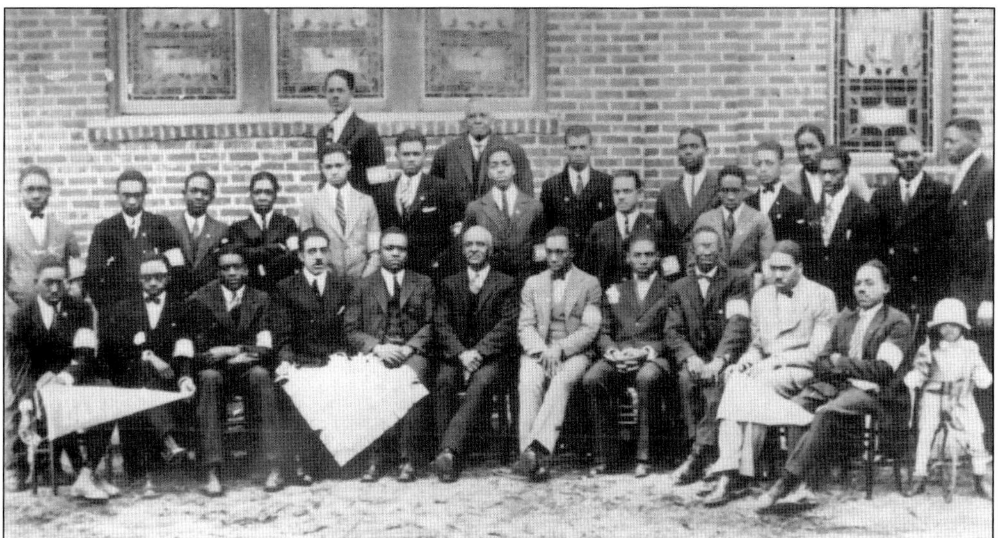

Members of the Baraca Club are pictured outside of the Shiloh Baptist Church in 1926. The Baraca Club was an all-male Bible class that met in the basement of the church. On the front row seated at the extreme right on the tricycle is Bessie Bullock, the daughter of the late Burwell Bullock and Adelaide Royster Bullock. Burwell Bullock is on the last row, standing in the center of the photo. Others persons noted in the photo include, in the front row, starting fourth from the left, Dr. L.C. Rogers; Dr. William S. Ravenell (1897–1966) pastor from 1925-1927; Deacon John E. Scott in the center; and the third from the right, holding the banner, is Asker Boyd Hawkins, pianist and teacher. (Courtesy of Alice E. Bryant and Bessie L. Bullock.)

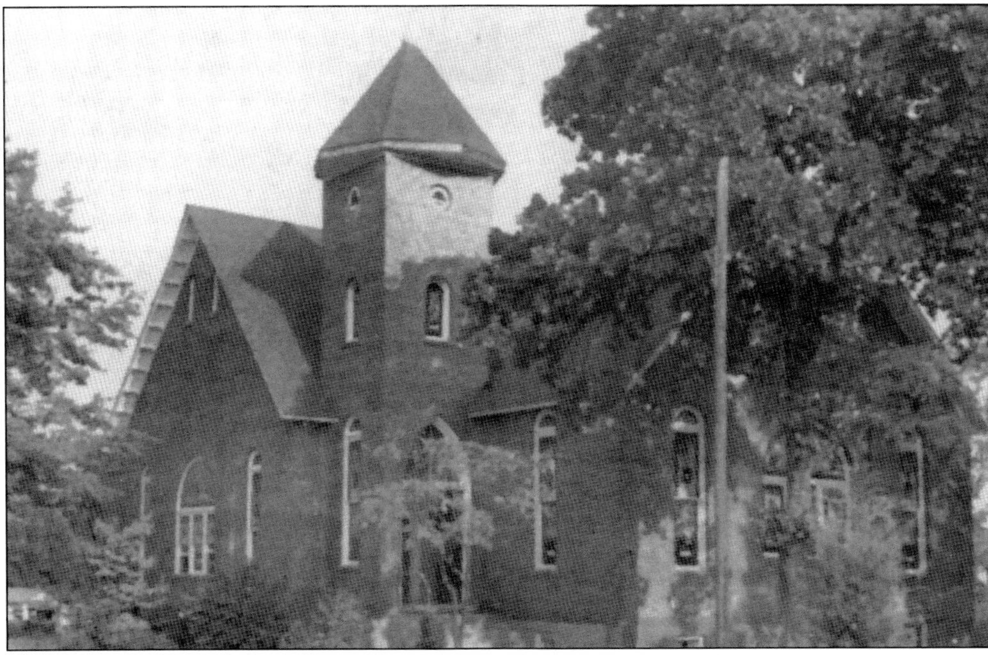

This is a 1940s photo of the Shiloh Baptist Church, located at 635 College Street on the edge of the Flint Hill Community. The church was formerly known as First Baptist Church of Henderson and begun in 1866. The first building was erected in 1868. The second building, seen above, was erected in 1895 and additions were made to the building in 1920. Sunday school rooms were annexed in 1950 and the entire auditorium redecorated in 1953 and 1954. (Photo courtesy of Andre D. Vann.)

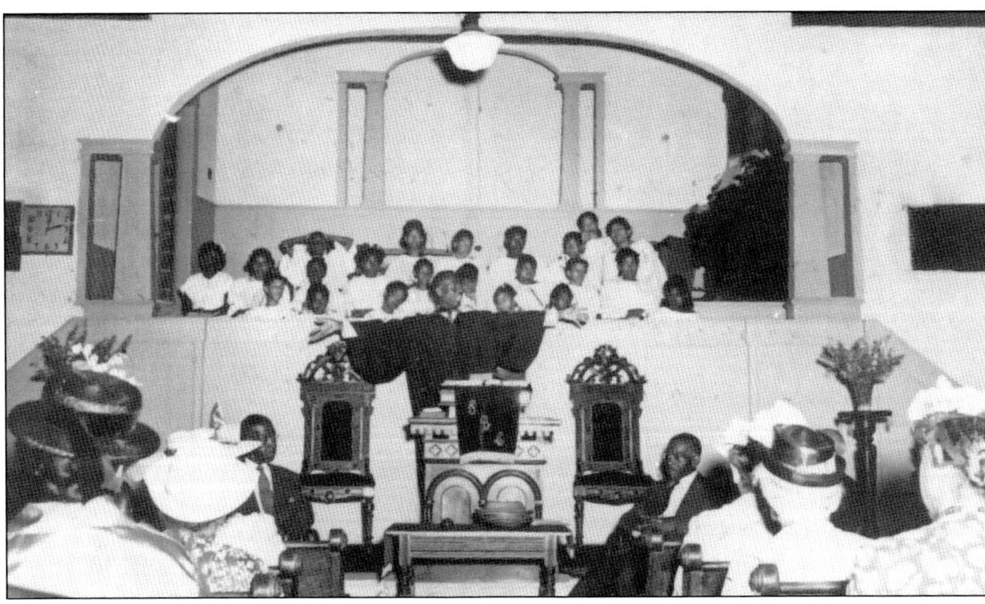

Taken in the 1940s, this photo shows Dr. Oscar B. Burson delivering a sermon at Shiloh Baptist Church in Henderson, where he was pastor from 1948 to 1963. (Courtesy of Andre D. Vann.)

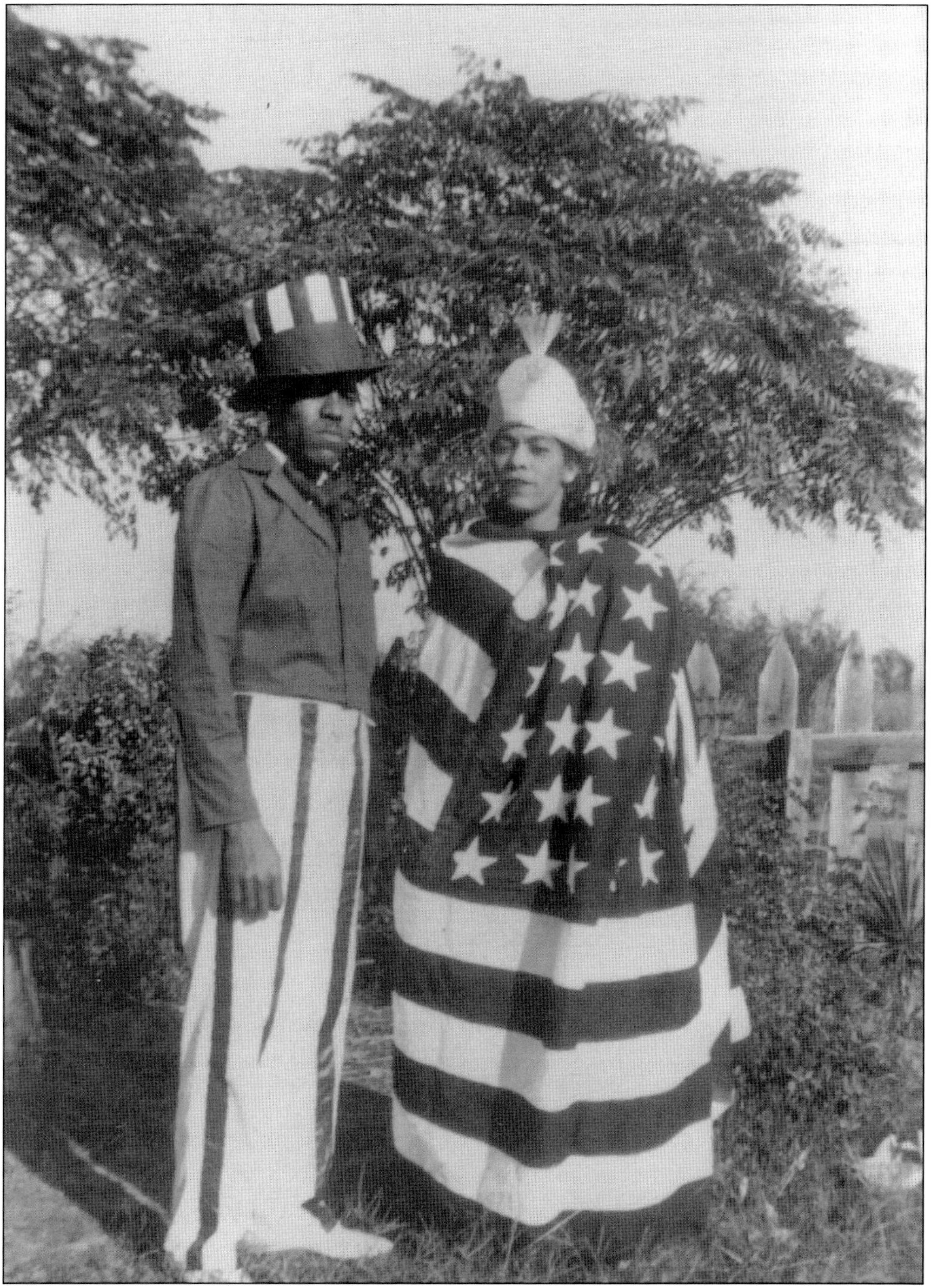

This *c*. 1948 photo is of participants in a play entitled *America* at the Shiloh Baptist Church; it was directed by Johnnie Y. Mims, who was assisted by Queen E. Davis. The participants, Asker Boyd Hawkins Sr. (left) and Carrie Hawkins Sewell Marable, are a sister-and-brother team, both members of Shiloh Baptist and educators in the Vance County School System. (Courtesy of Queen E. Davis and Andre D. Vann.)

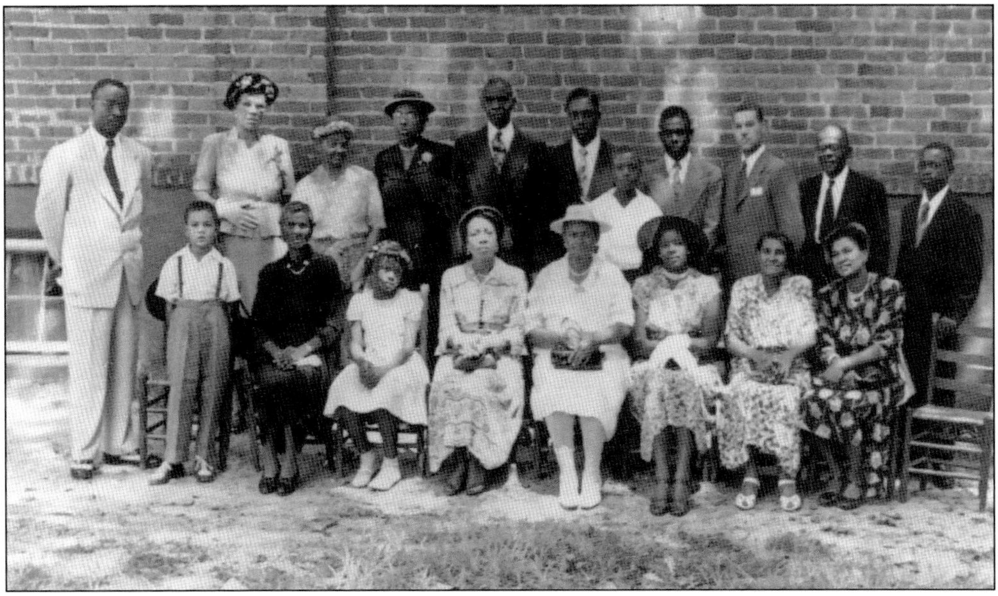

This 1950s photo shows members of the Flint Hill Club at the Shiloh Baptist Church. From left to right are as follows: (front row) Zollie Harris Jr., Lula Young, Mildred Crews, Lucile Brodie, Ozema Reid Kee, Jessie Crews, Audie Hicks, and Johnnie Young; (back row) Dr. Oscar B. Burson, Minnie Goode, Sallie P. Eaton, Josephine Yarborough, Ira Allen, Abraham Crews Jr., Melvin Crews, Irvin Crews, Zollie Harris Sr., Sam Williams, and Randolph Crews. (Courtesy of Andre D. Vann.)

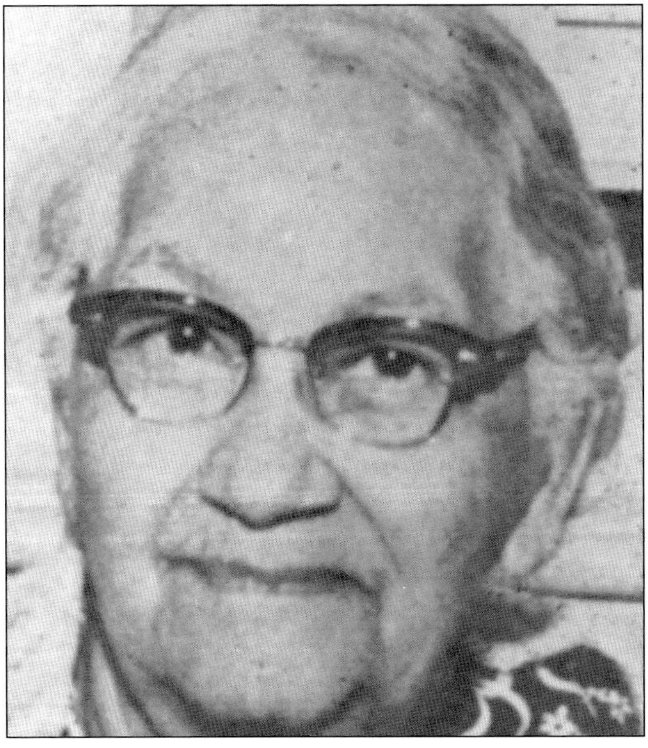

This is a 1950s photo of Sallie Walden Eaton (1875–1957), a noted local, state, and national missionary. She journeyed to Henderson and later joined the Shiloh Baptist Church, where her uncle, Dr. Richard Isaac Walden, was pastor. She married Thomas Eaton and also taught in the Vance County School System for over 36 years. For around 50 years she was a Sunday school teacher at the Shiloh Baptist Church, where she was also treasurer of the missionary circle. Upon her death in 1957 she bequeathed an annual sum to Shiloh in her will. (Courtesy of Andre D. Vann.)

Rev. Dr. Augustus Shepard (1847–1911) was born to slave parents Richard and Flora Shepard in Raleigh. In 1869, he enrolled in Shaw University, and in 1880 graduated from Shaw's Theological Department. In 1877 he assumed the pastorate of the Shiloh Baptist Church of Henderson. During this time he was appointed general Sunday school missionary and colporteur for North Carolina by the American Publication Society. He returned to the church, served from 1882 to 1887, and proposed the formation of the Colored Orphanage Association, which would go on to become the Colored Orphan Asylum of North Carolina. Shepard married Harriet Shepard and was the father of 12 children. He is interred in Beechwood Cemetery in Durham. (Courtesy of North Carolina Collection, University of North Carolina Library at Chapel Hill.)

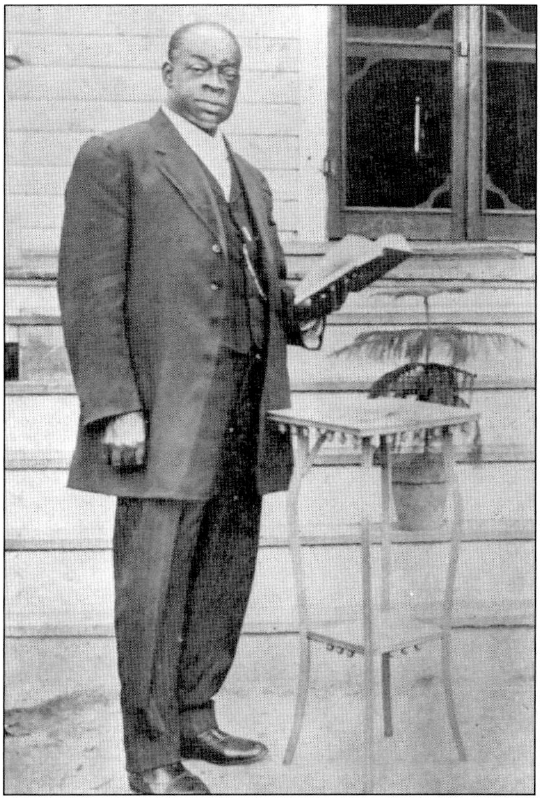

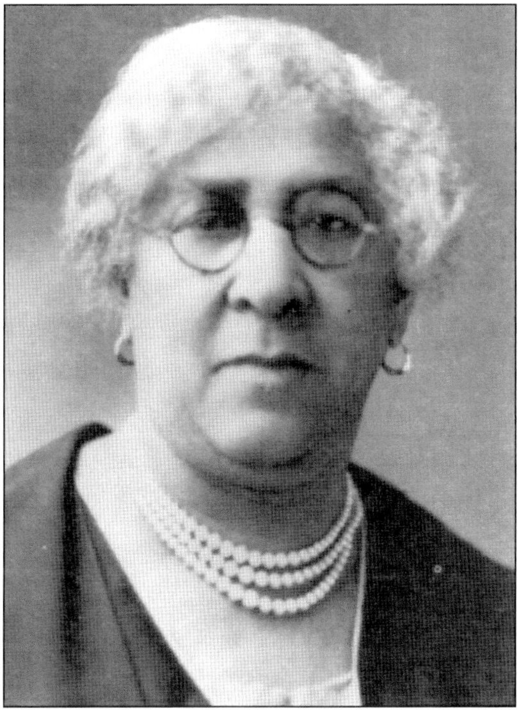

Seen here in 1940, Hattie Whitted Shepard (1858–1947) was born in Hillsborough, NC, one of the daughters of Austin Annie Whitted. She received her early training at Hampton Institute in Virginia. She worked faithfully with the missionaries in Vance County and served as president of the Woman' s Home and Foreign Missionary Convention of the State of North Carolina from 1930 to 1933. She was married to Dr. Augustus Shepard, was the mother of 12 children, and was the great-grandmother of Dr. James P. Green and Carolyn Smith Green of Henderson. (Courtesy of Andre D. Vann.)

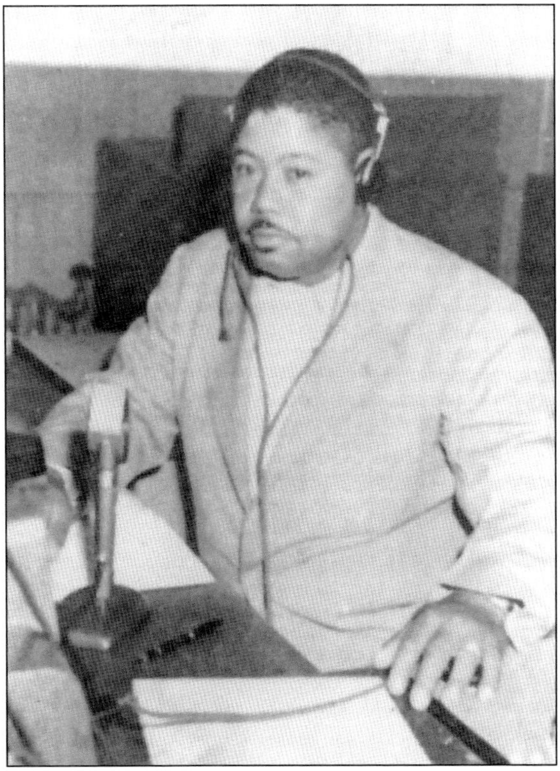

Clifford James David (1911–1976) was born in Columbus, GA, and was a World War II veteran. He later moved to Henderson and joined the Shiloh Baptist Church. In 1948, he married Margaret Gooch and became the father of Davida V. David. He joined the staff of WHNC radio and served for 26 years as the "Gospel Voice" for the station. David served as master of ceremonies for numerous church, school, and community programs. He was a Boy Scout leader and a Sunday school teacher. He was instrumental in assisting several individuals and groups in launching their careers in the gospel music industry. (Courtesy of Andre D. Vann.)

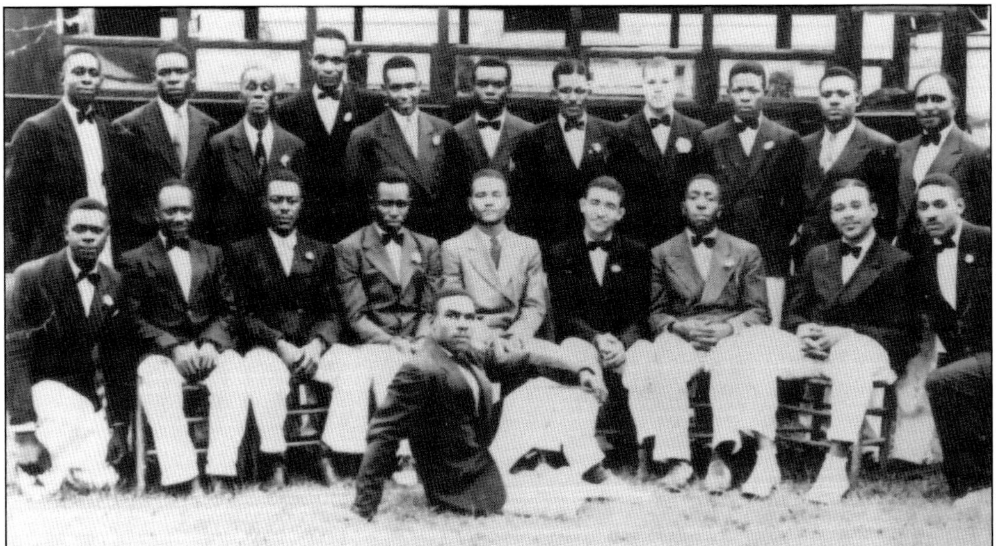

A 1943 photo shows the New Bethel Baptist Church Men's Chorus. Sitting down is David Brown, pianist and director. The others are, from left to right, as follows: (front row) E.C. Martin, Otha Lewis, Robert Cook, William Vass, Jackie E. Jones, Willie M. Grant, Joseph Nicholson, Willie M. Ramey, and Charlie Ellison; (back row) Willie Johnson, John Alston, Rev. Olandis Hicks, C.H. Brown, B. William, Vernie Carroll, Zollie Harris, L.T. Davis, Edward Davis, and Charlie Mason. (Courtesy of Bryan Solomon Simmons.)

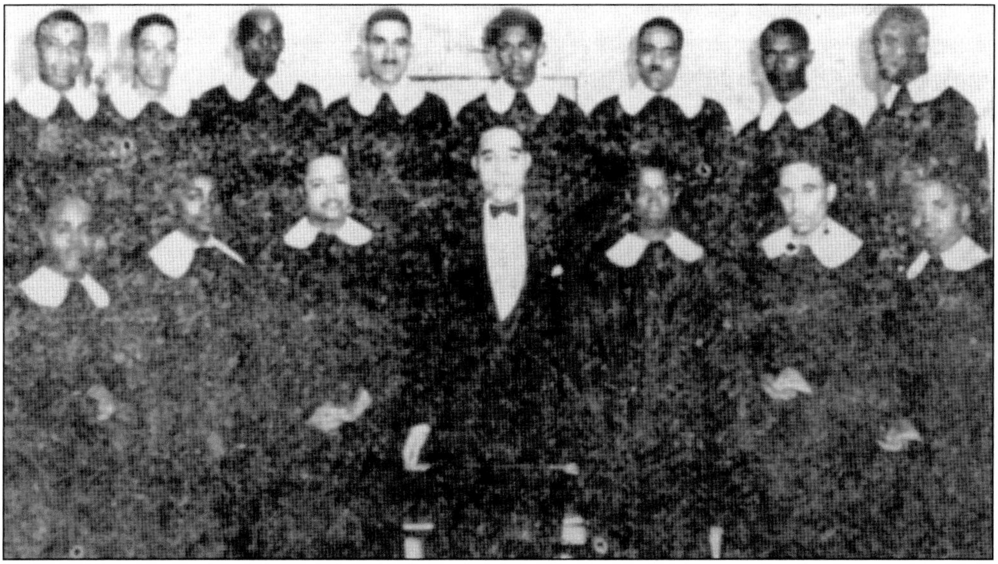

The Henderson Choral Club, seen here in the 1940s, was organized in 1939 by Dr. John Dewey Hawkins and his brothers. Hawkins is seen in the front row in the center, and his brother David Smith Hawkins is second from the right in the same row. In the back row, second from the left, is Frederick D. Hawkins; fourth from the left is Phillip A. Hawkins; third from the right is Asker B. Hawkins; and last in the same row is Herman A. Morrison, noted mortician and civic leader. (Courtesy of Andre D. Vann.)

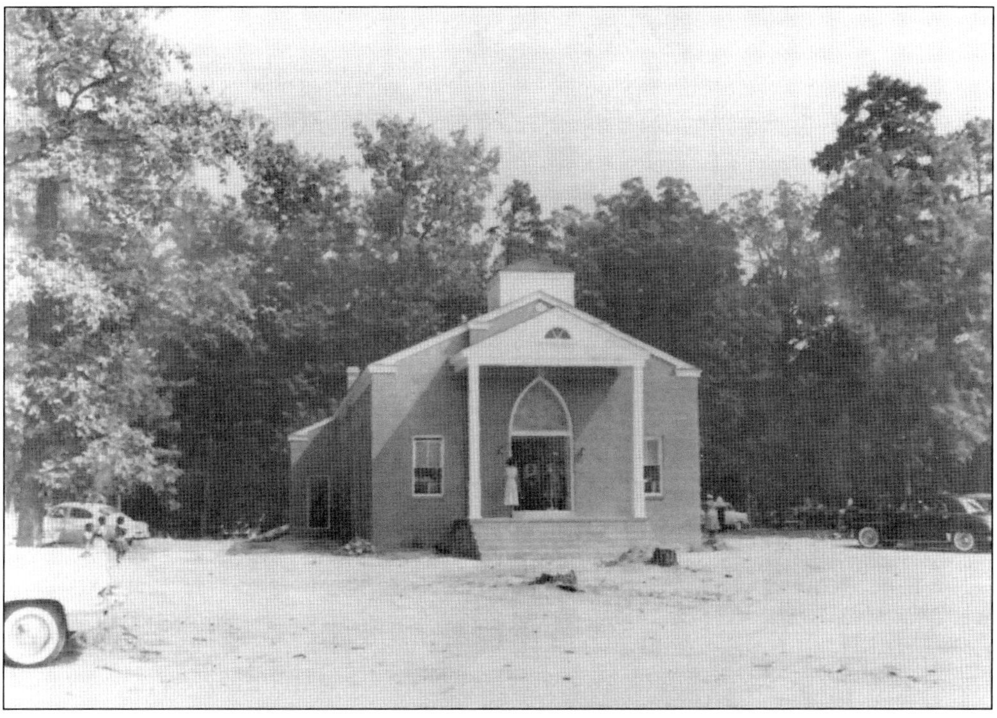

This is a 1940 photo of the Flat Creek Baptist Church of Williamsboro, begun in 1866 and named for the Flat Creek stream near the church. (Courtesy of Andre D. Vann.)

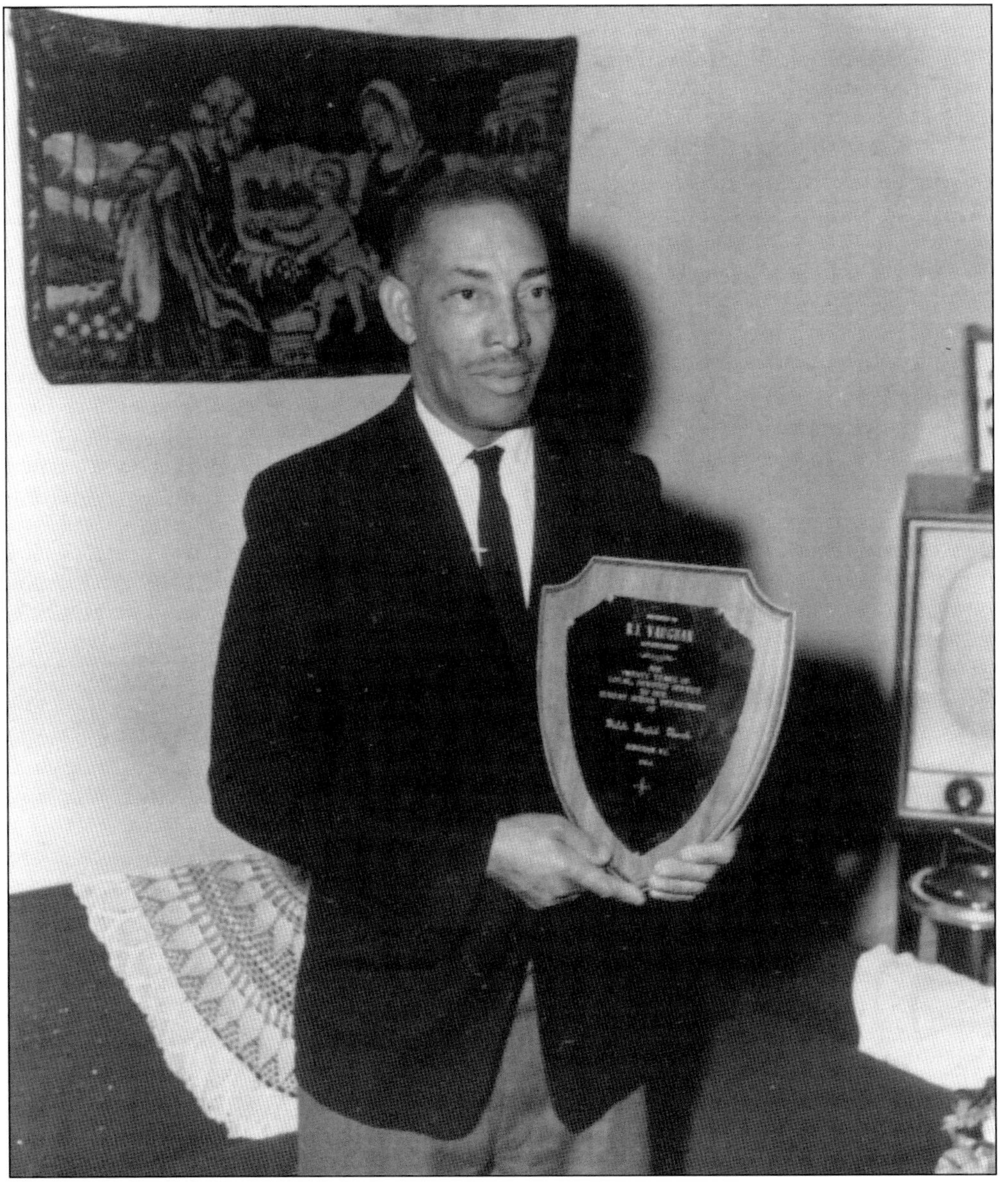

Richard Isaac Vaughan Sr., a resident of 611 East Winder Street, was a longtime community activist, churchman, businessman, and leader. He was a native of Vance County and the son of Deacon John D. and Gertrude Cooke Vaughan. He graduated from Henderson Institute and attended Shaw University, majoring in theology and education. He served as a school counselor in the recreation department of the Central Colored Graded School in Henderson. An entrepreneur, he later became self-employed for over 40 years as a painter and contractor. Vaughan was a member of the Vance County NAACP, the Democratic Club, and East Henderson Precinct No. 1. He was among the early black candidates for public office in Vance County. He was married to Tessie Bobbit Vaughan, and the father of Gertrude Dickerson, Barbara R. Vaughan, Laura Stokes, Linda Williams, Richard I., David S., and Samuel E. Vaughan. He is interred in the Vaughan plot in Blacknall Cemetery. (Courtesy of Tessie Bobbit Vaughan.)

Rev. Arthur Poole (1898–1987), a resident of Patton Circle, attended Kittrell College and received his A.B. degree at United Christian College. He and his wife moved to Henderson on July 4, 1919, and in 1922 joined the Shiloh Baptist Church. Soon after, he joined Holy Temple Church, where he served as associate pastor. After seeing a need for a transportation system in Henderson, he formed, owned, and operated Poole Cab Company for over 41 years; the cabs still bear his name. Poole was a charter member and past president of the Vance County NAACP, and was named "Man of the Year" by Omega Psi Phi fraternity, Inc. in 1957. He was married first to Harriet Debnam, and in 1972, he married Rosa Williams. He was the father of Oriel Poole Dillard. He is interred in the Union Grove Baptist Church Cemetery, Warren County, NC. (Courtesy of Rosa Williams Poole.)

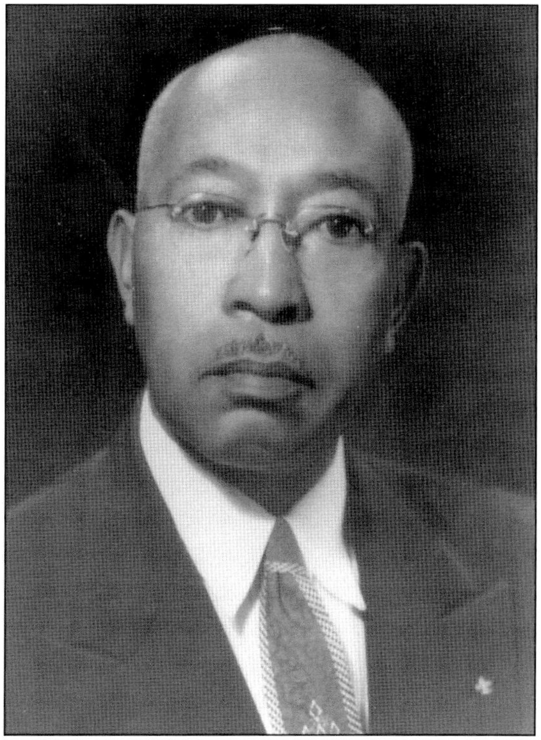

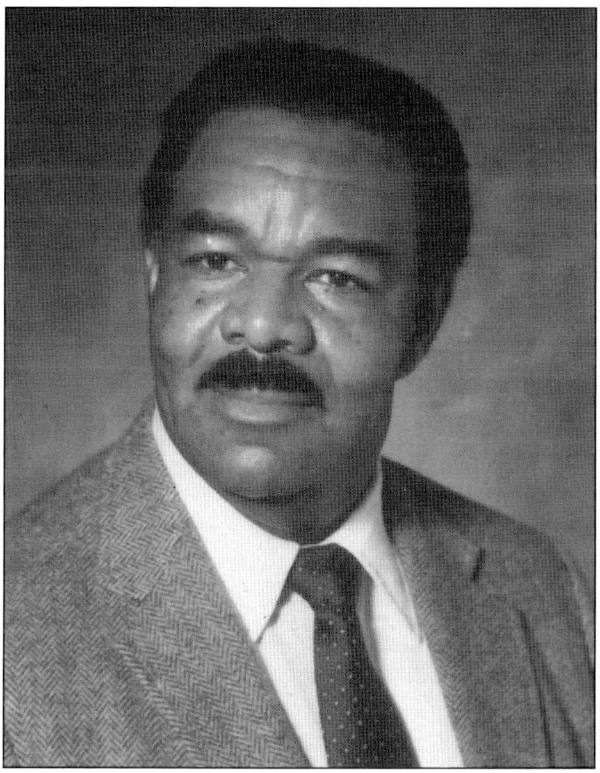

Rev. Roosevelt Alston, a native of Wilson County, graduated from Springfield High School and received a B.S. degree in theology and religion at Shaw University and an M.A. degree from North Carolina Central University. He received an honorary doctor of divinity degree from the James E. Teacher School of Religion. He taught for 36 years in Wilson and Warren Counties. He has been pastor of the Holy Temple United Holy Church since 1951 and serves as a general elder and trustee for the United Holy Church of America. Alston is married to Valeria Alston, and they are the parents of three children. (Courtesy of Valeria Alston.)

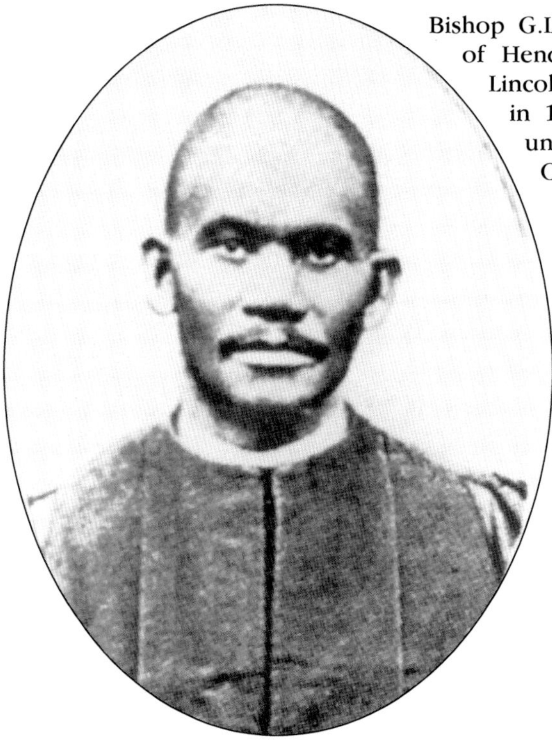

Bishop G.L. Blackwell (1861–1926) was a native of Henderson and a graduate of HNII and Lincoln University. He was elected a bishop in 1908 of the AMEZ Church and served until his death in 1926. (Courtesy of AMEZ Church Archives.)

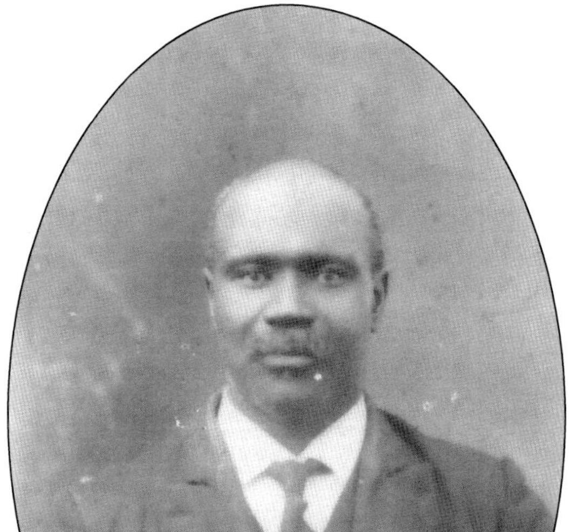

Rev. Thomas B. Hicks (1862–1920) was the son of Chainey Hicks, who was born on an African slave ship in the early 1820s en route to the Americas. Reverend Hicks attended the Boydton Institute and taught and preached in Vance County. He was married to Hattie Sommerville Hicks and was the father of Ethel C.R. Smith, Alma R. Faison, and Rosa Lillian Hicks, as well as eight other children from a previous marriage. He was a Mason and pastor of several churches in Granville County—including the Huntsville Church, Olive Grove Baptist, and Davis Chapel in Stovall—for 29 years. He also served as pastor of the Aberdeen Church in Aberdeen, NC, and the First Calvary Baptist Church in Durham, NC. (Courtesy of Ethel C.R. Smith.)

Rev. Frank Draper Brown (1902–1977), a native of Randolph County, was an ordained minister of Baptist churches for 55 years. He served as pastor of eight different churches and was pastor of the Concord Baptist Church in Kittrell at the time of his death. He is interred in the Beechwood Cemetery in Durham. (Courtesy of Andre D. Vann.)

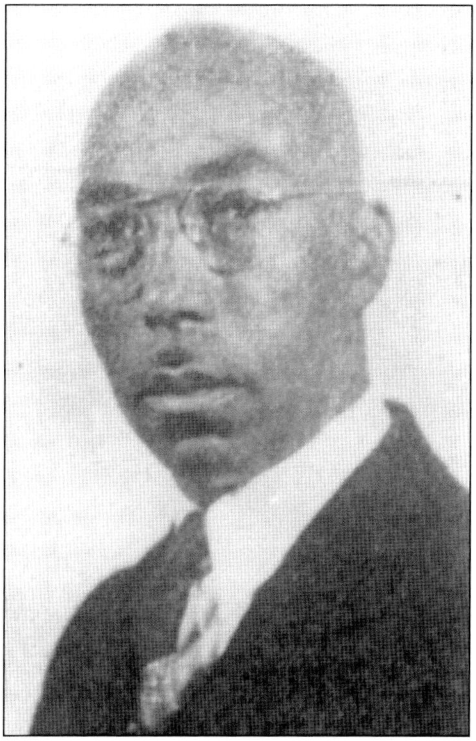

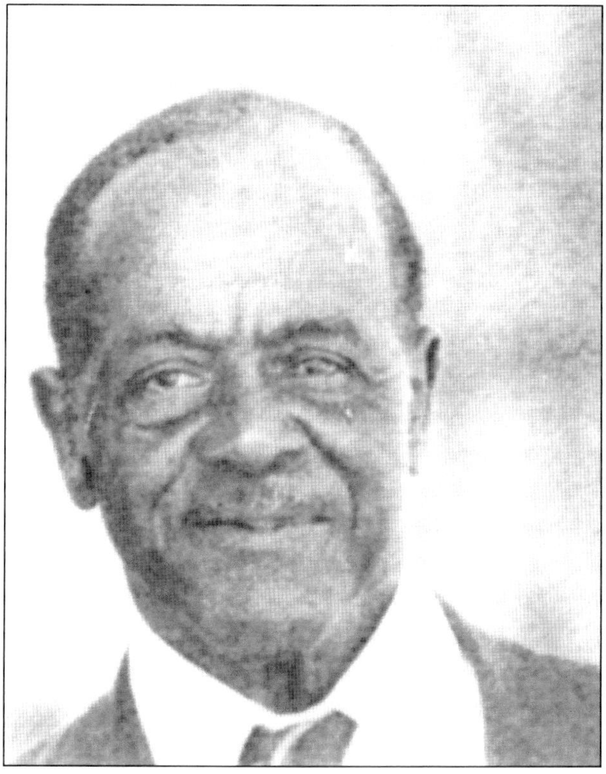

Rev. James Arthur Watson (1906–1977) a native of Warren County, accepted the call into the ministry at the age of 18. He received the bachelor of theology degree from Kittrell College and continued his studies at Shaw University and Hampton Institute in Virginia. He was pastor of several churches and was a member of the Middle Baptist Association, the Shiloh Association, and the Vance County Ministerial Alliance. He was married to Hattie Hunt and had two sons, John and Harold. Watson is interred in Allen Chapel Church Cemetery. (Courtesy of Andre D. Vann.)

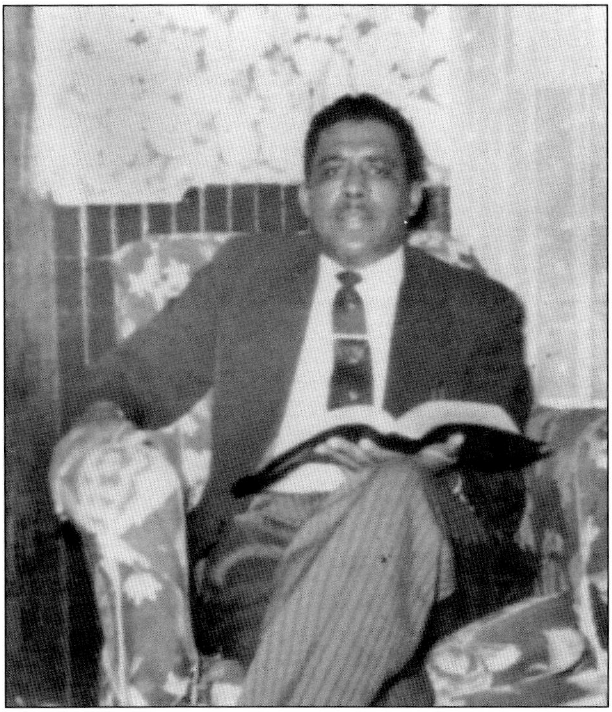

Rev. James Frank Ashe (1911–1960) was a native of Vance County and the son of James R. and Susie Roberts Ashe. He was educated in the local schools and was also an employee of the Carolina Bagging Mill. He served as a pastor of both the Goshen and Mountain Springs Baptist Churches in Granville County. For over 25 years he performed numerous weddings in Mobile, Henderson, and surrounding areas. He was married to Elnora McKnight Ashe and was the father of James, Minnie R., Alice, Mary, Ethel, Johnny, and Susie Ashe. He is interred in the Welcome Chapel Baptist Church. (Courtesy of Johnny Ashe.)

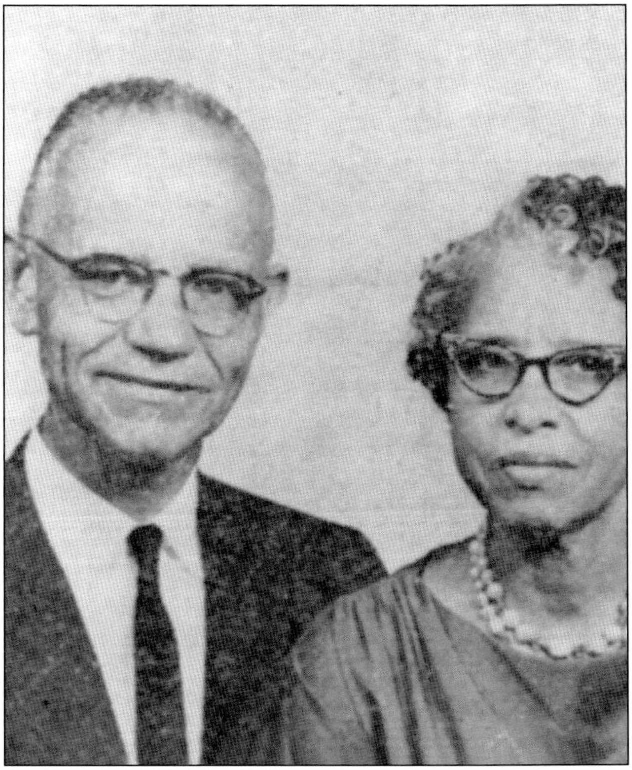

Dr. John Riley Dungee Jr. and his wife, Alethia, are pictured in the 1960s. He journeyed to Henderson in the 1930s to serve as minister of the Townsville United Presbyterian Church, the assistant minister of the United Presbyterian Church of Henderson, and as the instructor of Bible and history at HI from 1936 to 1942. In 1942 he was commissioned as chaplain in the Army. He returned with the rank of captain in 1946. From 1946 to 1968 he served as minister of the United Presbyterian Church of Henderson, now known as the Cotton Memorial Presbyterian Church. Alethia Anderson taught for 38 years in South Carolina and Vance County. (Courtesy of Andre D. Vann.)

Rev. Dr. Roland W. Perry (1924–1997) was a native of Sanford, NC, attended the Chatham County Schools, and graduated from Shaw University. Dr. Perry served as pastor of Shiloh Baptist Church of Henderson for 23 years. He was moderator of the original Shiloh Association, president of the Vance and Adjacent Counties Ministerial Alliance, chairman of the Vance County Health Care Coalition, chairman of the Henderson-Vance Human Relations Commission, and a member of the NAACP. He was married to Doris Perry and was the father of Tywanna Perry, Beverly West, Teresa Rainey, Michael Perry, Roland W. Perry II, Dexter Perry, and Gregory Perry. He is interred in Pittsboro, NC. (Courtesy of Andre D. Vann.)

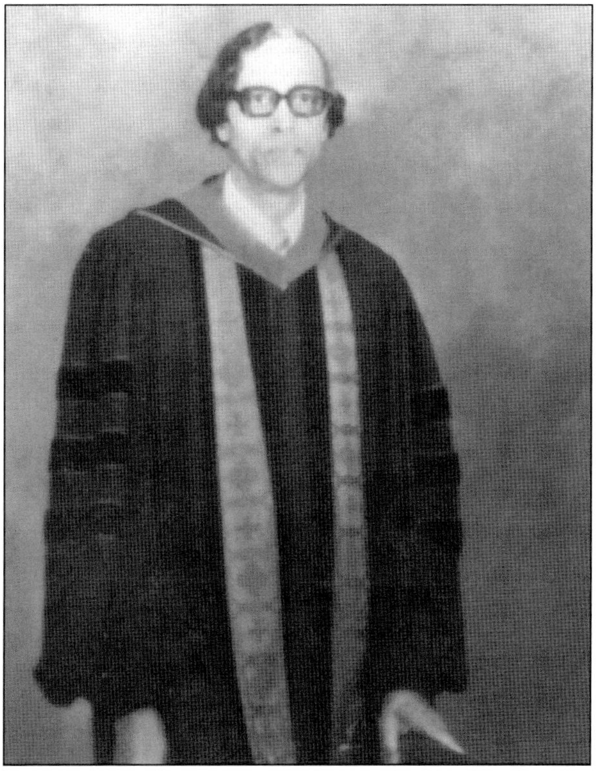

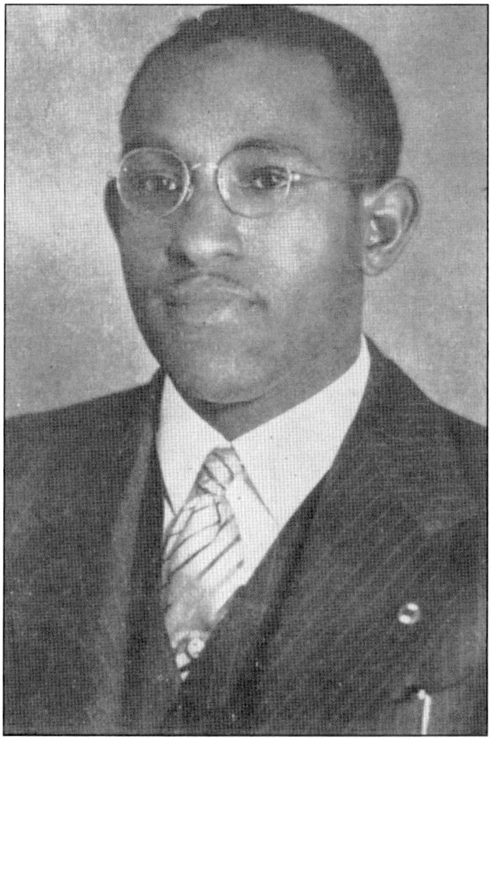

This is a 1940s photo of Rev. Simon Peter Cooke (1905–1991), the son of William Haywood and Kayte Harris Cooke. He received his high school training at Henderson Institute, and further studied at Kittrell College and Virginia Union University in Richmond, VA. He was a licensed barber with 65 years of experience and a minister with over 50 years of service in the Central North Carolina Conference of the A.M.E.Z. Church. Among the churches in Vance County where he served as pastor were Taylor' s Chapel, Kesler Temple, and Cooke's Chapel. He was married to Elvira B. Cooke and was the father of Rebecca C. Hunt. Cooke's Chapel, which is named in his honor, was built on the outskirts of Mobile in 1927, with Rev. S.P. Cooke as pastor and James Reed as trustee of the church. The church was rebuilt in 1962 and is still in operation in the Vance County community. Reverend Cooke is interred in the Ilong Baptist Church Cemetery. (Courtesy of Rebecca C. Hunt.)

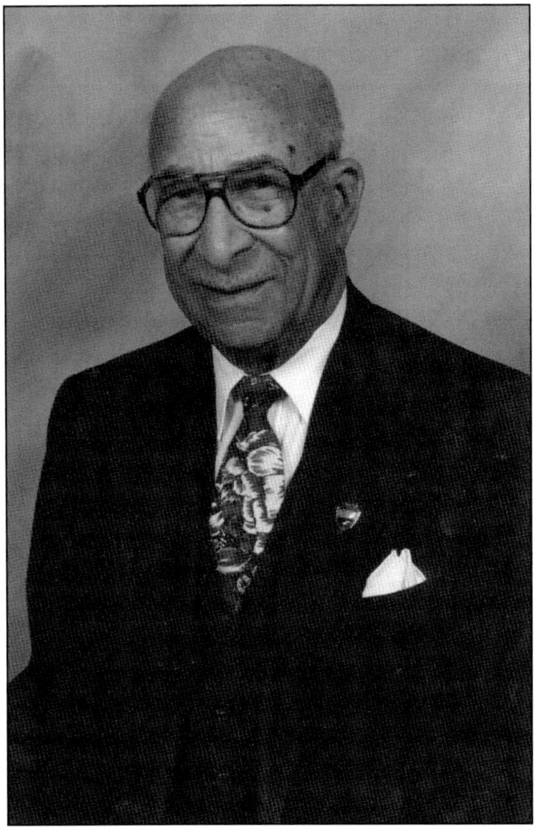

Rev. Clifton Lee Faison (1903–1999), a native of Seaboard, NC, migrated to Henderson in the 1930s. He graduated from Shaw University and Shaw Divinity School in Raleigh in 1937. He taught for a number of years in both Vance and Warren County schools. During his lifetime, he served as pastor of Edward's Grove Baptist Church in Warrenton, the First Baptist Church of Louisburg, St. John Baptist Church of Middleburg, and the Warrenton Baptist Church. He held active membership in the NAACP, the Vance County Human Relations Committee, the United Shiloh Association, and was a member of the Shiloh Baptist Church of Henderson for over 25 years. Faison was known for reciting poetry and had a great passion for black history. He is long remembered for his famous quote "Go slow so you can go some more; If you go too fast, you may not last." He was married to Susie L. Joyner for over 60 years and was the father of Brenda G. Faison. He is interred in Garysburg, NC. (Courtesy of Sophia Russell Ramey.)

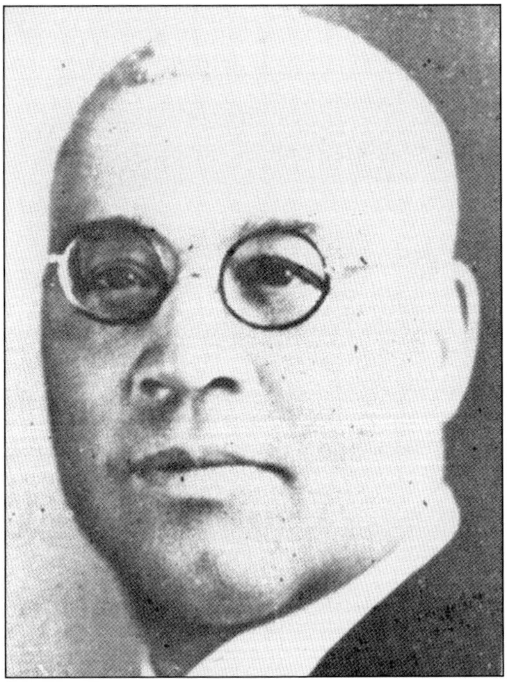

Dr. Oscar Sidney Bullock (1878–1966) was born in Vance County, the son of Horace and Emma Bullock, and received his early training at Henderson Normal School and Lincoln University, PA. He served as pastor of the Brookston Baptist Church for a number of years. His early professional career was spent as a mathematics teacher in High Point, NC. From 1921 to 1958 he served as pastor of the First Baptist Church in Raleigh. He also was an early executive with the General Baptist State Convention. On the national level, he was president of the Lott Carey Baptist Foreign Missionary Convention and traveled extensively in Africa. In Liberia, Africa, there is a building named in his honor as a result of his mission activities. He was married to Mahelia M. Bullock and was the father of Nancy B. McGhee. (Courtesy of Andre D. Vann.)

Five

Black Leadership

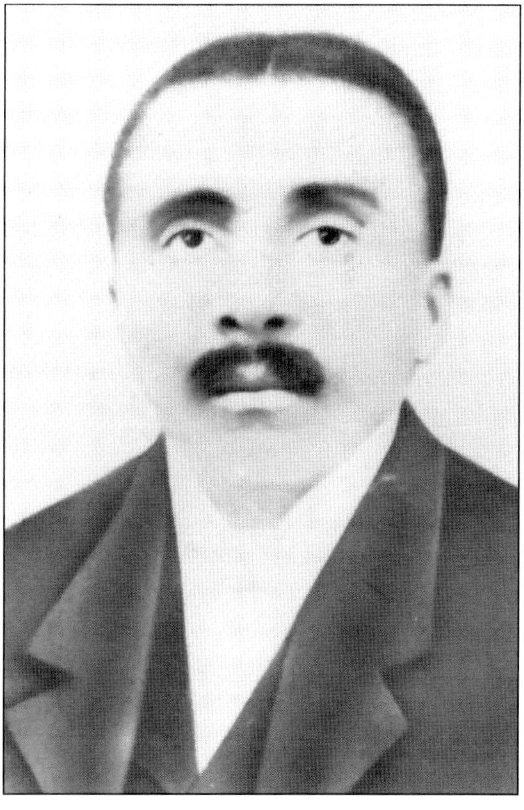

David Brame (1855–1943) born a slave in what is today Vance County and was freed at the age of 16 by his master. He was hired out to a white man for $5 a month, and he used this money to pay a school teacher to teach him to read and write. In the county he held many offices before a constitutional amendment disfranchised blacks in the state. As a Republican he ran for the state legislature and was defeated by only two votes in the general election. He owned a farm and a great deal of land, was married to Jennie Brame for 62 years, and reared a family of 10 children. (Courtesy of Andre D. Vann.)

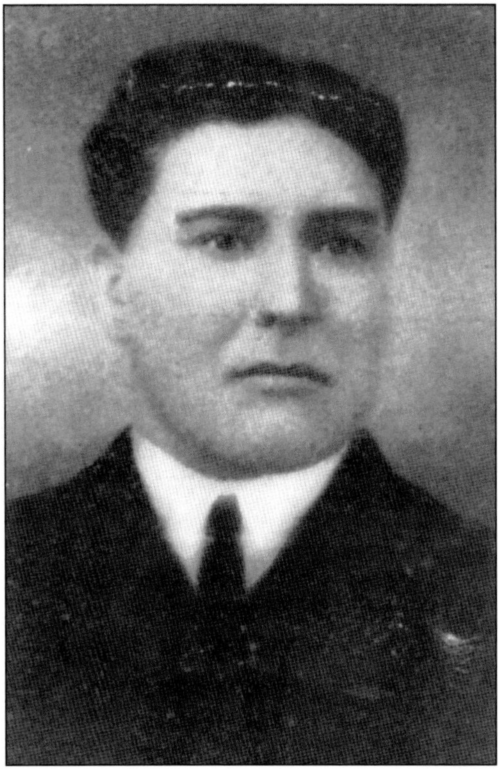

Henry Plummer Cheatham (1857–1935) was born the son of a slave on a plantation near Henderson. He attended Shaw University and graduated in 1883. In 1884, he was elected register of deeds of Vance County on the Republican ticket, where he earned the respect of both black and white citizens. He was elected to Congress from the Second Congressional District, served in the House of Representatives from 1889 to 1893, and in the 52nd Congress he was the sole black member representing the plight of blacks and rural whites. While in Congress he amassed a great deal of land tracts in Vance and Warren Counties, and purchased land in Washington, D.C. In 1901 he returned to North Carolina and eventually led the Colored Orphan Asylum from 1907 until his death in 1935. He was married to Louise Cherry; after her death, he married Laura Joyner. There was a total of five children born to these unions. (Courtesy of NC Division of Archives and History.)

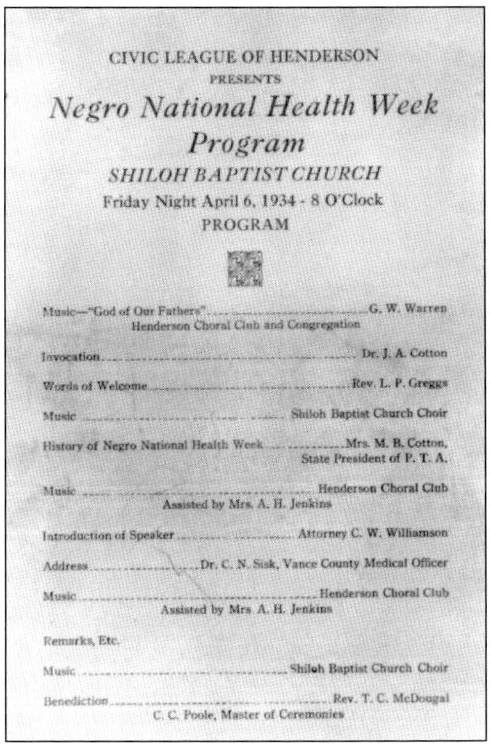

CIVIC LEAGUE OF HENDERSON
PRESENTS
Negro National Health Week
Program
SHILOH BAPTIST CHURCH
Friday Night April 6, 1934 - 8 O'Clock
PROGRAM

Music—"God of Our Fathers" .... G. W. Warren
Henderson Choral Club and Congregation

Invocation .... Dr. J. A. Cotton

Words of Welcome .... Rev. L. P. Greggs

Music .... Shiloh Baptist Church Choir

History of Negro National Health Week .... Mrs. M. B. Cotton, State President of P. T. A.

Music .... Henderson Choral Club
Assisted by Mrs. A. H. Jenkins

Introduction of Speaker .... Attorney C. W. Williamson

Address .... Dr. C. N. Sisk, Vance County Medical Officer

Music .... Henderson Choral Club
Assisted by Mrs A. H. Jenkins

Remarks, Etc.

Music .... Shiloh Baptist Church Choir

Benediction .... Rev. T. C. McDougal
C. C. Poole, Master of Ceremonies

This early 1930s program, "Negro National Health Week," was hosted by the Civic League of Henderson at the Shiloh Baptist Church. (Courtesy of Andre D. Vann.)

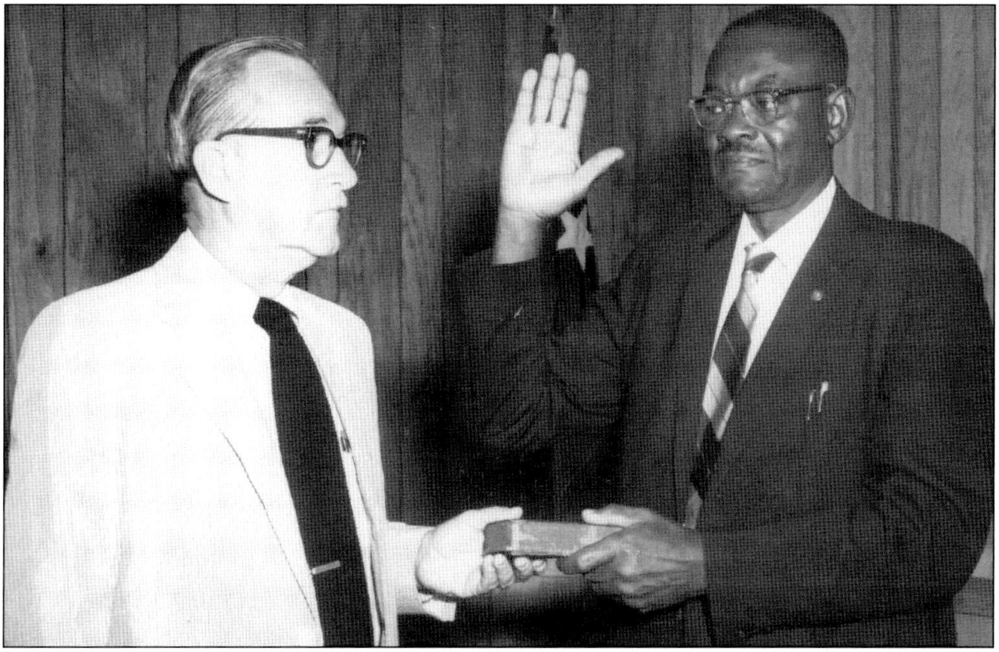

On September 1, 1971, David L. Mims (1908–1979) took the oath of office as the first black alderman in Vance County history. He was a member of the Henderson City Council, where he was named to several work areas, including the journal, cemetery, recreation, and water and sewer committees. He later served as a member of the Henderson City Planning Board. Mims was an executive with the NC Mutual Life Insurance Company. He was married to Johnnie Y. Mims, a Vance County educator and music leader. (Courtesy of Henderson *Daily Dispatch*.)

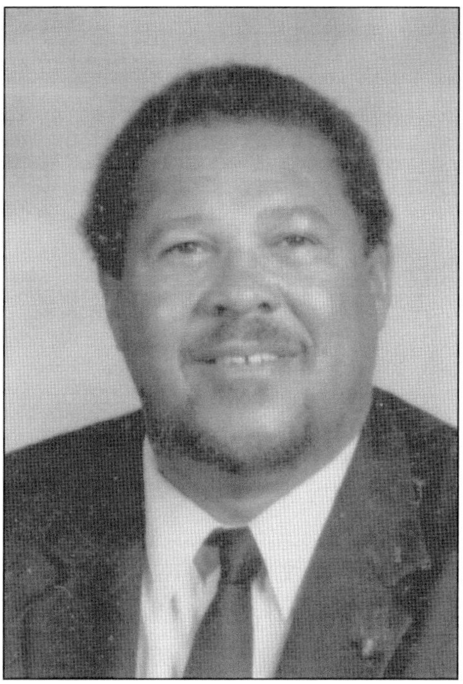

Emeron J. Cash Sr., a resident of 1220 Alpha Street, is a native of Granville County. He served as a teacher and coach in Granville County and at the former Henderson Institute from 1964 to 1967. He then taught at the Pinkston Street School before returning to the Henderson Institute ninth grade campus. In 1973 joined the faculty at Henderson Junior High School (presently Henderson Middle School) where he taught and coached until 1988. Cash retired in 1991 after 31 years of service and then opened the first commercial driving school in Vance County. He was elected to the Vance County Board of Education in 1992 and was recently reelected to a third term on the board. He is married to Patrica Parker Cash, a retired educator and school counselor, and they are the parents of Emeron Jr., Christopher, and Candy Cash. They are members of the Shiloh Baptist Church. (Courtesy of Emeron and Patricia Cash.)

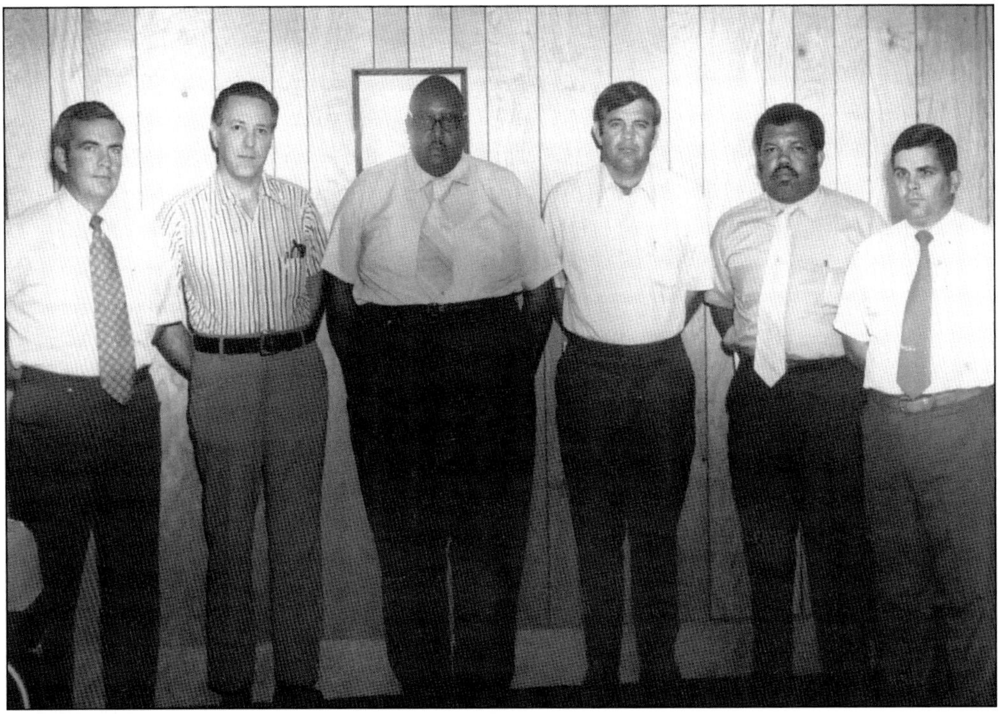

This is a 1971 photo of members of the Henderson-Vance Parks and Recreation Commission, with two black members representing the interests of the black population. They include James E. Wilson (middle) and Lonnie Davis (second from right), now a member of the Henderson City Council. (Courtesy of Henderson *Daily Dispatch*.)

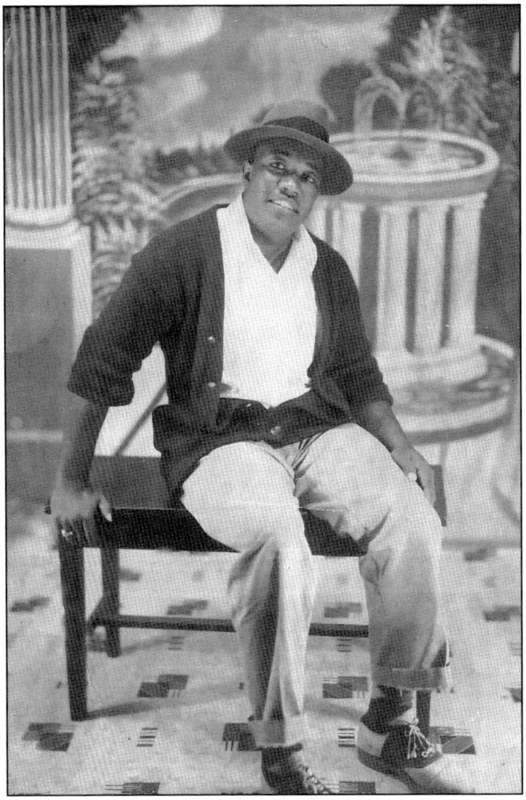

Jesse J. Butler, a native of Clinton, NC, is seen in this 1940s photo. He attended E.E. Smith High School, Fayetteville State University, St. Augustine College, and North Carolina Central University. He was instrumental in such organizations as the Assembly of Vance, Black Caucus, NAACP, and the Gateway Community Development Corporation and Credit Union. A member of the Vance Elks Lodge #1263 and the Cotton Memorial Presbyterian Church, Butler was married to Virginia Dare Knight Butler. He is interred in Elmwood Cemetery in Henderson. (Courtesy of Virginia K. Butler.)

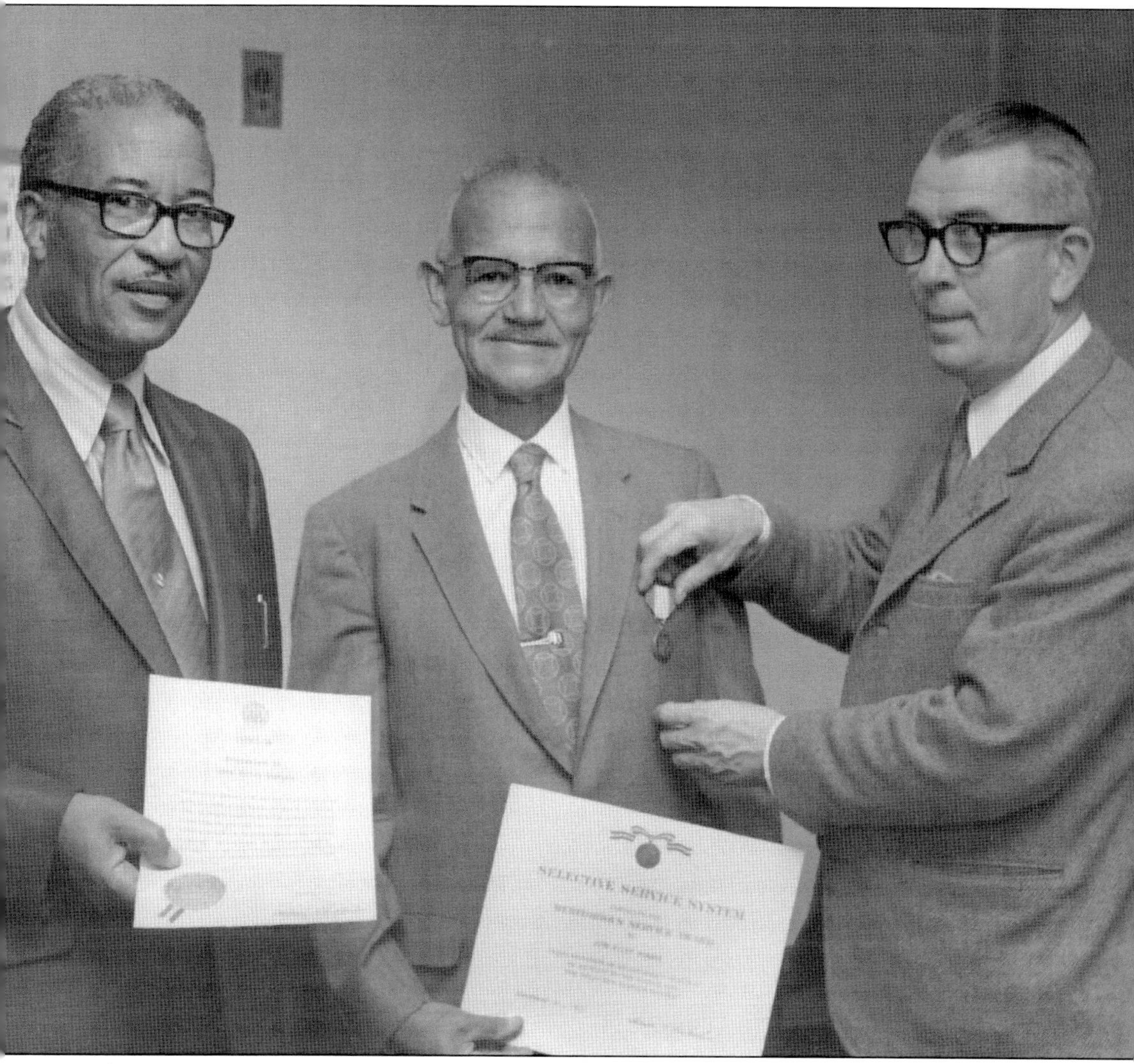

Dr. John Riley Dungee, eminent pastor and civic leader, was commended in 1972 with a Meritorious Service Award from the Selective Service System. To the extreme left of the photo is Allen Williams, a noted businessman, mortician, and the first black member of the Vance County Technical Institute (the forerunner of Vance Granville Community College). (Courtesy of Henderson *Daily Dispatch*.)

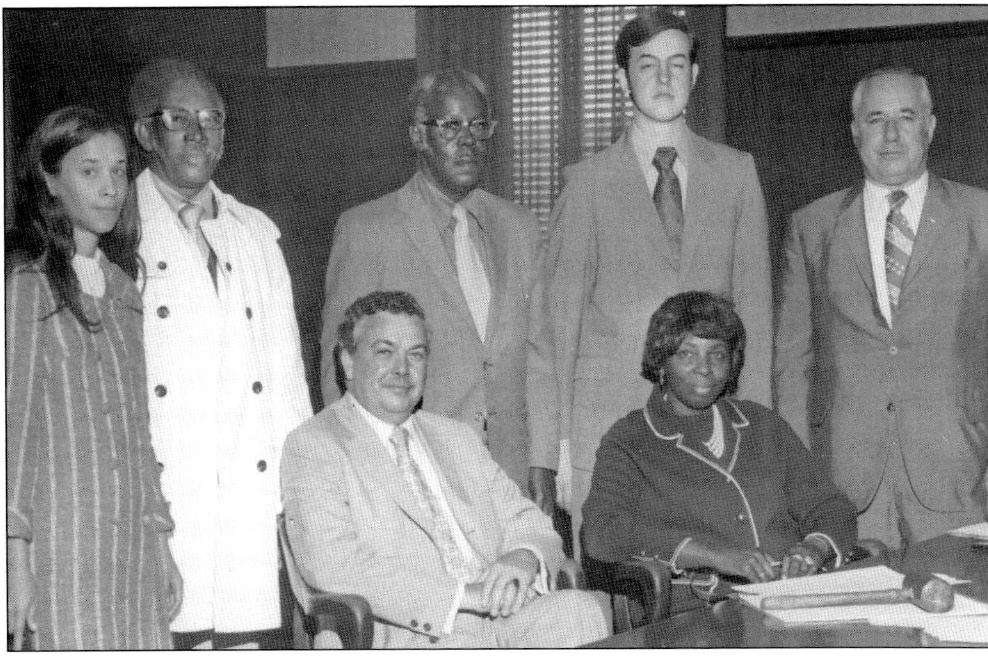

This is a 1972 photo of the Vance County Executive Committee Officers. Seated in the front row is Mary Bing Hawkins; standing second from the left is Richard I. Vaughan Sr. (1913–1990); and in the center is Leo McPherson Hatton (1912–1979). (Courtesy of Henderson *Daily Dispatch*.)

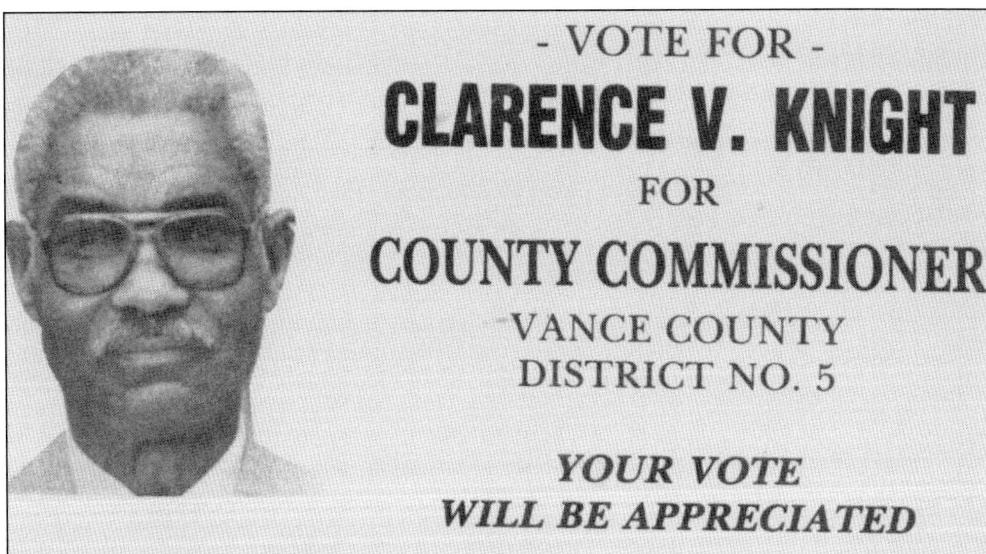

Clarence V. Knight (1919–) was successful in his campaign as county commissioner for district number five. He and Terry Garrison were the first two black county commissioners in the history of Vance County. Knight was elected in 1988 and served continuously until his term expired in 2000. A retired educator, Knight is a member of the NAACP, Masons, Order of the Eastern Star, Black Leadership Caucus, and the Beacon Light Housing Project. (Courtesy of Clarence V. Knight.)

This 1940s campaign literature was used by prominent dentist Dr. John Dewey Hawkins in his attempt to become alderman of the fourth ward in the city of Henderson. He was an active member of the Elks, Shriners, Masons, and Boy Scouts, a trustee of Shiloh Baptist Church, and a trustee of Palmer Memorial Institute in Sedalia, NC. Although he was unsuccessful in his bid, he did lay the groundwork for the election of competent black elected officials in the county. (Courtesy of Andre D. Vann.)

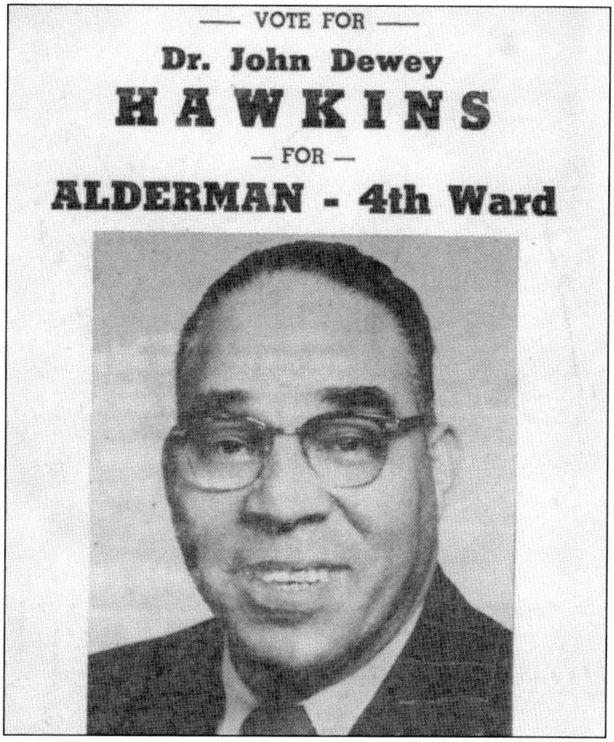

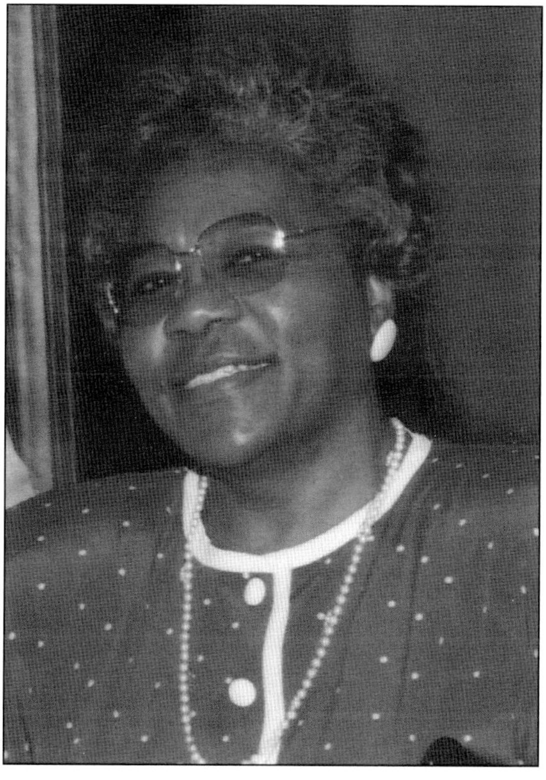

Margaret Ellis received her early education in the Franklin and Vance County Schools and an associate degree in criminal justice from Vance Granville Community College. In the 1970s she served as director of the Assembly of Vance, organizing every precinct in the county to address problems affecting African Americans. As a result she helped to substantially increase the number of registered voters in the county. Also, she was an advocate for black representation and gender equality on the board of the Maria Parham Hospital. She served as past president of the local NAACP chapter and currently serves as the vice chair of the Vance County Board of Education. A licensed disc jockey and gospel director for WIZS, she attends the Union Grove United Church of Christ. She is the mother of Michael, Curtis, Eddie ,and Carolyn Ellis. (Courtesy of Margaret Ellis.)

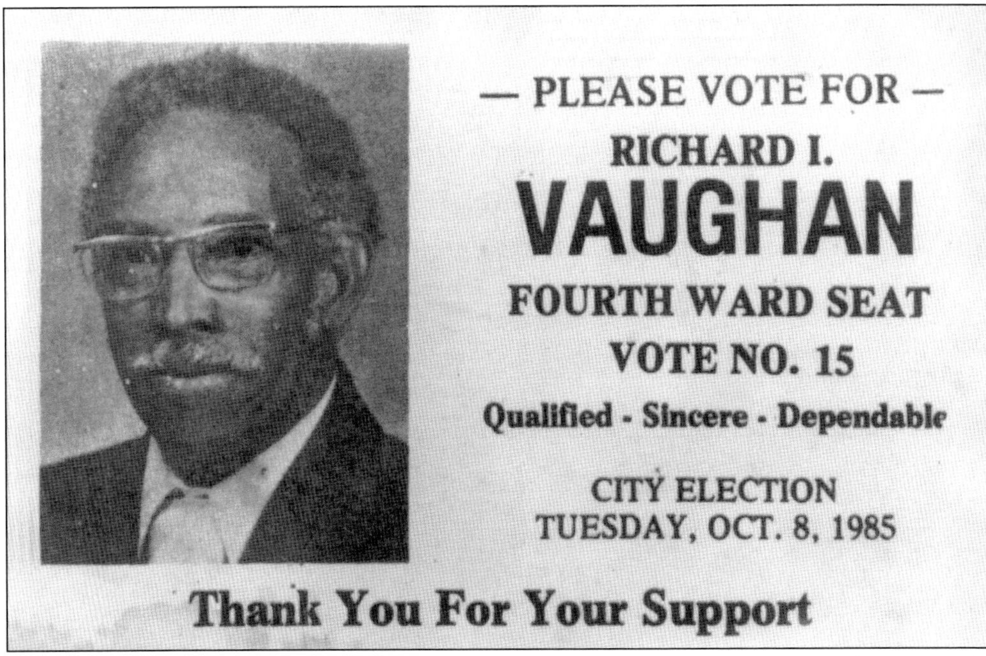

This campaign literature was used by prominent civic leader Richard I. Vaughan Sr. as he attempted to run for the fourth ward city council seat in 1985. Although he was unsuccessful in his attempt he still remained active in the political process, and served as a precinct captain until his death. (Courtesy of Tessie Bobbit Vaughan.)

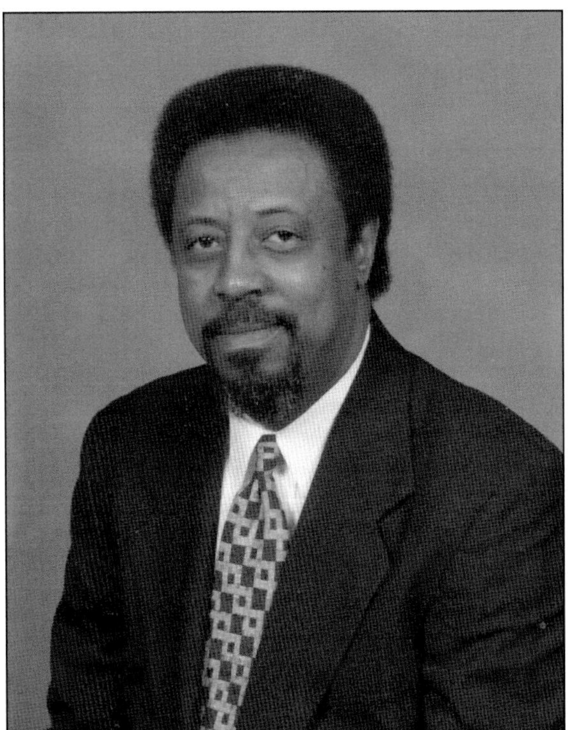

Attorney Randolph Baskerville, son of Charlie and Sallie Baskerville, is a native of Vance County and graduated from Middleburg High School in 1967. He graduated from Fayetteville State University in 1971, and received his law degree in 1976 from NC Central University. He was a practicing attorney in Henderson prior to becoming the first African-American assistant district attorney in the ninth judicial district from 1979 to 1985. Also, he was the first African American to serve on the local board of directors of North Carolina National Bank in Henderson, from 1985 to 1994. Currently he is in private practice in Henderson. (Courtesy of Randolph Baskerville.)

Dr. James Preston Green (1925–), a native of Vance County, was the son of William and Annie Henderson Green. He graduated from HI in 1944, Johnson C. Smith College in Charlotte in 1948, and received a medical degree from Meharry Medical College in Nashville, TN. After his residency he came to Henderson, where he has been in continuous practice since 1960. He established the Beckford Medical Center, served eight years on the Henderson City Council, and served from 1993 to 1995 as a member of the North Carolina House of Representatives. His maternal grandfather, William B. Henderson Sr., was a senator representing Vance and Warren Counties from 1896 until 1900. An entrepreneur, Green was also a founder and co-owner of Pine Crest Manor Nursing and Rest Home and Green Acres Terrace housing complex, all in Henderson. He is married to Carolyn Smith Green of New Bern, NC. (Courtesy of Carolyn G. Boone.)

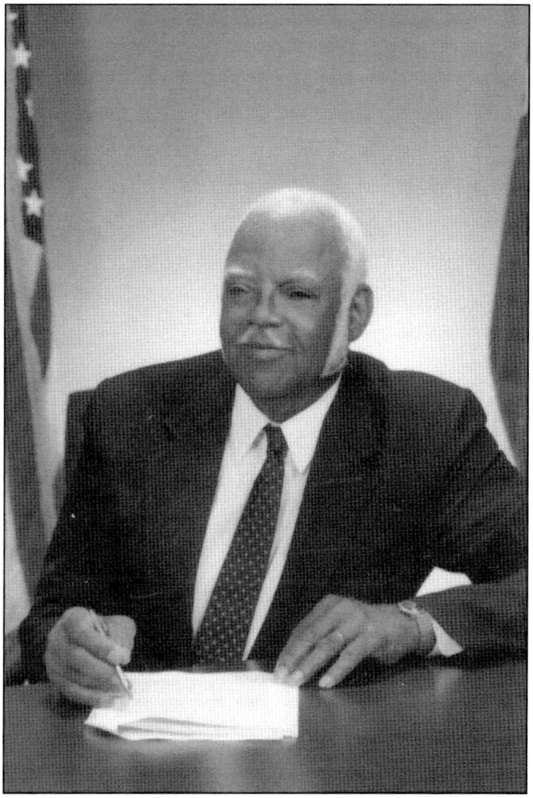

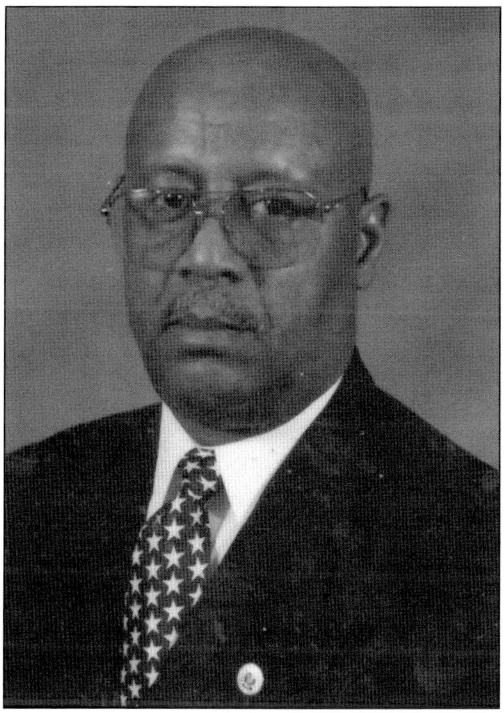

Ernest Carlton Terry (1948–) was born on Horner Street on the West End, the son of Raymond and Ethel Boyd Terry. He attended Eaton-Johnson Elementary School and graduated in 1966 from HNII. He entered Saint Augustine's College in Raleigh, NC, joined the Marine Corps, and served in Vietnam. He returned to Henderson and was among one of the early blacks to integrate the Henderson Police Department. He later attended Gupton-Jones Mortuary College and was employed by Garnes Funeral Home. He established Terry's Funeral Service and became active in civic affairs in Henderson. In 1992, he was elected to the Henderson City Council as alderman of ward one, and presently serves as a Henderson City Councilman. He was married to Costelle B. Terry and is the father of Enesa C. Terry. He is a member of the Kesler Temple AMEZ church and numerous civic groups. (Courtesy of Ernest C. Terry.)

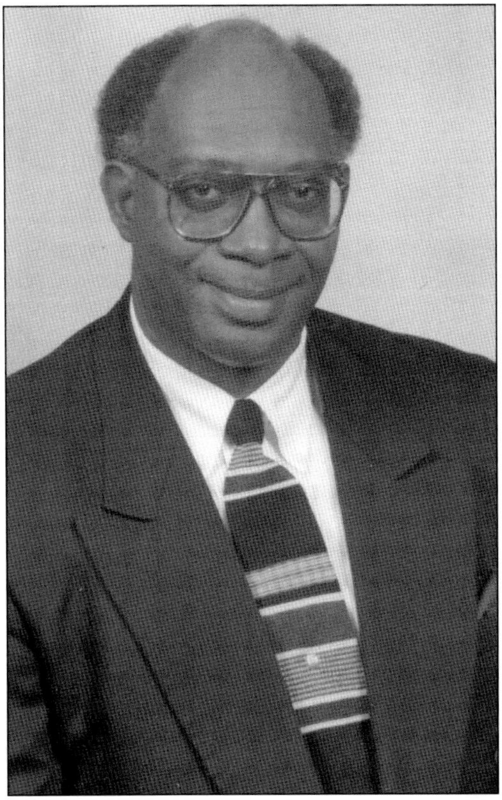

Terry E. Garrison, a native of Bayboro, Pamlico County, NC, attended Pamlico Central School and graduated from NC Central University with a B.A. in 1971. He received a masters degree from NC A&T State University in Greensboro, and attended the Bacon School of Real Estate in 1980 and Vance Granville Community College. He is a licensed real estate broker and is the owner and operator of Tegarris Associates Realty since 1980. He also has been employed with Vance Granville Community College since 1973. From 1988 to the present, he has been a member of the Vance County Board of County Commissioners, serving as chairman in 1991 and 1996, thus becoming the first black chair of this governing body in Vance County history. He also held membership on the First Citizens Bank Board of Directors, the Henderson-Vance Chamber of Commerce, the NAACP, and is an active member of the Shiloh Baptist Church. He is the father of Terrence E. Garrison. (Courtesy of Terry E. Garrison.)

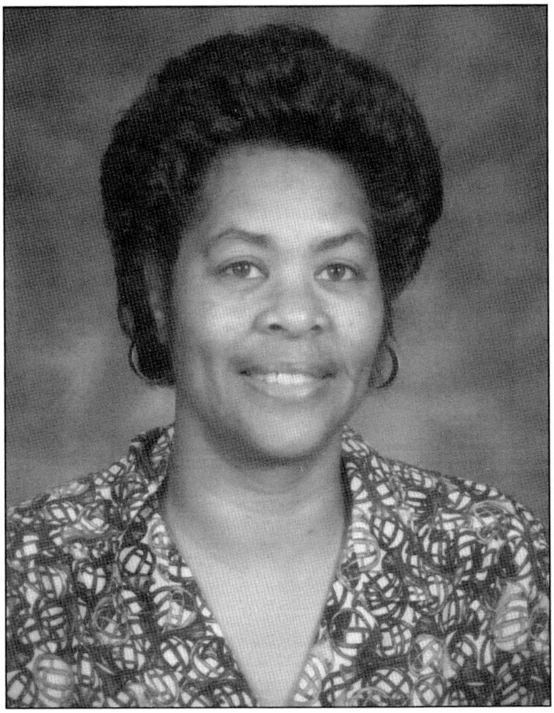

Annie Ruth Bullock (1942-2000) is a native of Granville County and a graduate of the Mary Potter High School and Fayetteville State University. In 1967, she became the sixth African American and the first African-American female to receive a master's degree (in education) from Duke University. Bullock was an educator in the Vance County School System for over 31 years. She was also the second female and the first African-American female elected as a member of the Henderson City Council, where she served for the last five years until her untimely death. She was married to Edd A. Bullock and was the mother of Edd A. Bullock Jr. and Shelly B. Watson. She was a member of the Mt. Moriah A.M.E.Z. Church and is interred in the cemetery. (Courtesy of Edd Bullock.)

Deborah Jefferson Brown (1951–), a native of Vance County, graduated from HNII in 1968 and from the Temple Business School in Washington, D.C., in 1970. She worked for 15 years with the Interstate Commerce Commission and the Internal Revenue Service, served with the US Naval Reserve in Washington, D.C., and later returned to Henderson. She became the owner of the Mercury Restaurant in Williamboro and has been a licensed real estate salesperson and broker for 15 years. Currently, she is the owner of Choice Realty in downtown Henderson. In 1988, she was elected a member of the Vance County Board of Education and served uninterrupted until elected in May 2000 to the Vance County Board of County Commissioners. She is a member of the Mt. Zion United Church of Christ, the NAACP, and the Black Leadership Caucus. Brown is married to Lunsford Brown and is the mother of Lunsford II, Dana, and Jason Brown. (Courtesy of Deborah J. Brown.)

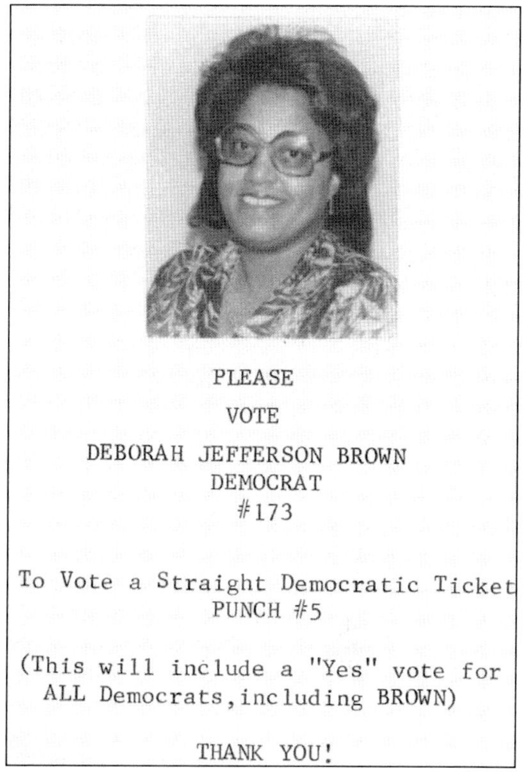

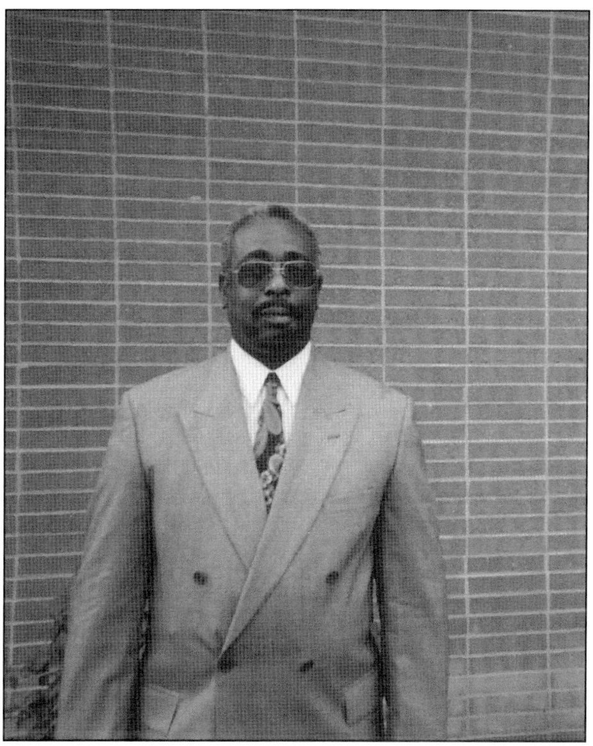

On May 2, 2000, Harold Thompson Sr. was named the local extension director and the first African American to the lead the North Carolina Cooperative Extension program in Vance County. Thompson began his career with the Cooperative Extension in 1979, when he was named an associate agricultural agent with responsibilities for 4-H youth and horticultural crops programming. In 1984, he was promoted and assumed duties related to the agency. He is married to Clara Williams Thompson and is the father of Harold Jr. and Desmond, who are both educators in the Vance County School System. They are members of the Shiloh Baptist Church of Henderson. (Courtesy of Harold Thompson.)

Congresswoman Eva M. Clayton (D-NC), First Congressional District Representative for the State of North Carolina, is serving her third term. The district represents Vance County and other eastern counties that have been referred to as the old "Black Second" because of the large black electorate and population of African Americans. In 1992, Clayton became the first African-American woman in North Carolina elected to Congress, where she became an advocate for education and vocational training, economic development, rural health, and the minimum wage. Prior to her election she served as a member of the Warren County Board of Commissioners. She received her bachelor's degree from Johnson C. Smith University in Charlotte and master's degree from NC Central University at Durham. She also attended law school at the University of North Carolina, Chapel Hill. She is married to attorney T.T. Clayton and is the mother of Joanne, Theaoseus Jr., Martin, and Reuben Clayton. She is a member of the Alpha Kappa Alpha Sorority, Inc. (Courtesy of Eva Clayton for Congress Committee.)

Six

HENDERSON INSTITUTE

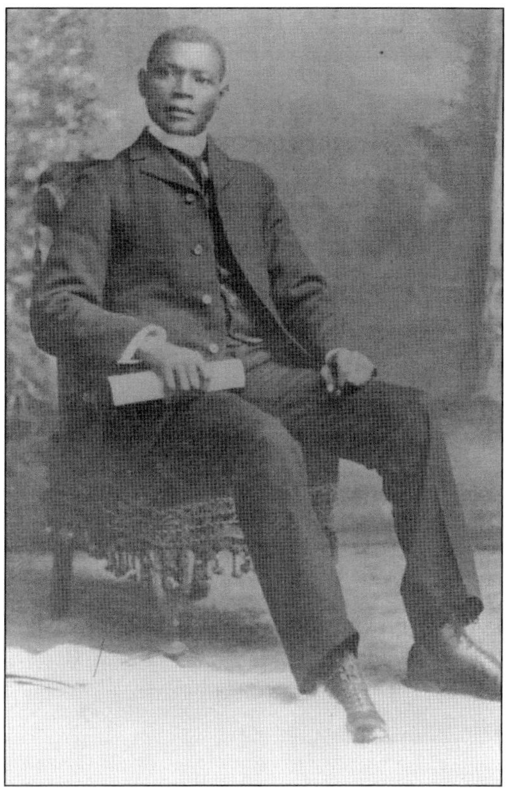

Rev. Jacob L. Cook served from 1900 until 1903 as the first black minister and head of an all-black teaching staff at HNII. He was born in Tennessee and was educated at Knoxville College. He went on to graduate from the theology department at Monmouth College, and was appointed principal of the United Presbyterian Mission School at Athens, TN. Next he was appointed president of HNII by the United Presbyterian Board of Home Missions. Reverend Cook was assisted by his wife, Anna Floyd Cook, a teacher at HNII. (Courtesy of Andre D. Vann.)

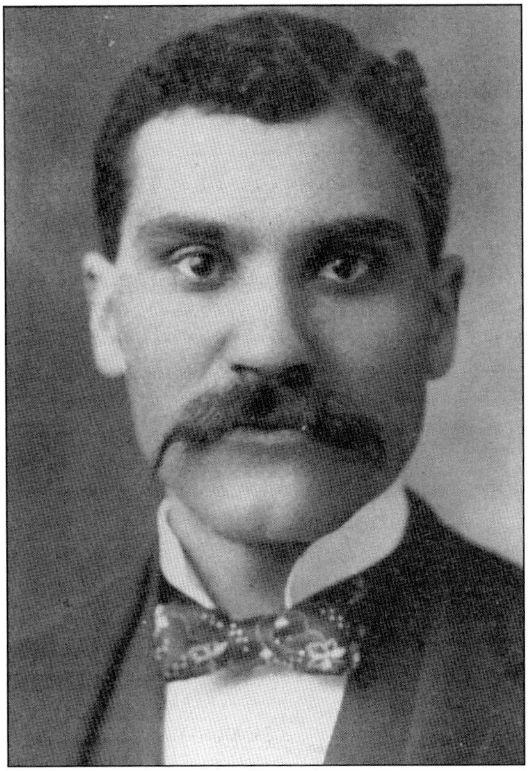

Rev. Dr. John Adam Cotton (1865–1943), seen here in the early 1900s, was born near Manchester, KY. He began his education at Berea College and entered Knoxville College in 1893. After teaching two years he began theological study, graduating from Pittsburg Theological Seminary in 1898. In 1900 he was married to Maude Brooks; after the death of Reverend Cook (previous page), the Cottons were sent to Henderson in 1903.

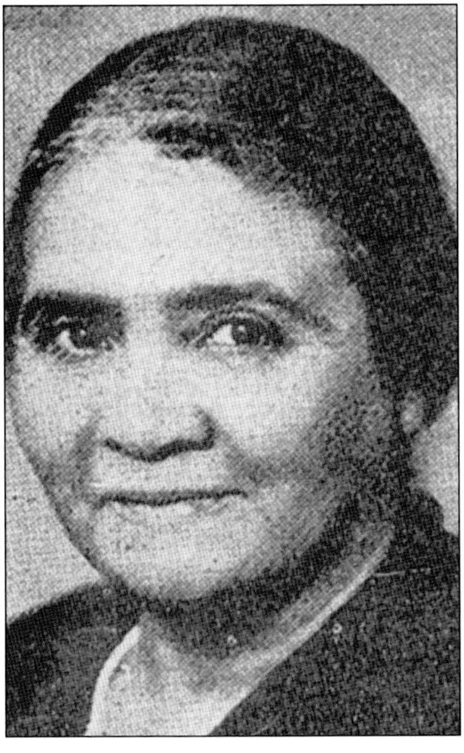

Maude Brooks Cotton (1872–1945), a native of Oberlin, OH, received her early school training at Knoxville College. Later she enrolled at the Oberlin Conservatory of Music, where she received a Mus. B. degree in 1896. In 1900 she was married to Rev. John Adam Cotton and immediately journeyed in the mission field for the United Presbyterian Church. In 1903, she joined her husband in Henderson, NC, where he was called to pastor and serve as president of the Henderson Normal School. She was an active member of the N.C. Federation of Negro Women's Clubs, where she was a charter member of the organization and also wrote the words and music for the Federated Song, "We Are Lifting as We Climb." Cotton was a charter member and local and state president of the Parent-Teachers Association. In 1943, she accompanied her husband to Knoxville College, where he was named the first black president and served until his death. She was the mother of Dr. Carol C. Bowie, an educator. She is interred on the grounds of Jubilee Hospital. (Courtesy of Andre D. Vann.)

This is a 1960s photo of Oliver "O.T." Robinson (1900–1981), a resident of Route 5 in Henderson and a native of Camden, AL. A graduate of Thyme Institute in Chase City, VA, Knoxville College in Knoxville, TN, and Hampton Institute in Hampton, VA, Robinson joined the faculty of HI in 1923. In 1934, he assumed the duties as principal under Dr. John A. Cotton, who remained general supervisor and in charge of finances until 1940. He retired from active service in the education field in 1965 after serving at the Franklin County Training School in Louisburg. An active member of Cotton Memorial Presbyterian Church, Robinson was married to Frankley Turner Robinson. He was also the brother of Sadie R. Gaither, who was married to the legendary football coach Alonzo S. "Jake" Gaither. (Courtesy of Frankley Robinson and Carolyn Green Boone.)

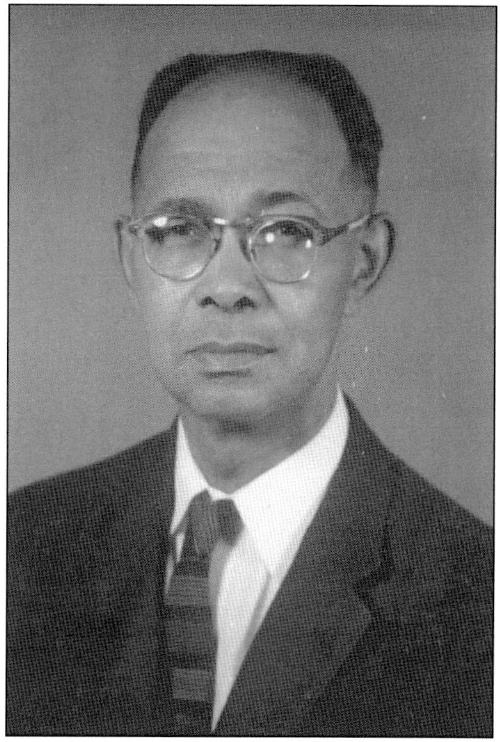

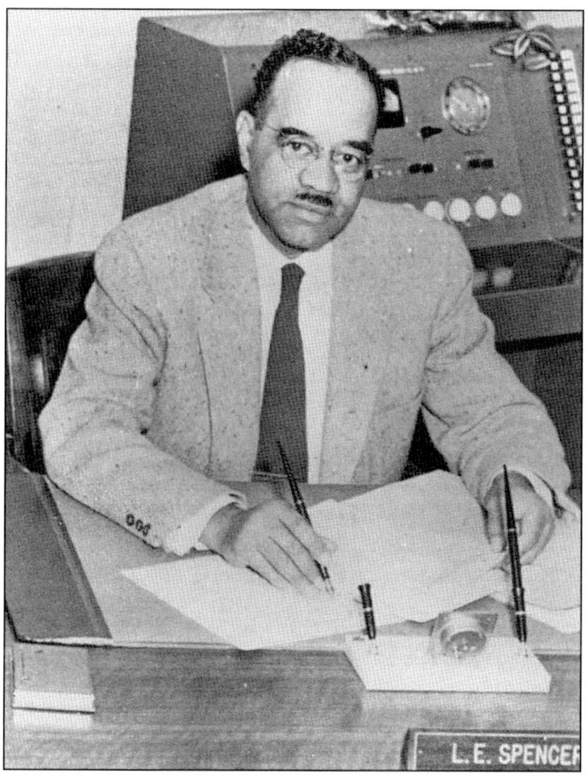

This is a 1950s photo of Leander Essex Spencer (1908–1973), a resident of Delta Place and a native of Ossining, NY. A graduate of Morgan State College (now Morgan State University), he received his master's degree and professional diploma from Columbia University. He served as principal of HI from 1947 until 1969. Spencer was married to Alma D. Spencer, and was the father of Leandra S. Toms and Emogene C. Spencer. He is remembered as a substantial landowner and was the developer of a middle-class black neighborhood on NC 39, which includes Omega Street, Alpha Place, Delta Place, and Cannady Streets. He is interred in the Alpha-Omega Cemetery in Henderson. (Courtesy of Andre D. Vann.)

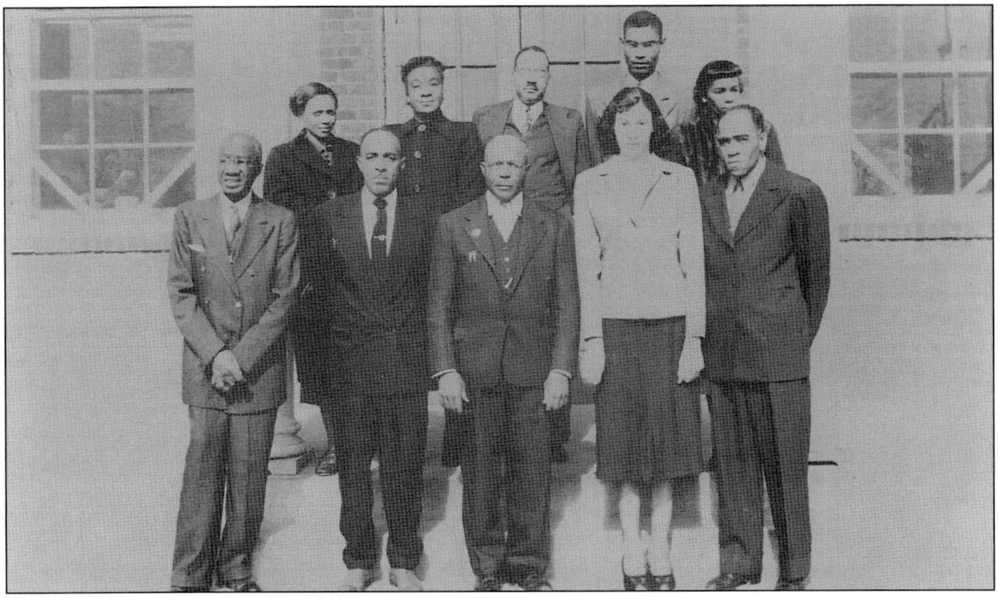

This is a 1940s photo of the faculty of HI with principal Leander E. Spencer standing in the center on the back row. Others in the photo include Asker Boyd Hawkins (front row, far right) and in the back row, from left to right, Clarence Knight and Melvina Simon Bulluck. Knight served as principal of HI from 1969 to 1970. He would later go on to serve as a member of the Vance County Commisioners. (Courtesy of Courtney Eisbey and Andre D. Vann.)

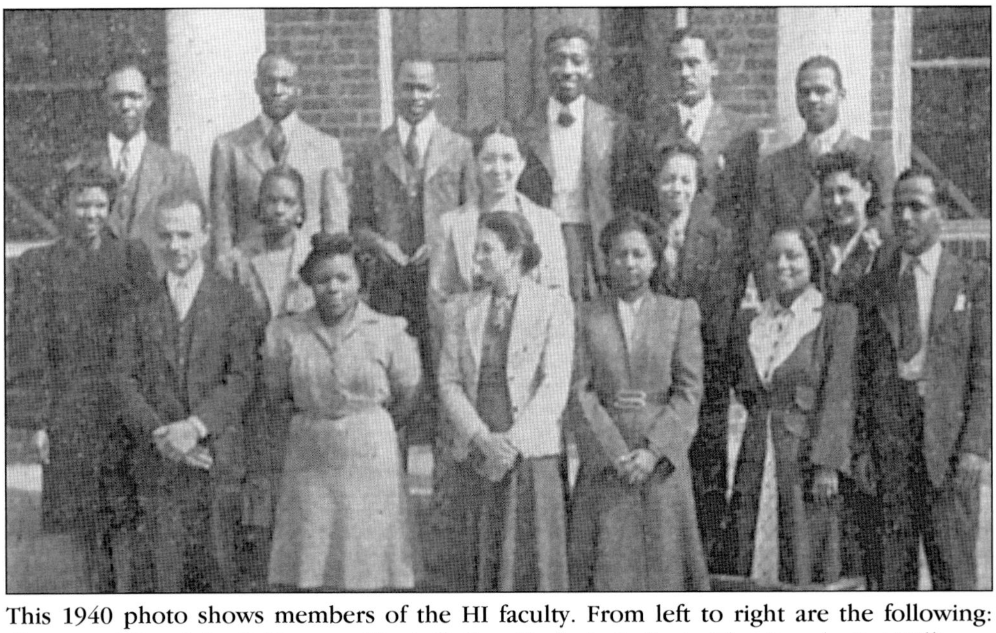

This 1940 photo shows members of the HI faculty. From left to right are the following: (front row) Rev. John R. Dungee, Hattie Bailey, Marjorie Bullock, Cleo People, Roi Williams, and S.E. Cary; (middle row) Mable Bryant, Melvina Simon, Frankley Robinson, Reba Reaves, and M.S. Williams; (back row) Oliver T. Robinson, Irvin Mitchell, Jesse Mayes, Julian Jordan, S.H. Brown, and P.C. Taylor. (Courtesy of Andre D. Vann.)

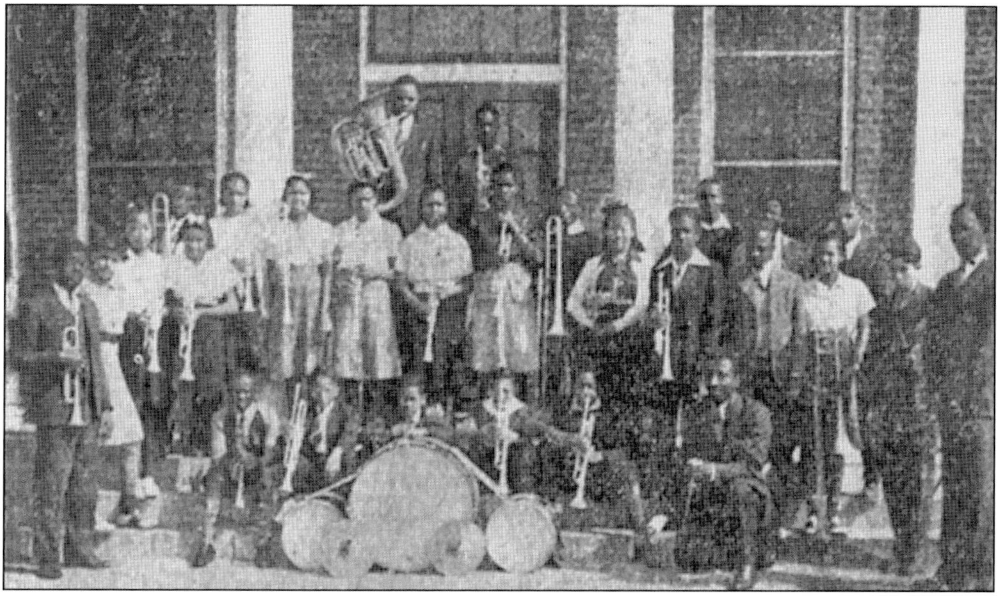

This 1940 photo captures members of the first school band standing outside of the HI auditorium. They hosted their first annual Spring Concert on May 6, 1941, under the direction of Julian B. Jordan, seen standing at the extreme right of the photograph. (Courtesy of Andre D. Vann.)

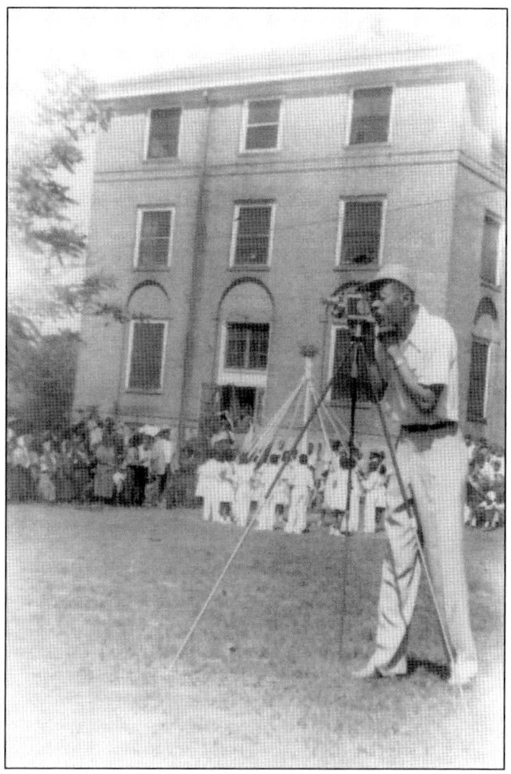

This *c*. 1950s photo shows James Rufus Barnes (1914–1996), an educator in Vance County, videotaping the May Day celebration at HI. Barnes provided motion pictures to the black segregated schools in Henderson and throughout Vance County before desegregation. (Courtesy of Andre D. Vann.)

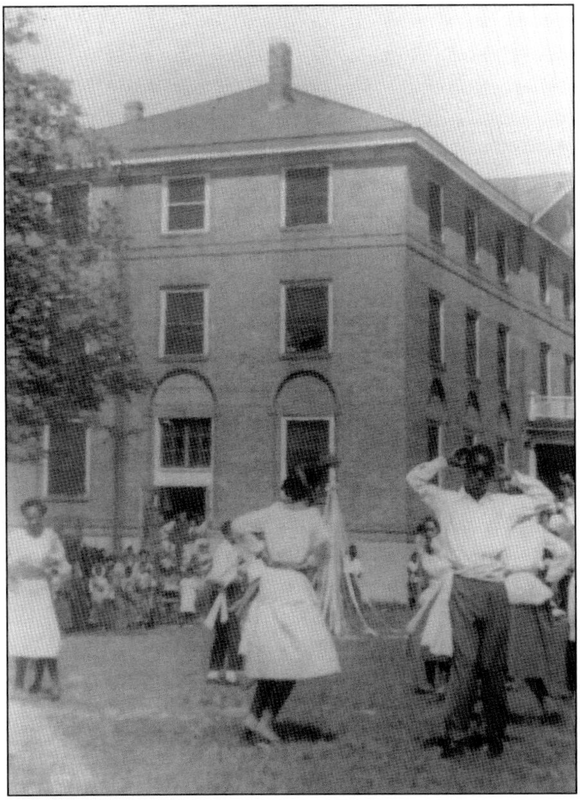

This scene shows students participating in the May Day celebration at HI. (Courtesy of Andre D. Vann.)

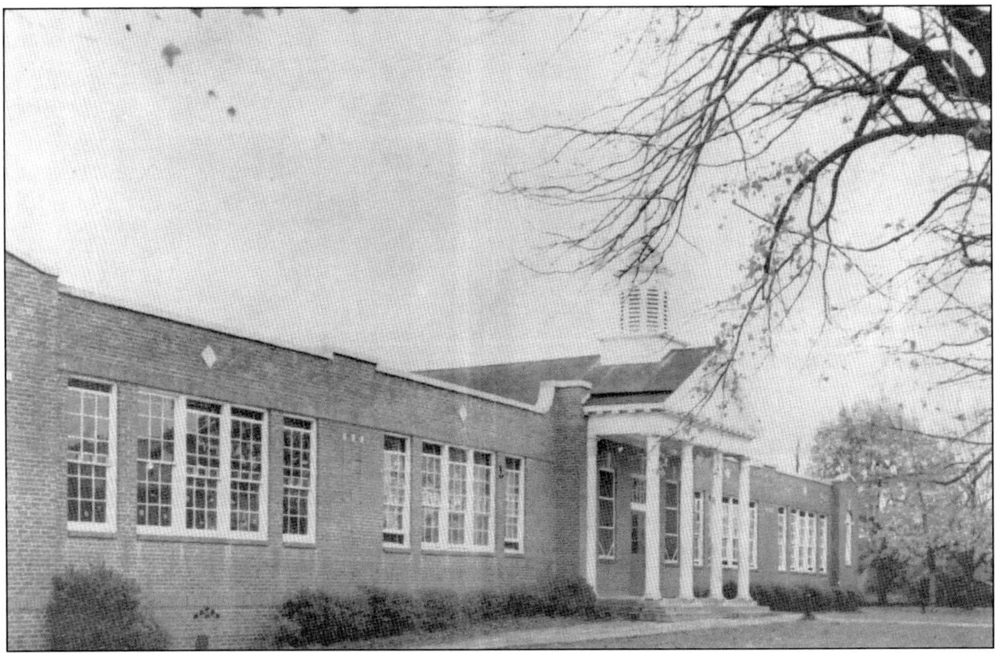

Pictured here is one of the modern buildings on the HI grounds that is now used as a classroom building for the Eaton-Johnson Middle School. (Courtesy of Andre D. Vann.)

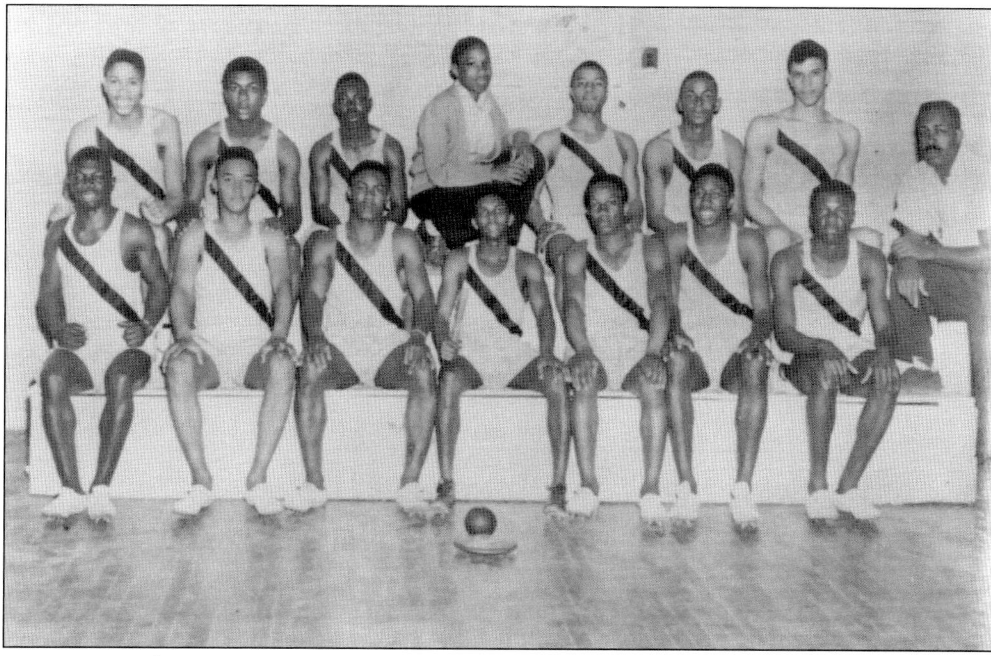

This is a 1956 photo of members of the men's track team at HI. From left to right are as follows: (front row) G. McKnight, L. Vann, W. Epps, L. Davis, H. Hawkins, E. Nicholson, F. Person, and Coach J.X. Miller; (back row) W. Alexander, R. Williams, S. Sanders, S. Davis, R. Davis, W. Sanders, and manager R. Bryant. (Courtesy of Andre D. Vann.)

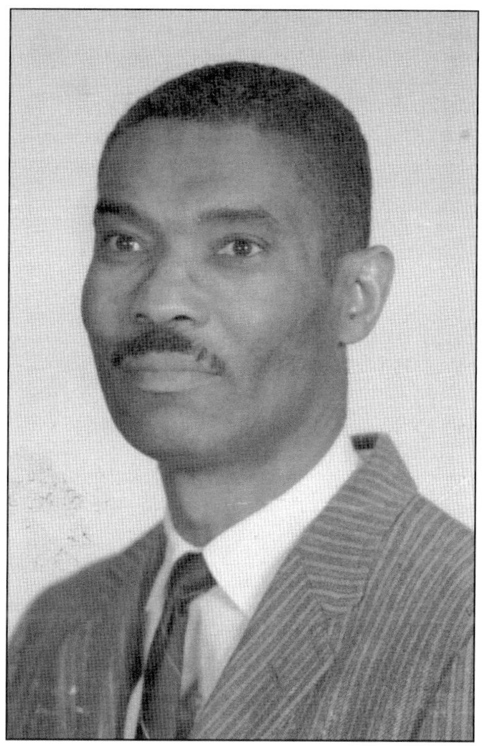

Clarence V. Knight (1919–), the son of Julius and Mary Knight, is a native of Halifax County and moved with his family to Henderson when he was three years old. He attended Central Colored Graded School and graduated from Henderson Institute in 1935. He received a B.A. degree in social studies from Hampton Institute (now Hampton University) in 1940. During World War II he served in the Armed Forces and was stationed in an all-black unit at Tuskegee Air Force Base, AL. He attained the rank of chief warrant officer and was honorably discharged in 1946. Knight received his master's degree from Pennsylvania State University in 1955. He was employed at Henderson Institute where he served as a teacher, girls basketball coach, dean of boys, assistant principal, and principal. He was later employed at Vance Senior High School from 1973 to 1979. From 1979 to 1986 he taught driver education throughout the county. (Courtesy of Clarence V. Knight.)

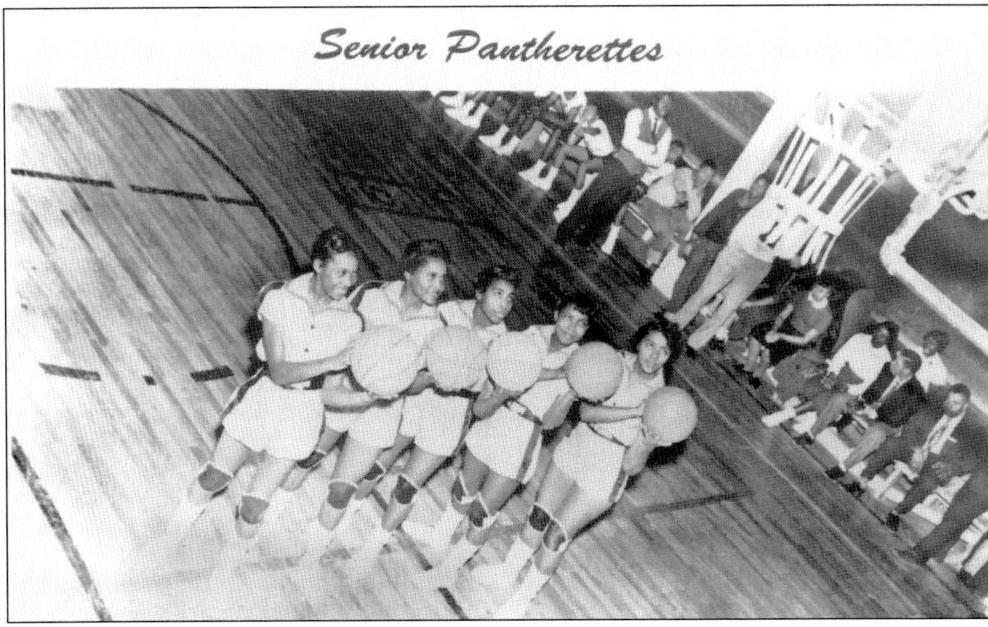

This is a 1956 photo of the senior Pantherettes women's basketball team at HI. From left to right are S. Mayfield, F. Brodie, M. Cooper, L. Kearney, and D. Chavis. (Courtesy of Andre D. Vann.)

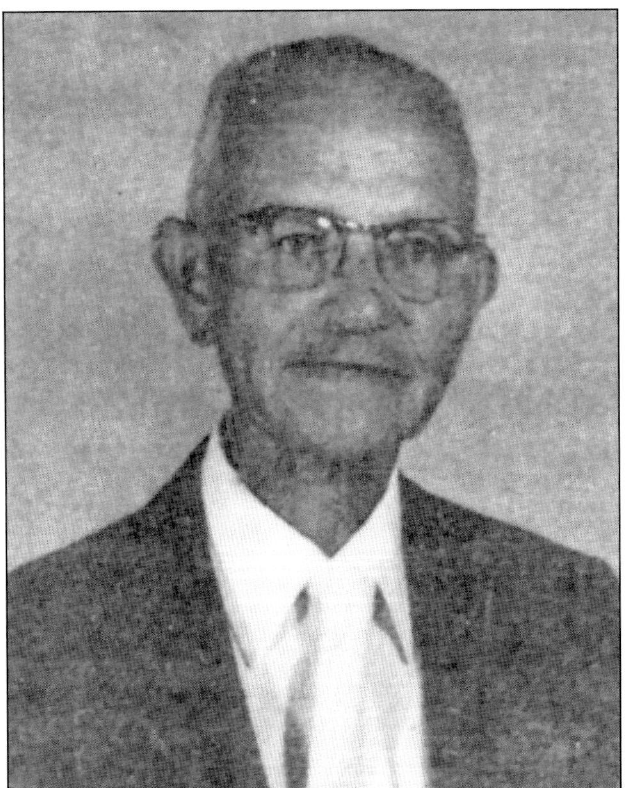

Dr. John Riley Dungee Jr. (1900–1983), a graduate of Johnson C. Smith University, came to Henderson in 1936 to serve as minister of the Townsville United Presbyterian Church. He also served as assistant minister of the United Presbyterian Church of Henderson, and as the instructor of Bible and history at HI from 1936 to 1942. (Courtesy of Andre D. Vann.)

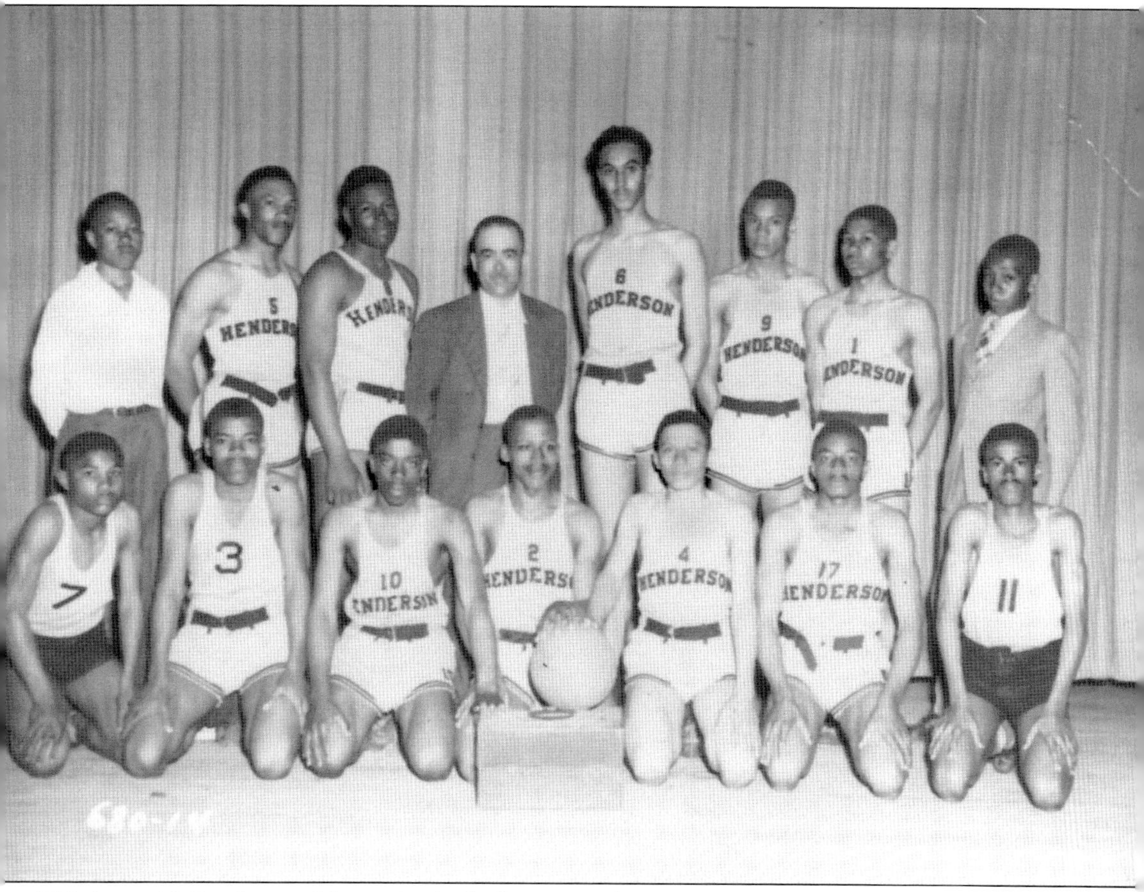

This is a *c.* 1940s photo of the HI Basketball Team with Coach James McDougle in the center of the back row. (Courtesy of Andre D. Vann.)

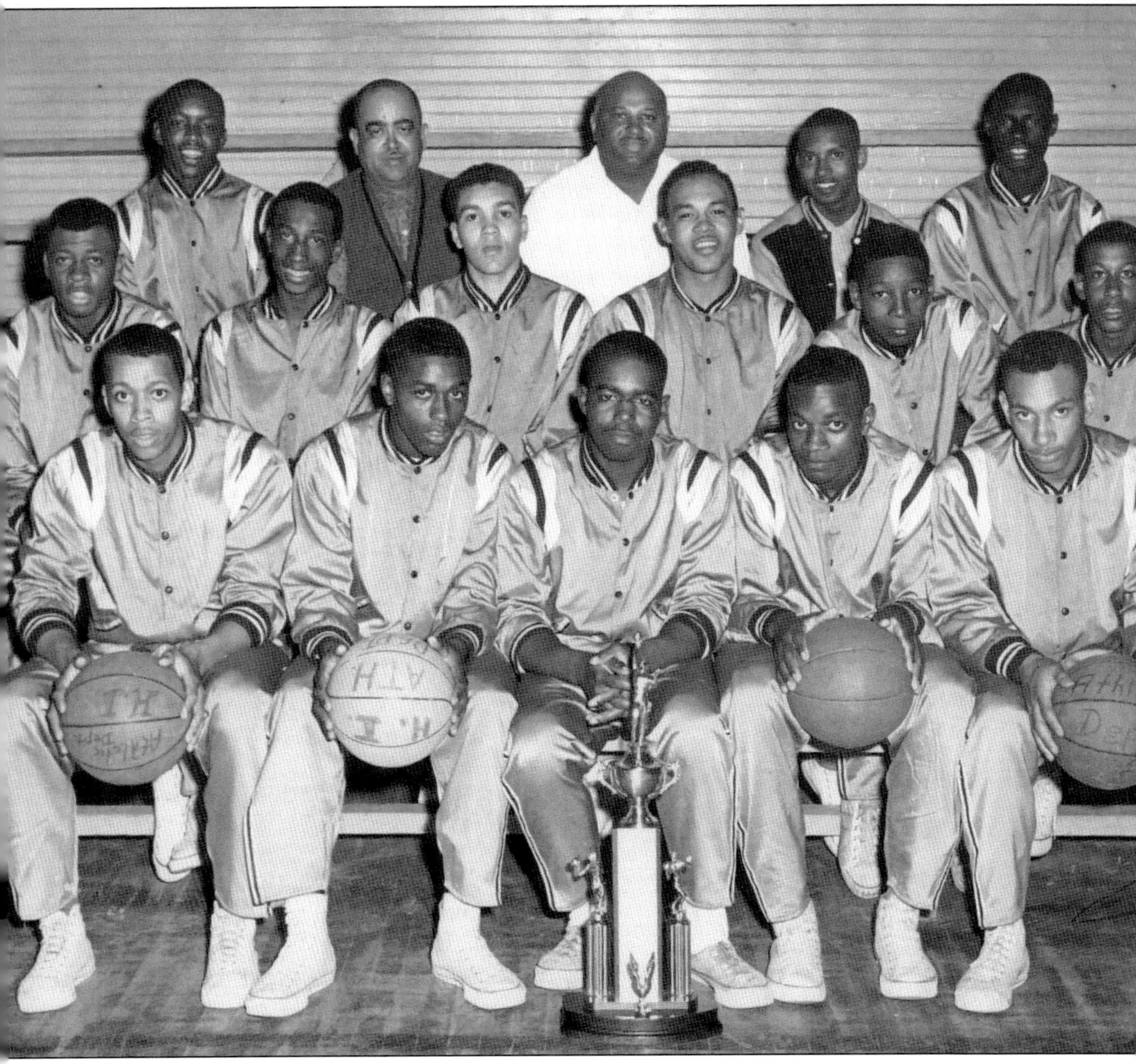

The HI Team won the District III Class AA Championship on March 16, 1961. (Courtesy of Henderson *Daily Dispatch*.)

Seven

Community Snapshots

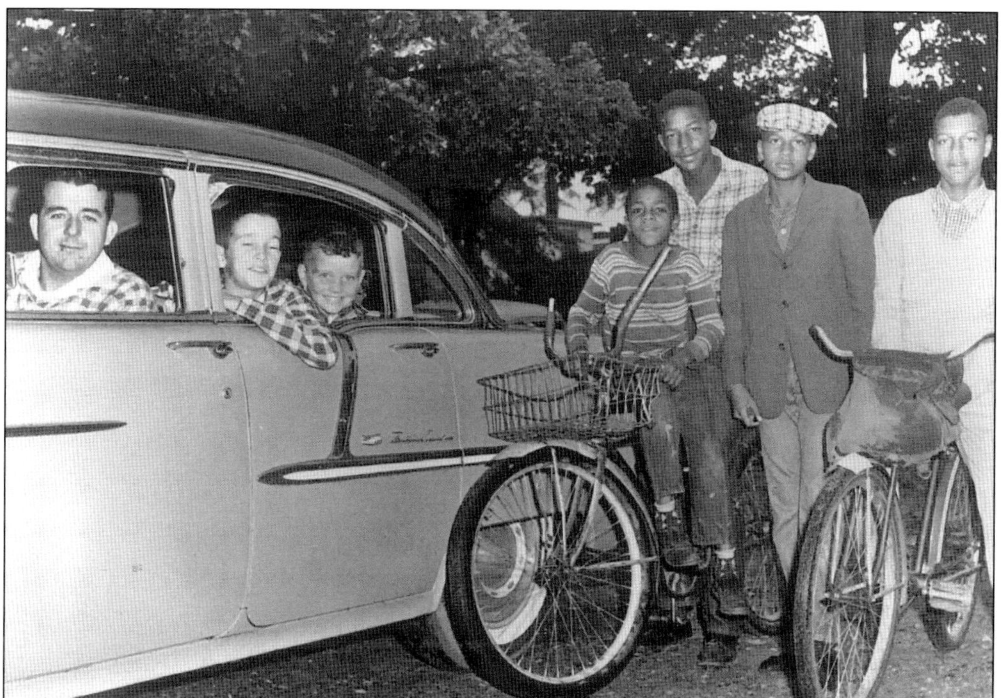

This 1958 photo shows a group of newspaper couriers of the Henderson *Daily Dispatch* after their daily route. (Courtesy of Henderson *Daily Dispatch*.)

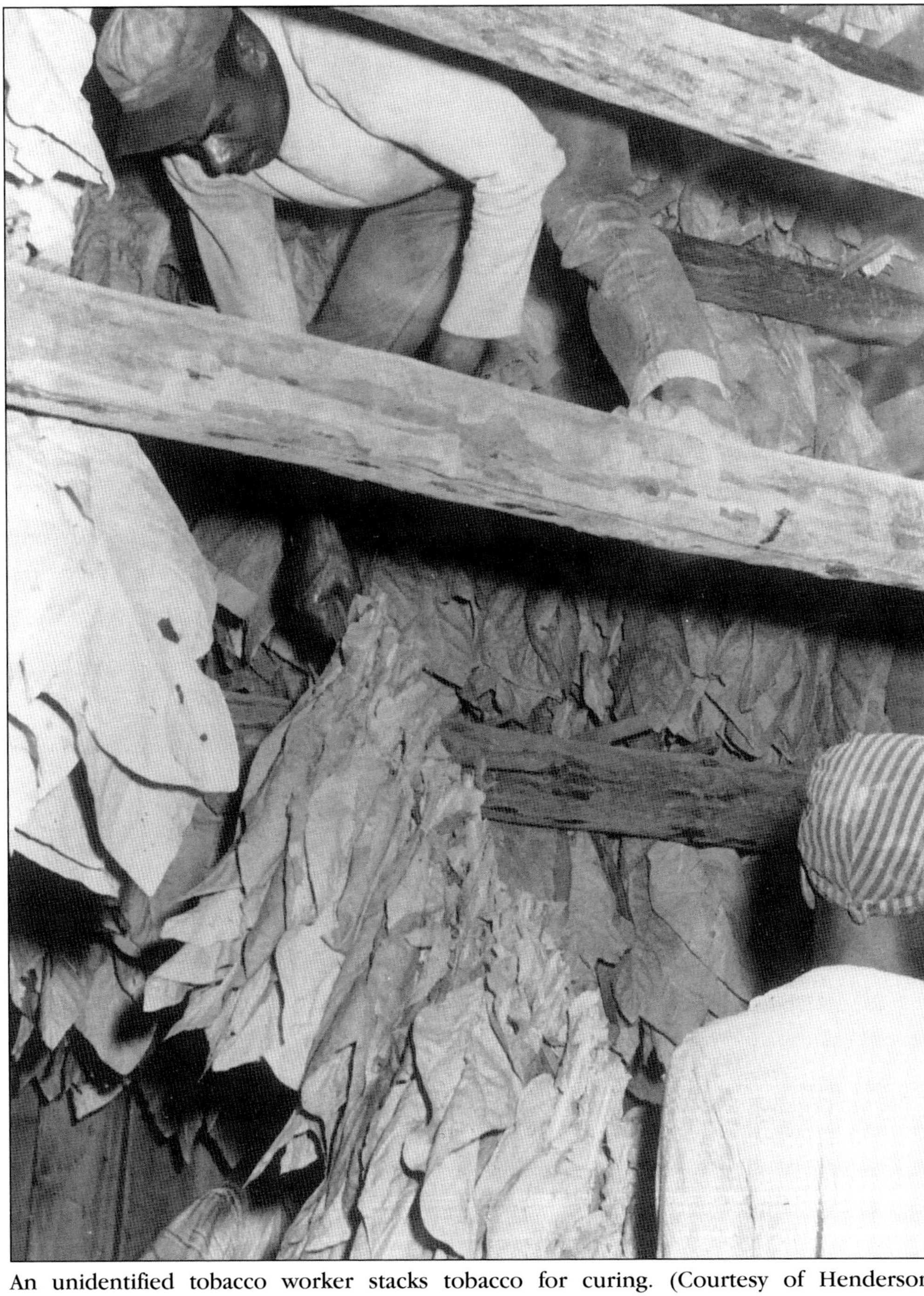

An unidentified tobacco worker stacks tobacco for curing. (Courtesy of Henderson *Daily Dispatch*.)

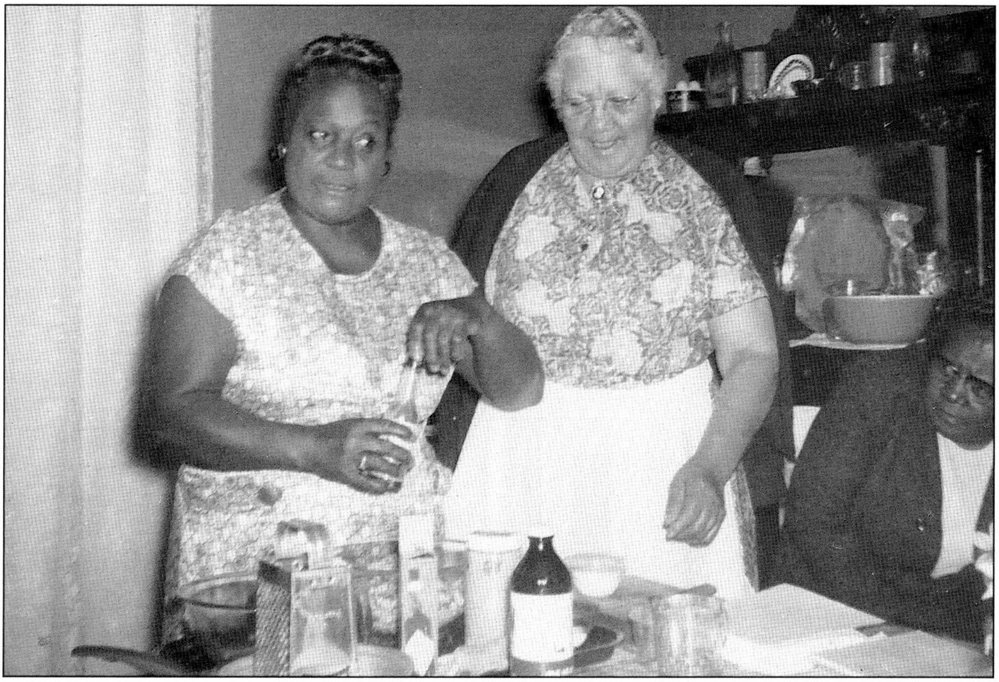

This is a 1950s photo of leaders of the Vance County Progressive Extension Homemakers Club. Pictured at a foods and nutrition workshop, from left to right, are Florence Bullock and Annie Henderson Green.(Courtesy of Henderson *Daily Dispatch*.)

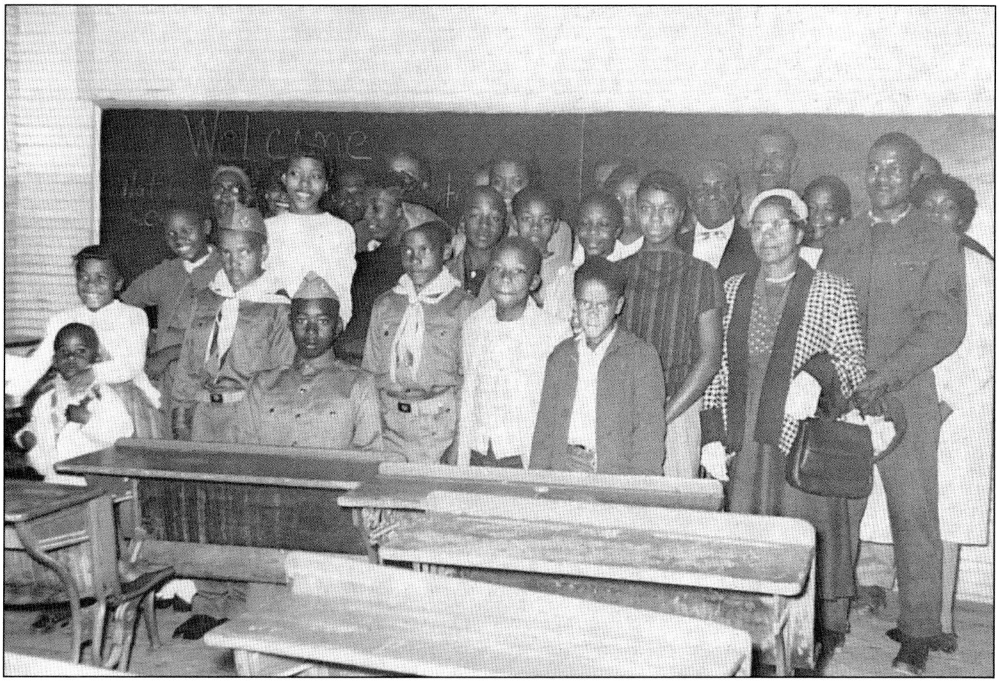

This is a 1960s photo of the Nutbush Negro Community Development Corporation. (Henderson *Daily Dispatch*.)

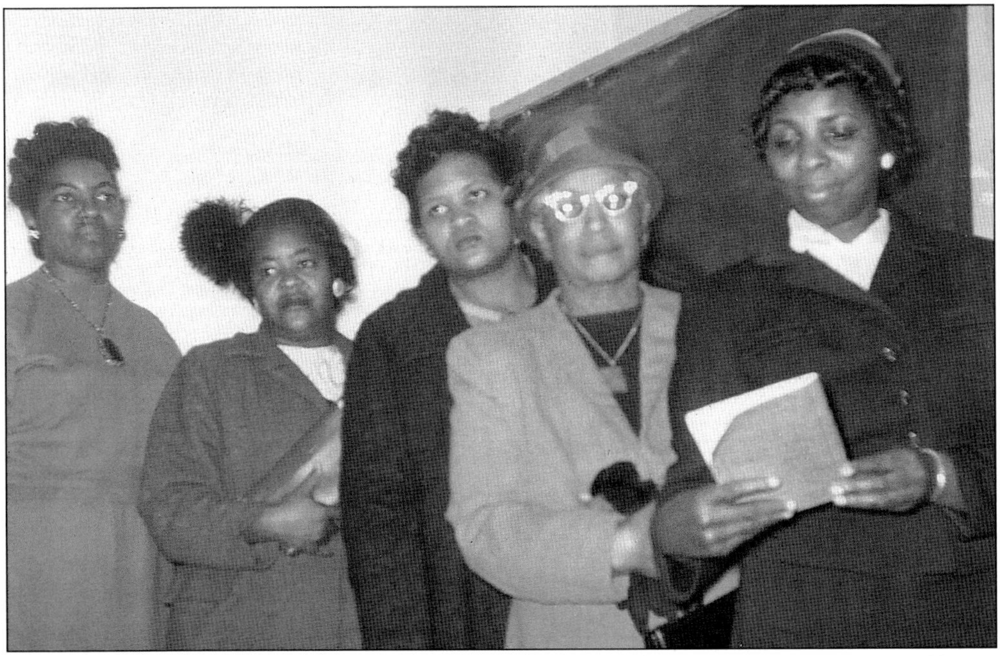

This is a 1960s photo of members of the Vance County Home Demonstration Council officers. To the extreme right of the photo is Mary Bing Hawkins, a great leader in the Homemakers Extension movement in the county. (Courtesy of Henderson *Daily Dispatch*.)

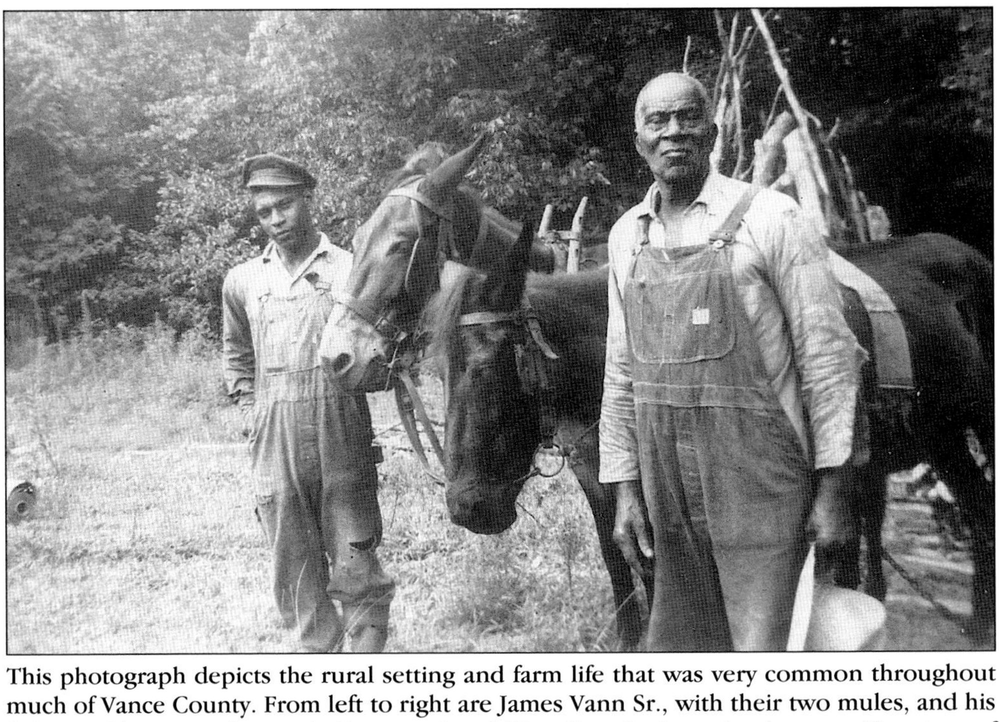

This photograph depicts the rural setting and farm life that was very common throughout much of Vance County. From left to right are James Vann Sr., with their two mules, and his father, Edd Vann, a farmer in Bearpond and Kittrell and a large landowner. (Courtesy of Andre D. Vann.)

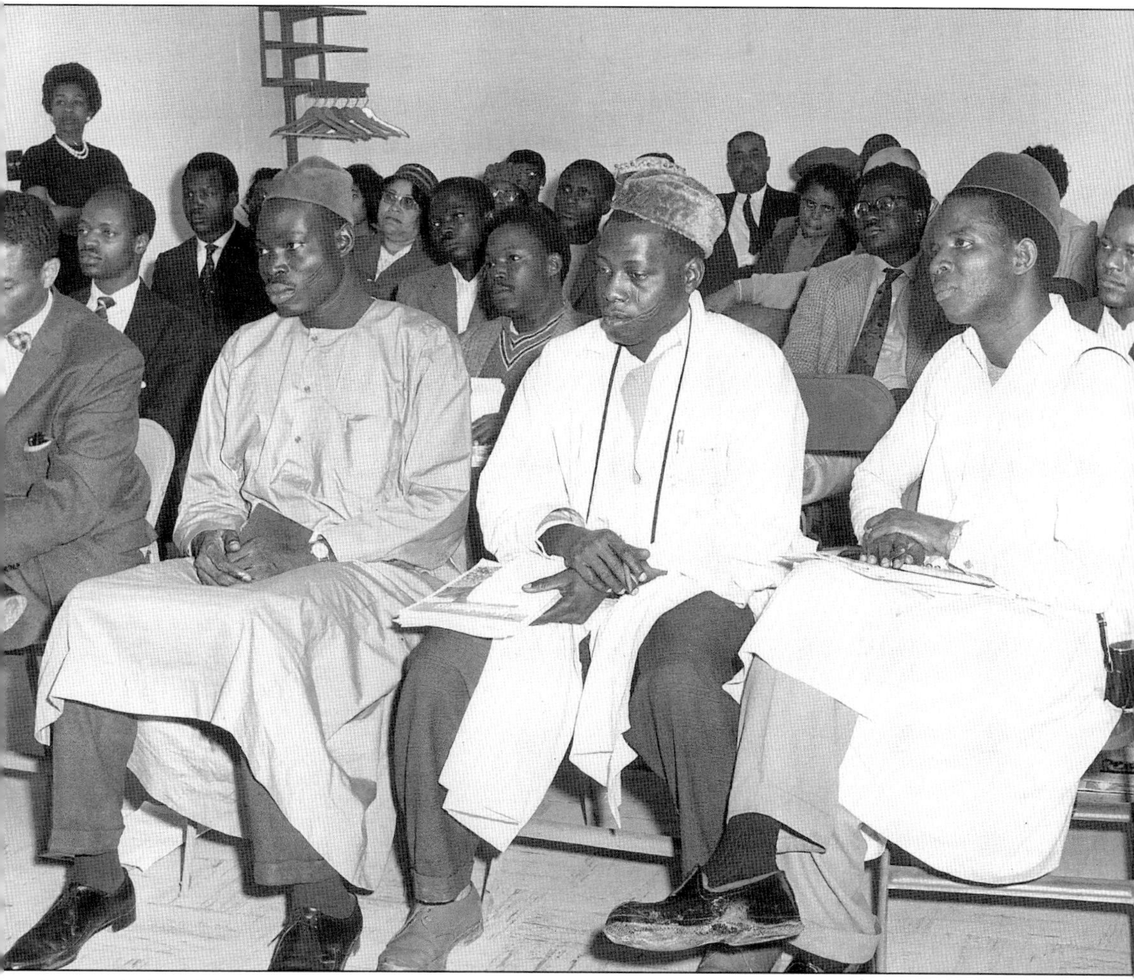

On April 14, 1961, Vance County farmers received a visit by a Nigerian delegation. The visit was intended to allow African farmers to learn of the farming practices of Vance County farmers. (Courtesy of Henderson *Daily Dispatch*.)

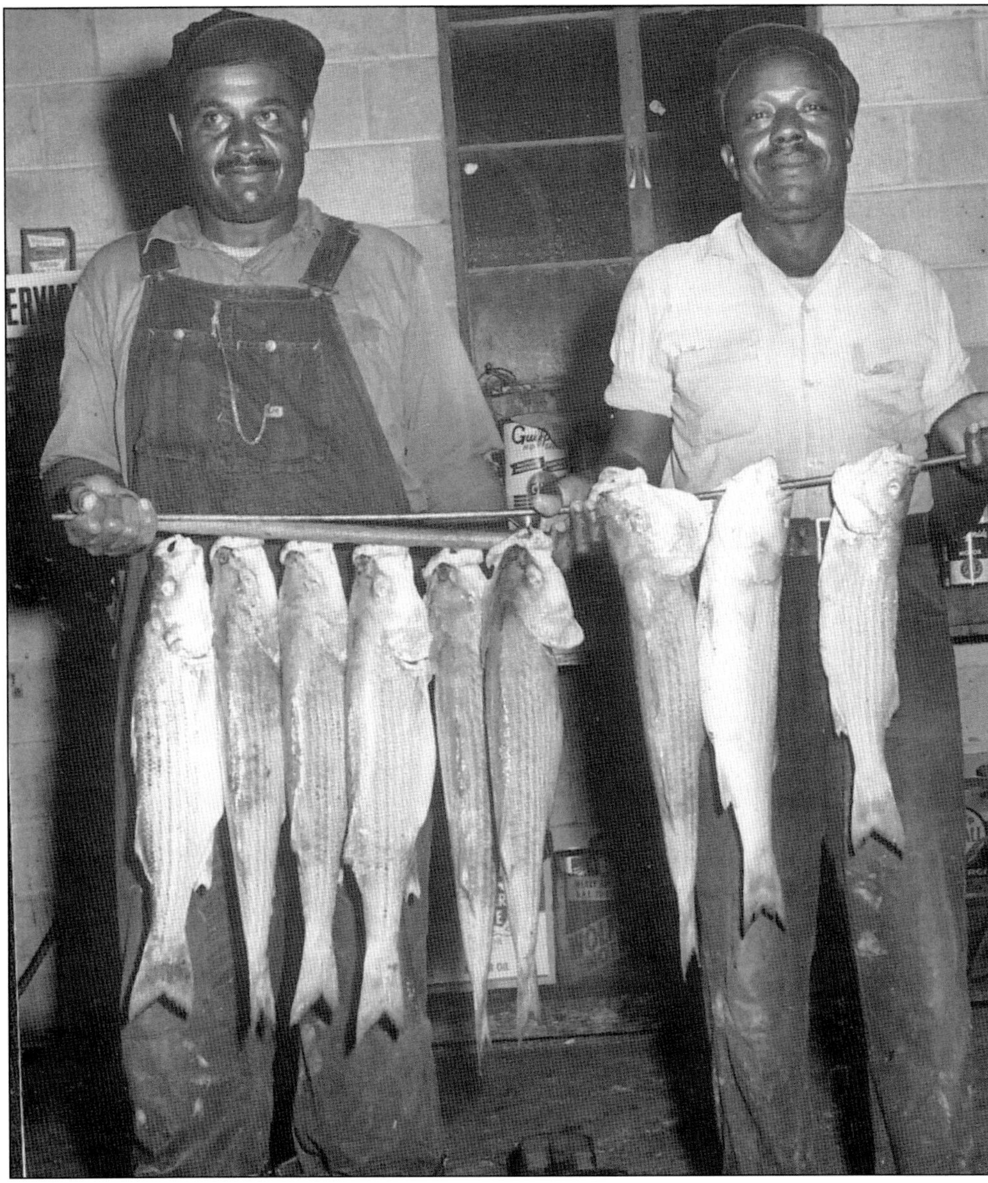

Pete Edwards (left) and LeRoy Reed display their daily catch of nine rockfish that weighed in at a total of 45 pounds. (Courtesy of Henderson *Daily Dispatch*.)

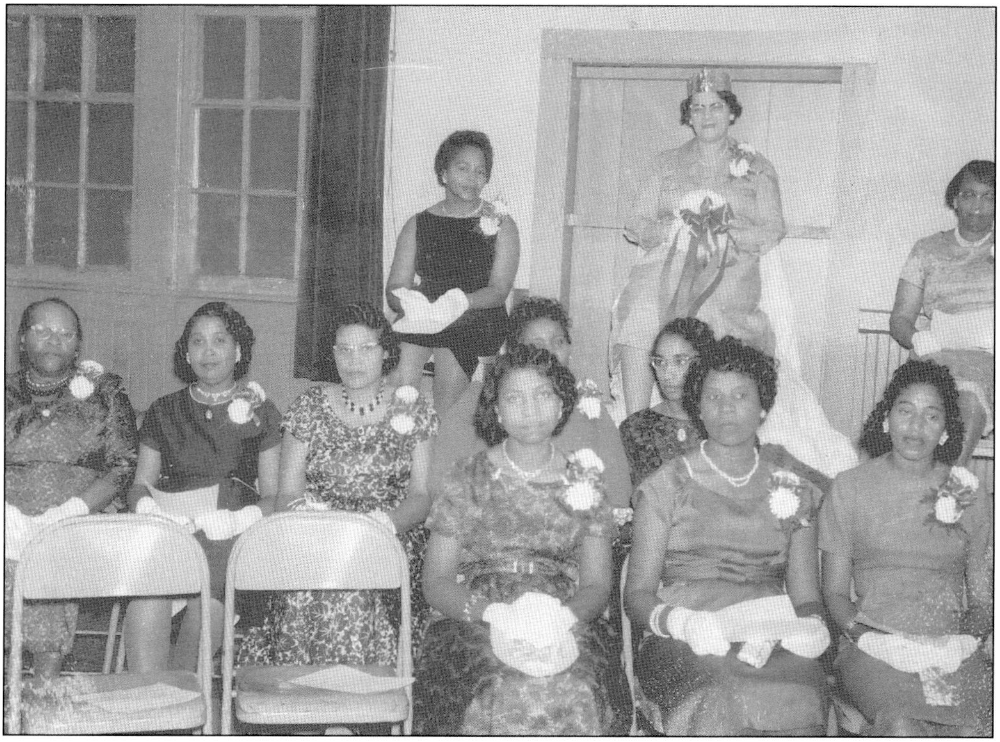

This photograph shows the crowning of an unidentified women and her court at the Kittrell Graded School. This event was used as an opportunity to raise funds for local community agencies. (Courtesy of Henderson *Daily Dispatch*.)

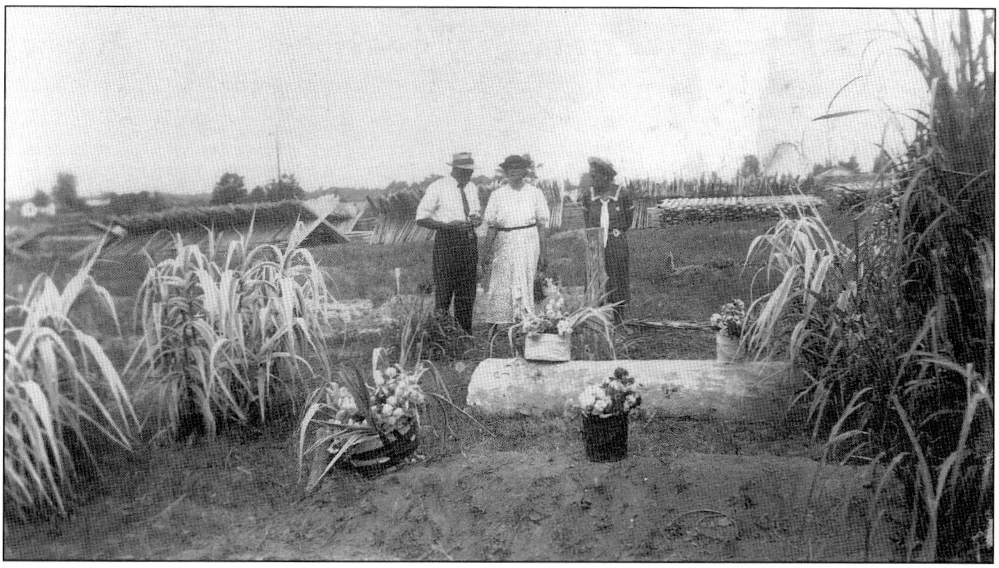

This 1940 scene shows Vance County residents visiting the grave of a deceased family member buried in the Blacknall Cemetery. This cemetery has served generations of blacks in Vance County. Among those interred in the cemetery are James Y. Eaton, Thomas Eaton, and Dr. James E. Baxter. (Courtesy of Andre D. Vann.)

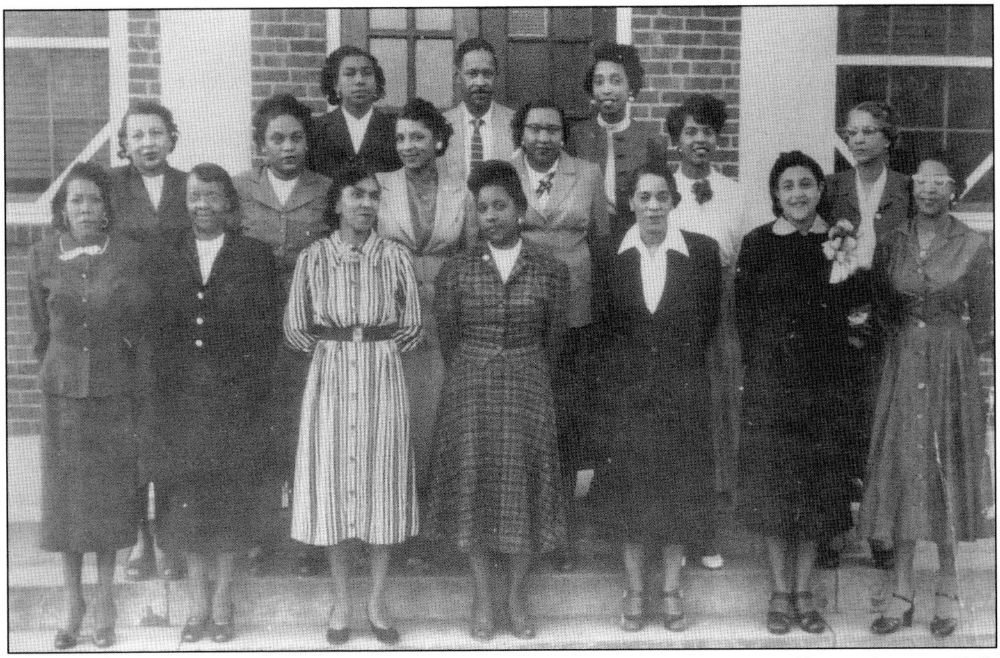

This is a 1940s photo of members of the Winston-Salem Teachers College Alumni Club (now Winston-Salem State University). From left to right are the following: (front row) unidentified, Mary Brame Henderson Reid, Mary L. Merrit Harris, Dorothy McGhee, Carrie Hawkins Marable, Ruth Hawkins Hughes, and Mary Clack Mitchell; (middle row) Elizabeth Burt Wilson, Fannie M. Plummer, Alice Green, Ruth Burt, Francine Hawkins, and Lottie Allen Parham; (back row) Clara Nelson Hunt, James R. Barnes, and Lena Bullock Howell. (Photo courtesy of Sherman G. Parham.)

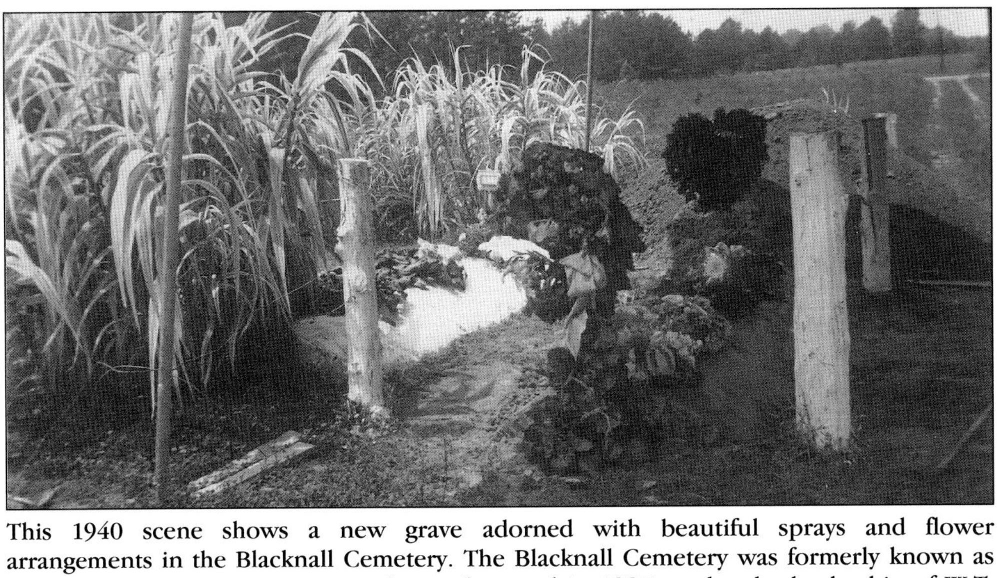

This 1940 scene shows a new grave adorned with beautiful sprays and flower arrangements in the Blacknall Cemetery. The Blacknall Cemetery was formerly known as the Union Cemetery Company and was chartered in 1887, under the leadership of W.T. Richardson, Thurston Brodie, W.M. Merriman, J. Cheek, and James R. Reavis. (Courtesy of Andre D. Vann.)

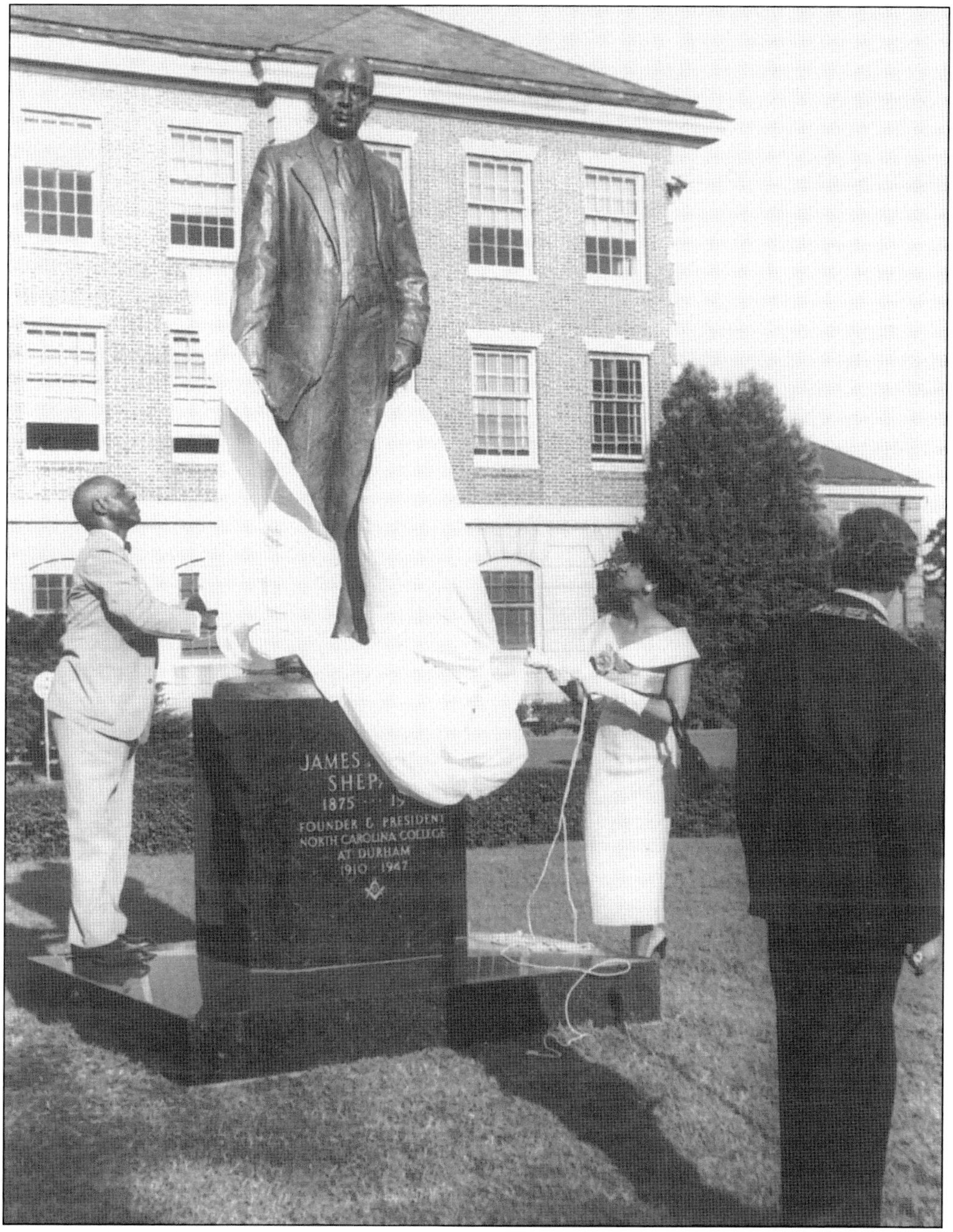

The unveiling of the James E. Shepard Statue took place in 1957. Shepard founded North Carolina College (now known as North Carolina Central University) in Durham. His granddaughter, Carolyn Smith Green, is the wife of Dr. James P. Green of Henderson. Dr. Shepard's father, Dr. Augustus Shepard, was pastor at Shiloh Baptist Church in Henderson in the 1880s and 1890s. His mother, Hattie Shepard, founded the black women's missionary movement in Vance County and the state. At left in the photo is James Taylor, a former student at NCC. (Courtesy of Alex Rivera and Andre D. Vann.)

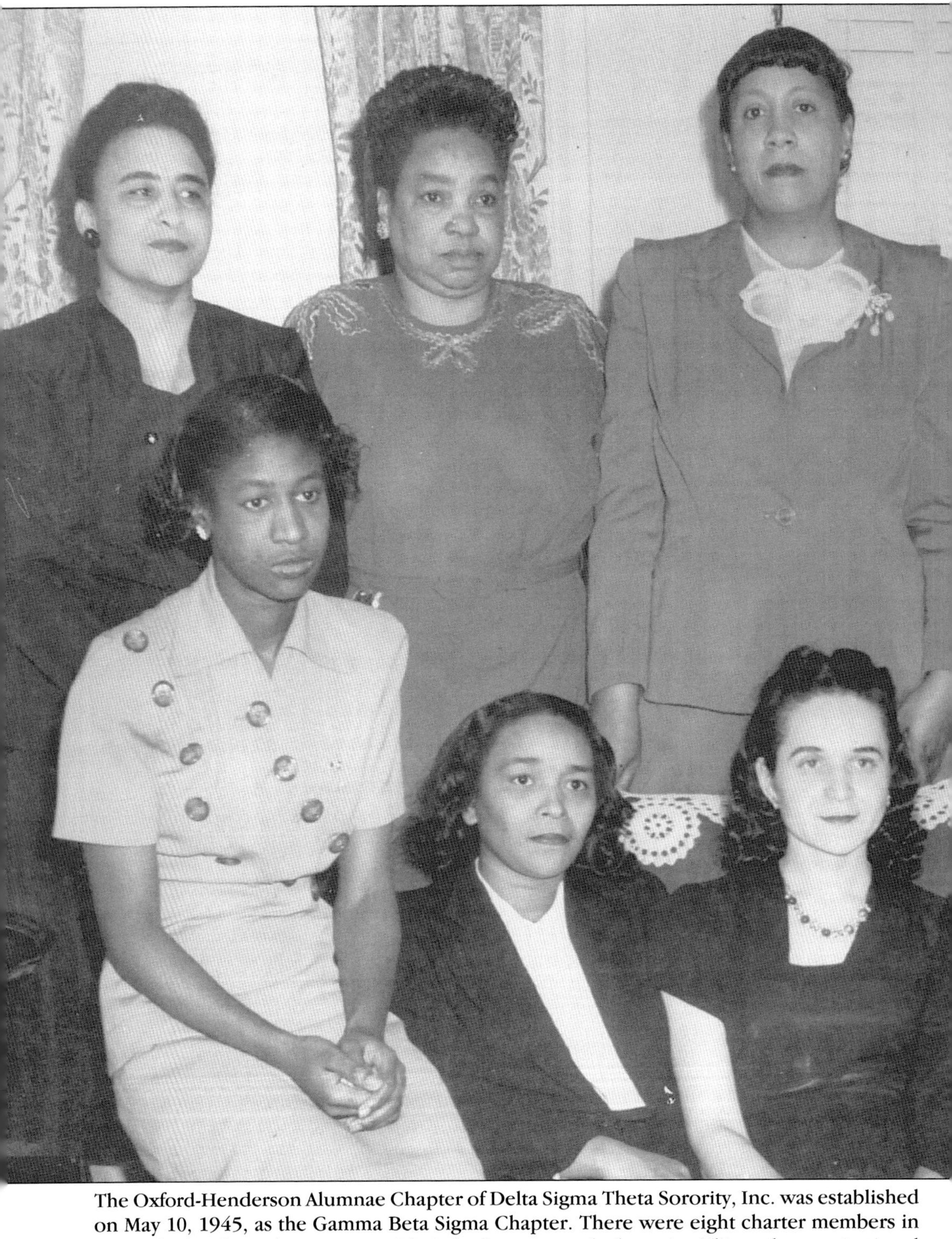

The Oxford-Henderson Alumnae Chapter of Delta Sigma Theta Sorority, Inc. was established on May 10, 1945, as the Gamma Beta Sigma Chapter. There were eight charter members in the Oxford and Henderson area, with Oxford serving as the host site. This early organizational photo shows members at their annual tea in 1947. From left to right

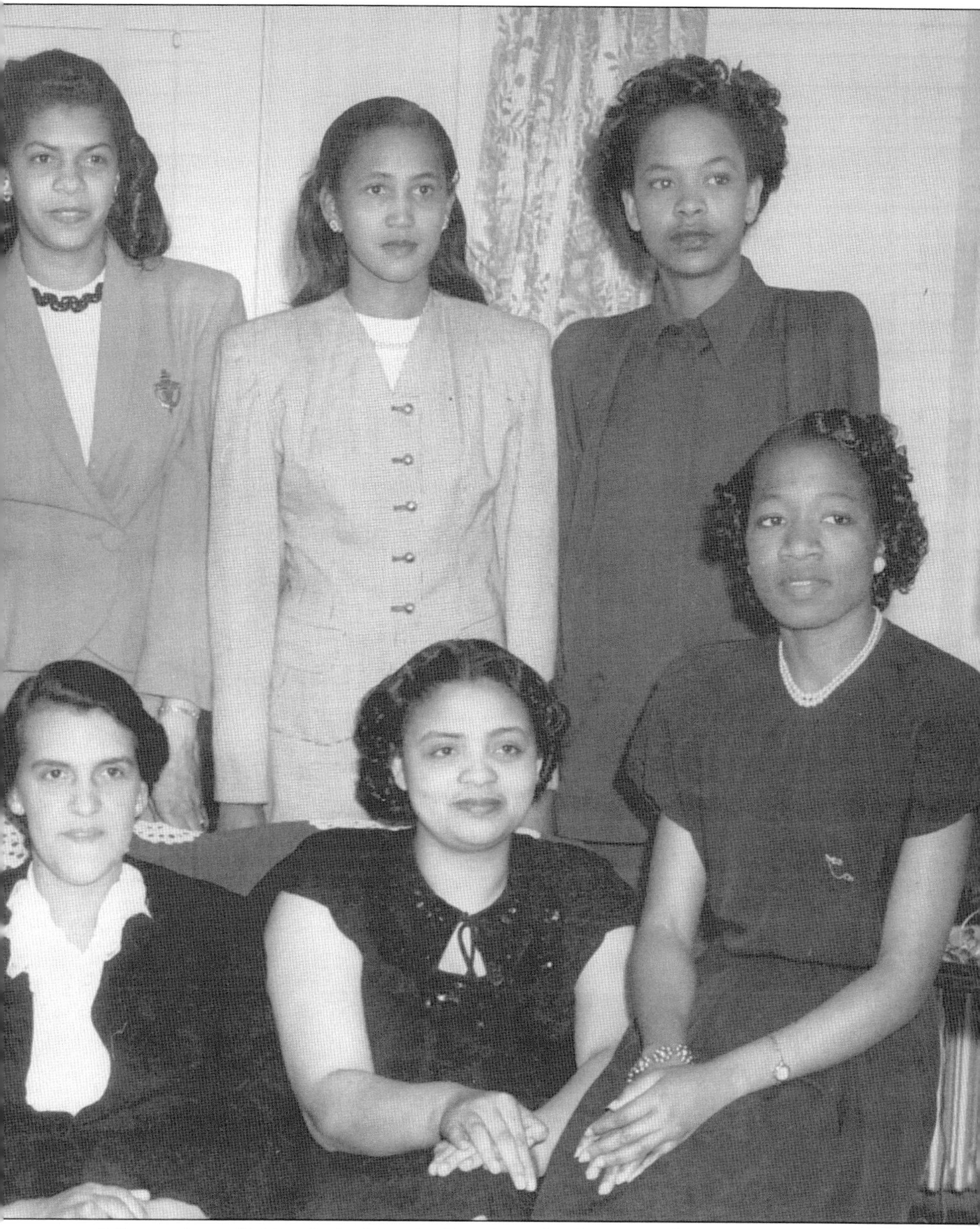

are as follows: (seated) Margie C. Morris, Era G. Littlejohn, Dorothy J. Roberson, Bessie B. Redding, Andolia O. Eaton, and Edith Scriven; (standing) Annie M. Rivera, Lillie Q. Hamme, Owena H. Davis, Irene Parham, Roberta E. Howell, and Mabel J. Bryant. (Courtesy of Andolia O. Eaton.)

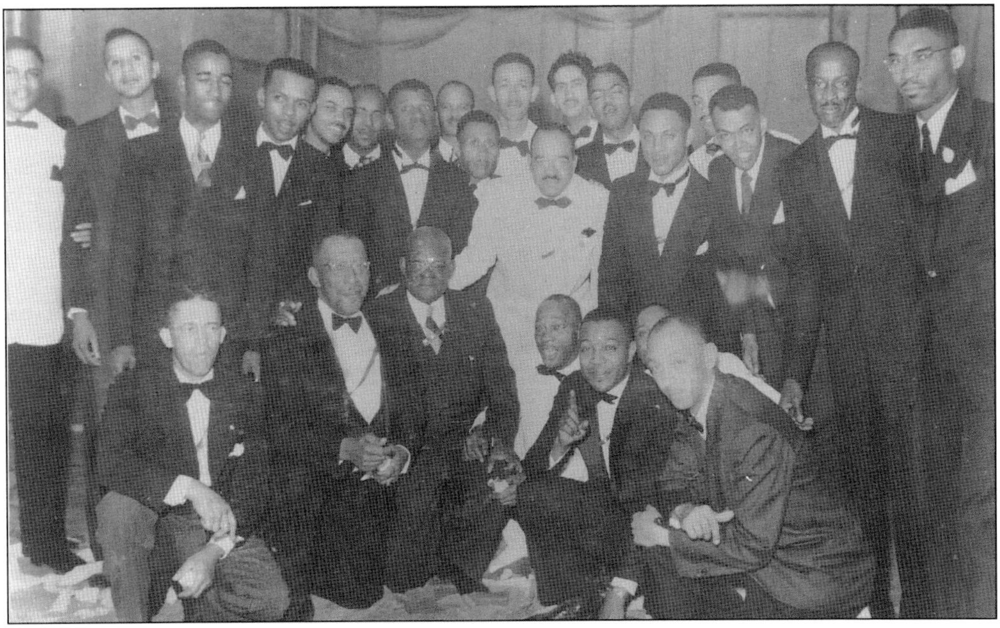

This 1940s photo shows members of the graduate chapter of the Zeta Alpha Chapter of Omega Psi Phi Fraternity, Inc., which was comprised of members from Henderson, Warrenton, and Granville Counties. Dr. James P. Green, who later became a state legislator, is visible in the back row. Clarence Knight, a former Vance County commissioner, is standing at the far right in the picture. The Omega Psi Phi House is located on Highway 39 in Henderson. (Courtesy of Andre D. Vann.)

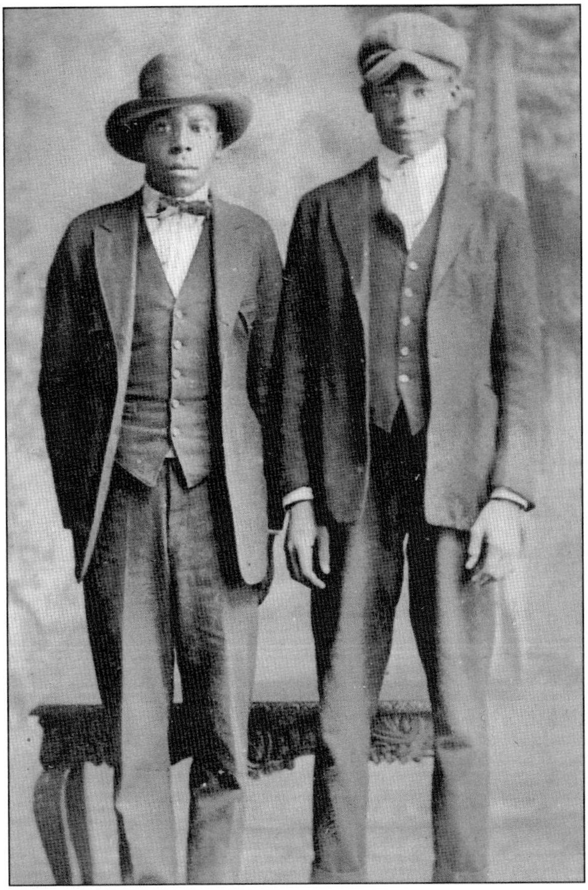

Edward Thomas Young (1901–1918), right, is pictured with an unidentified young man. He drowned during a church picnic in Rowland's Pond. (Courtesy of Johnnie Y.M. Sanders.)

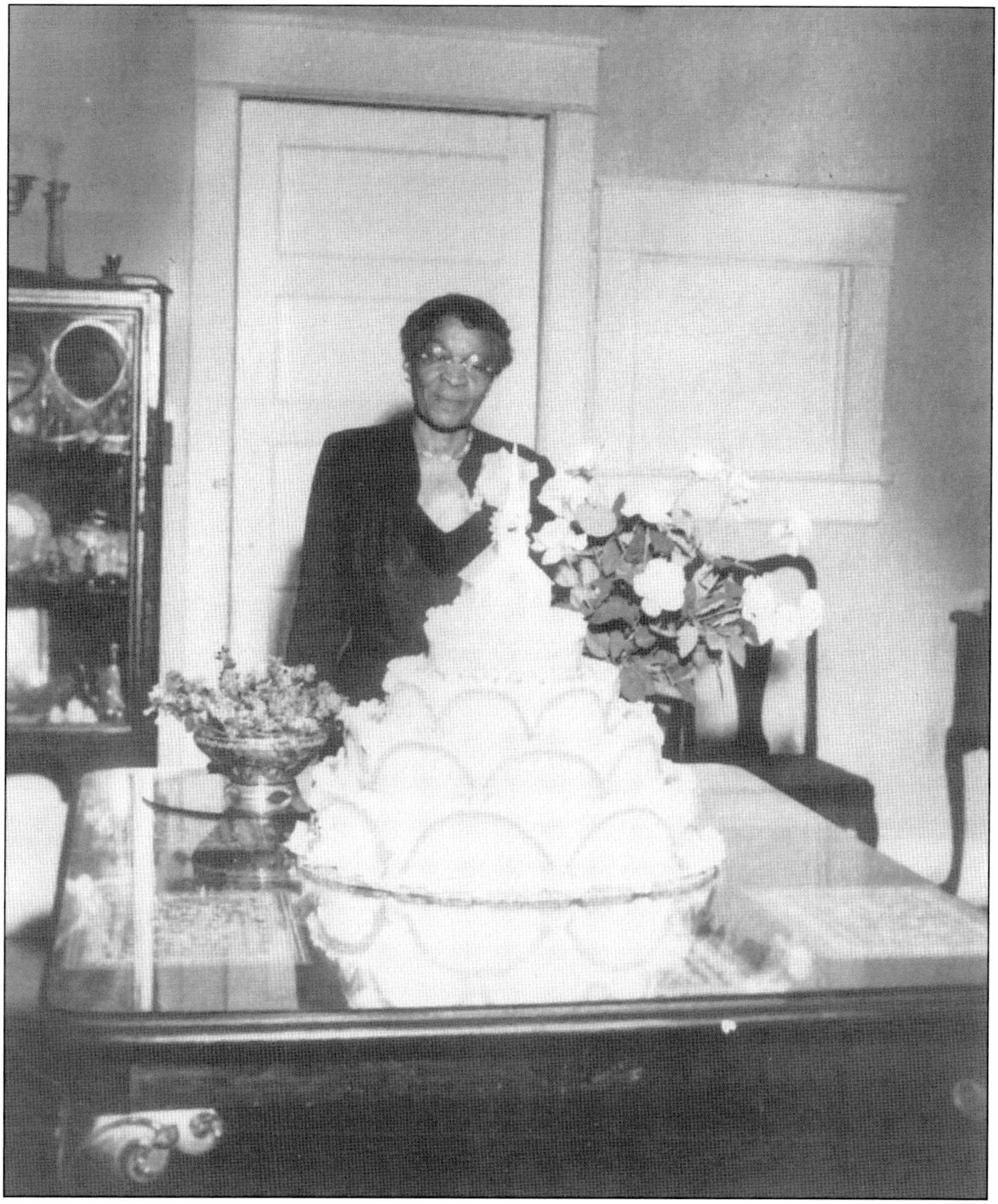

Dr. Charlotte Hawkins Brown (1883–1961) was born the daughter of Carrie Hawkins Willis in Mobile, and later migrated during the 1880s to Cambridge, MA. She attended the Alston Grammar School and graduated from the Cambridge English High School in 1900. Hawkins entered the State Normal School of Salem, MA, but left to teach at Bethany Institute in Sedalia, NC, in 1901. In 1902 she transferred to Palmer Memorial Institute, the nation's first boarding school for blacks. Brown served as president from 1901 to 1952. She is remembered as a noted educator, a school and women's club founder, social worker, author, lecturer, orator, and religious leader. The Palmer Site is now the Charlotte Hawkins Brown Memorial State Historic Site, dedicated in 1987. It is North Carolina's first state-funded historic site named for an African-American woman. She is interred on the grounds of the campus and site. (Courtesy of Andre D. Vann.)

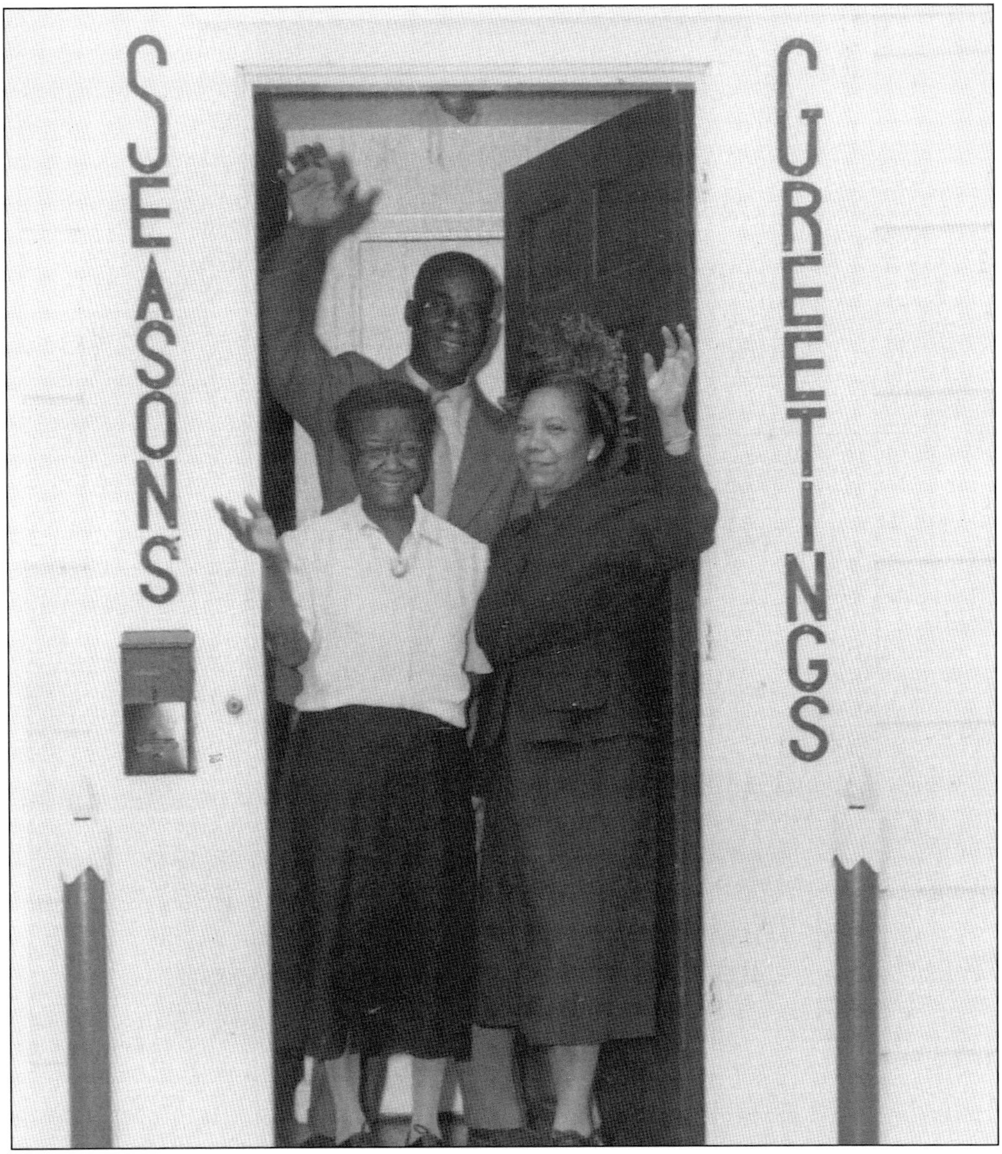

This 1950s Christmas photo shows, from left to right, Lydia Hatch Crutchfield, Oscar M. Thompson, and Dr. Mary Crutchfield Thompson (1902–1981). Dr. Thompson, a native of Henderson, was the daughter of William and Lydia Hatch Crutchfield. In 1908 the family migrated to Cambridge, MA, where her father could get a job as a mason and where other members of the Hawkins and Crutchfield family had settled in the late 1890s. She attended Cambridge High and Latin School, graduating in 1925. From there she went to Tufts Dental School, where she was the third black female student in its history. She graduated in 1930 and established a practice in Boston, MA, thus becoming the first black woman to practice dentistry in the Boston area. She also founded the Children's Dental Clinic, for disadvantaged children, in her home. She was active in Alpha Kappa Alpha Sorority, Inc., the NAACP, the YWCA, and the United Negro College Fund. She retired to Hyannis, MA, after 50 years of practice in the dental profession. A scholarship was established in her name at Tufts Dental School for black female students. (Courtesy of Andre D. Vann.)

Bettie Esther Parham Crosby (1906–) is the daughter of Rev. Samuel and Carrie Hawkins Parham. She graduated in 1923 from HI, attended Winston-Salem State Teacher's College , graduated in 1928 from Shaw University, and received her master's degree from Columbia University. With her training in the field of home economics, she became aware of the use of certain calories, nutrients, and vitamins and eventually developed a beauty product and founded Esther's Beauty Aids Company. She established shops in New York City and eventually her business spread to Lagos, Nigeria, Africa. Upon retirement she and her husband, Matthew Crosby, have spent their time at her mansion, Parham Place, at Croton on the Hudson. In 1990, she established the Bettie E. Parham Scholarship Fund with a $50,000 donation to Shaw University. (Courtesy of Andre D. Vann.)

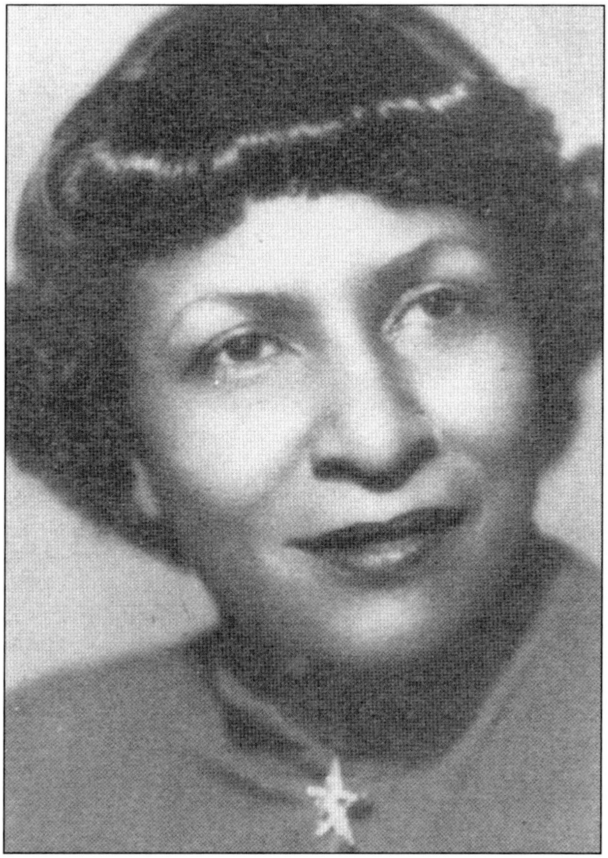

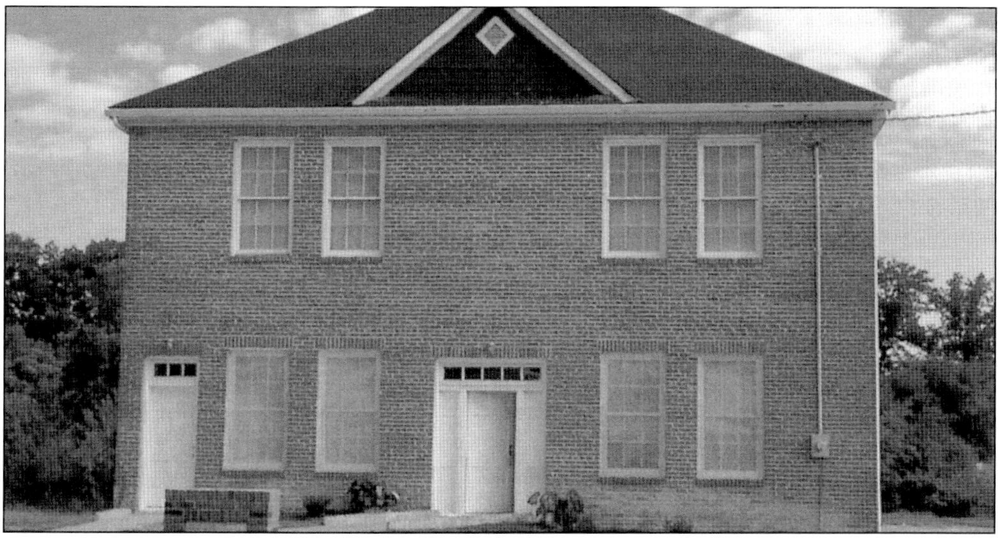

Henderson Institute Museum was established in 1986 to preserve the history of Henderson Institute and the citizens of Vance County. This is the former Henderson Institute Library and Laboratory that was built in 1928. It was placed on the National Register of Historic Places by the U.S. Department of the Interior. (Courtesy of Claude W. Brame.)

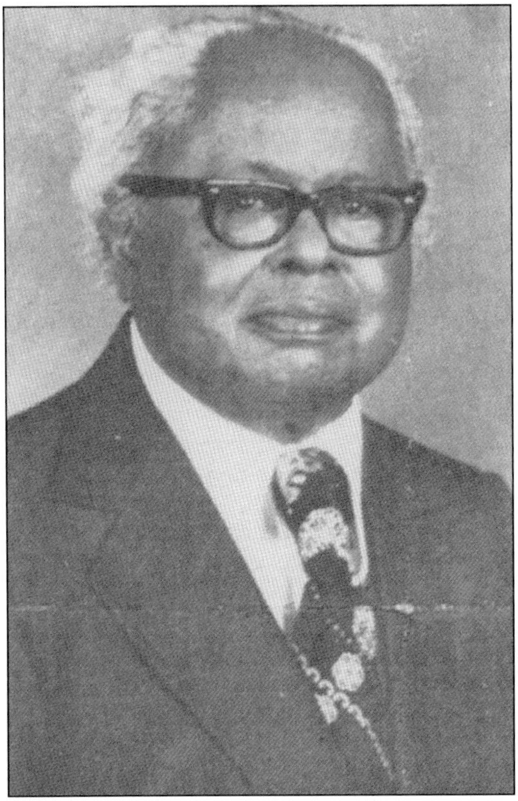

Dr. James Youman Eaton Jr. (1905–1983), son of J.Y. and Mary Eaton Sr., was a native of Vance County and a member of Shiloh Baptist Church. He attended Shaw University, Fisk University in Nashville, TN, and later transferred to Howard University, where he received a B.A. and M.A. degree. His first teaching position was at Kittrell College. Later, he settled in Washington, D.C., where he was employed with Blackwell Junior College. He taught business administration and later served as dean and chaplain of the college. Eaton also was employed as a psychologist with the federal government and met with government officials to discuss issues surrounding the invasion between Ethiopia and Mussolini. Upon retirement he settled in Henderson and lived in the Eaton mansion at 515 Orange Street on West End. He was married to Wilhelmina Fray and was the father of James Y. Eaton III. He is interred in the Eaton family plot in Blacknall Cemetery. (Courtesy of Andre D. Vann.)

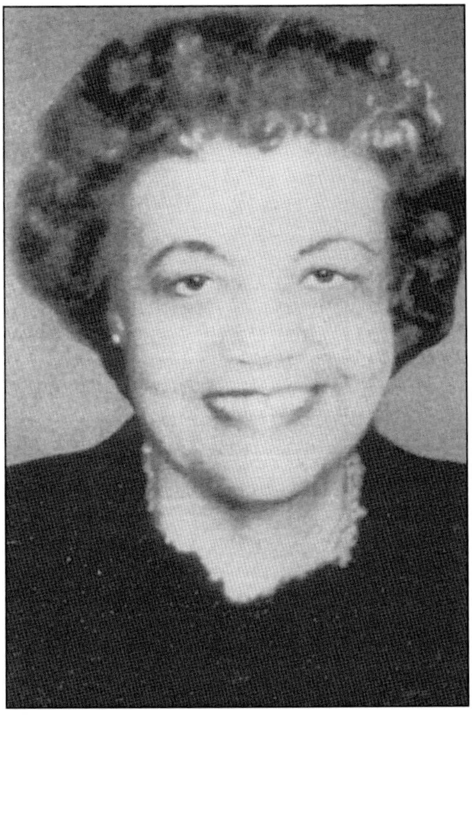

Dr. Dorothy Kendrix Hunt (1916–2000), daughter of Allen and Mabel B. Johnson, attended HNII and received a B.A. degree in education from Spelman College in Atlanta, GA. She did her graduate work at the Catholic University of America, American University, and the University of D.C. To her credit were two masters degrees and a doctorate degree in guidance and counseling. She retired as a psychologist from the District of Columbia Public Schools in 1981. Dr. Hunt and her husband, George L. Hunt, moved to Henderson where she became active in numerous civic organizations. Several of her books were published while in Henderson, including *Reaching for a Star Through Poetical Imagery* and *Miracle of Escape*. She spent her last years traveling as a visiting poet and author around the country. She was the mother of Brenda Alexander, Moss H., Alan L. Kendrix, and Blake Hunt. She is interred in Sunset Memorial Gardens. (Courtesy of Andre D. Vann.)

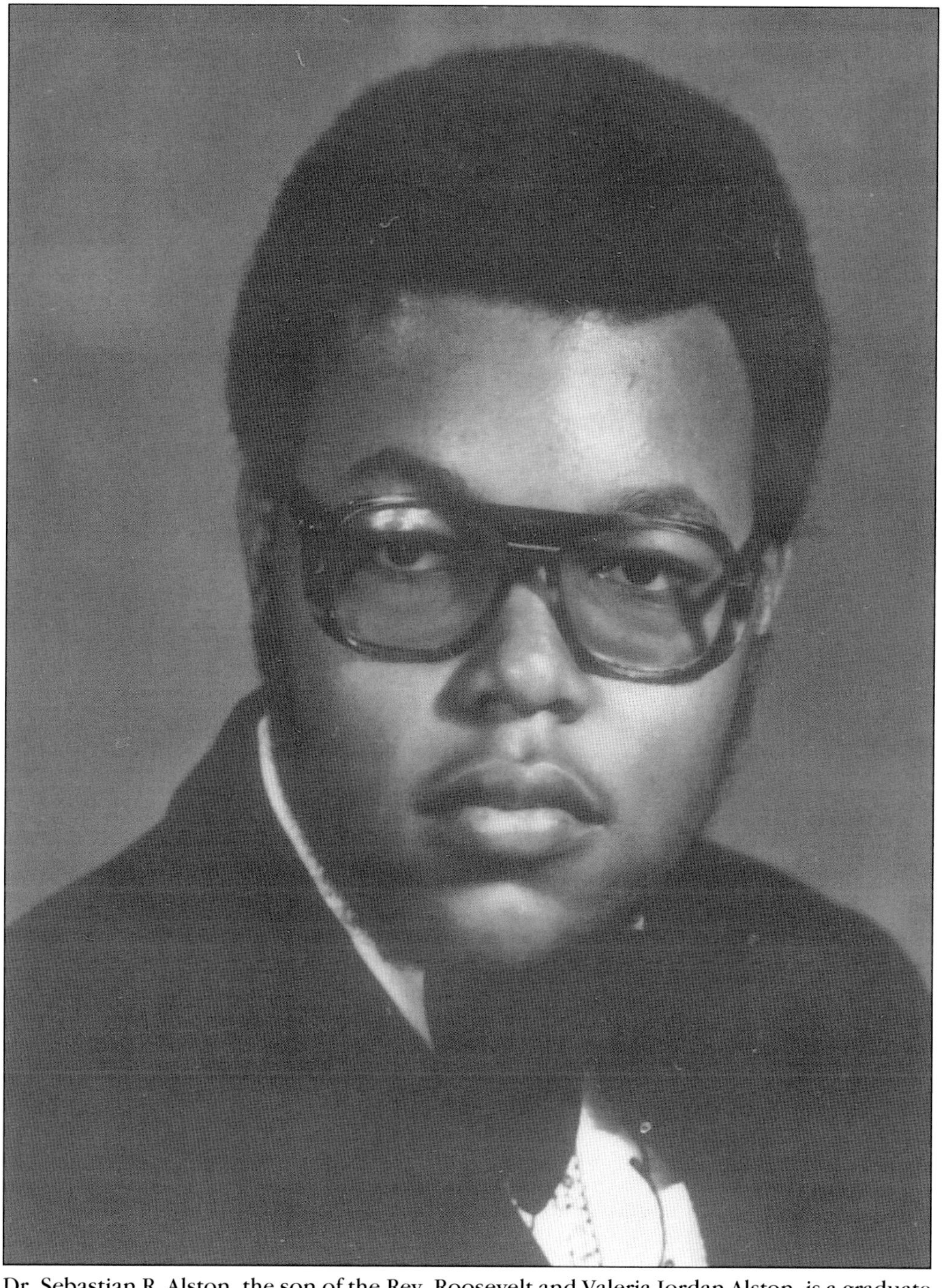

Dr. Sebastian R. Alston, the son of the Rev. Roosevelt and Valeria Jordan Alston, is a graduate of Northern Vance High School. A member of Phi Beta Kappa, he graduated from the University of North Carolina at Chapel Hill (UNC-CH) and received a Morehead Fellowship for the UNC-CH School of Medicine. Alston was the first black neuropathologist in the United States. He is associate professor of pathology at Mercer Medical School in Macon, GA. (Courtesy of Valeria J. Alston.)

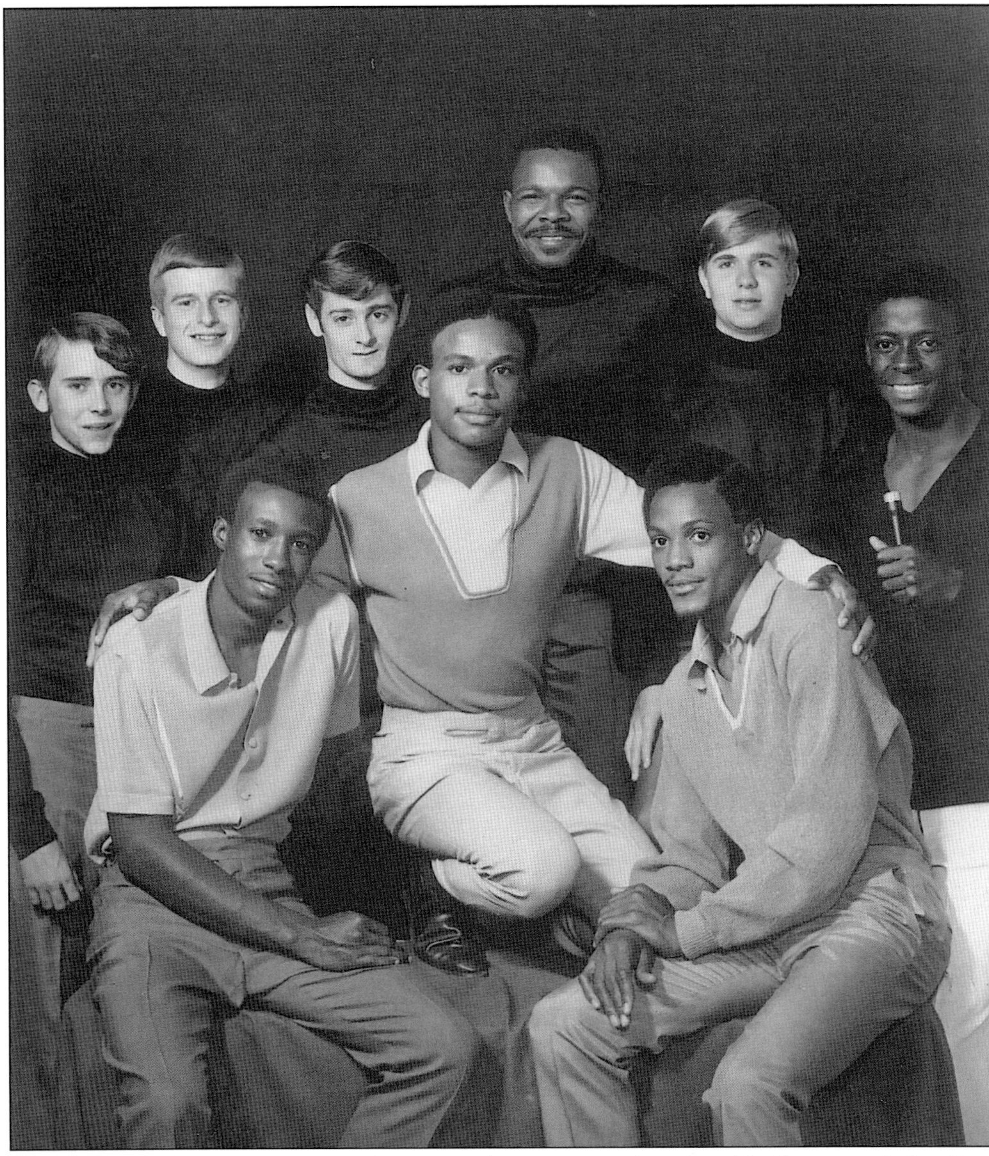

This early 1968 photo was used as an advertisement for Gerald Alston and the New Imperials. The group provided dance music in Vance County and surrounding areas, performing at numerous high schools, benefits, and private functions during the 1960s and 1970s. Also, the group provided music for college campuses in NC and VA. From left to right are as follows: (front row) Andrew Crews, James Smith, and Dwight Fields; (back row) Tony Braswell, Harry Hedgepeth, Donald Vaughan, Butch Turner, Bernie Long, and Gerald Alston. (Courtesy of Harry Hedgepeth.)

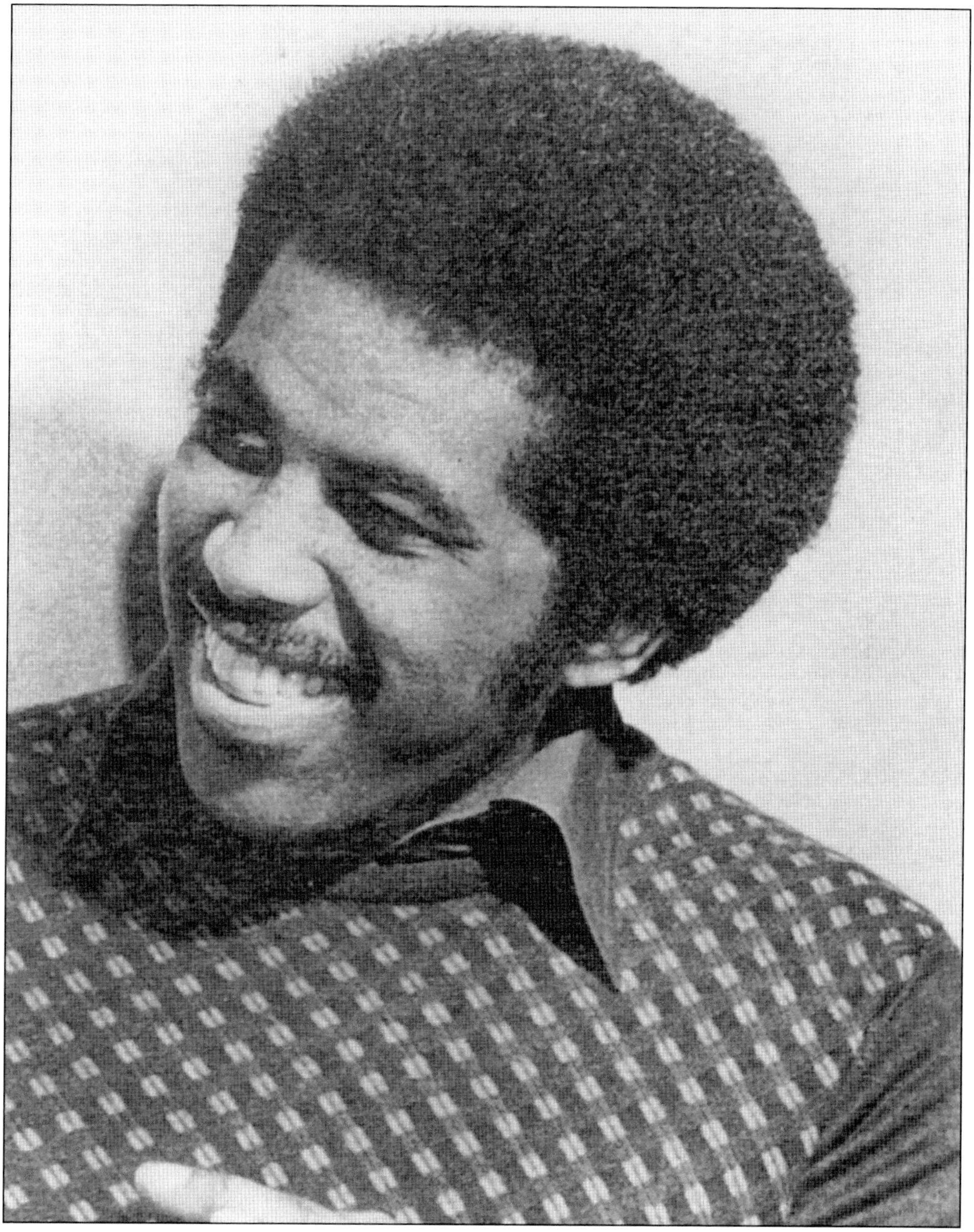

Ben E. King (1938–) was born Benjamin Earl Nelson in Henderson and was raised on Vaughan Street. The family later moved to New York City, but King often spent his summers in Henderson with family members and attended Davis Chapel Baptist Church. He recorded his first record at age 18, performing while still in high school in a singing doo-wop group called the Four B's. He later joined the Five Crowns, then the Drifters. He is best remembered as a solo vocalist and recorded such classics as "Stand By Me," his first record as a soloist, "There Goes My Baby," and "Save The Last Dance for Me." King is married to Betty Nelson King and they reside in New Jersey. (Courtesy of Paths Toward Freedom and NC Division of Archives and History.)

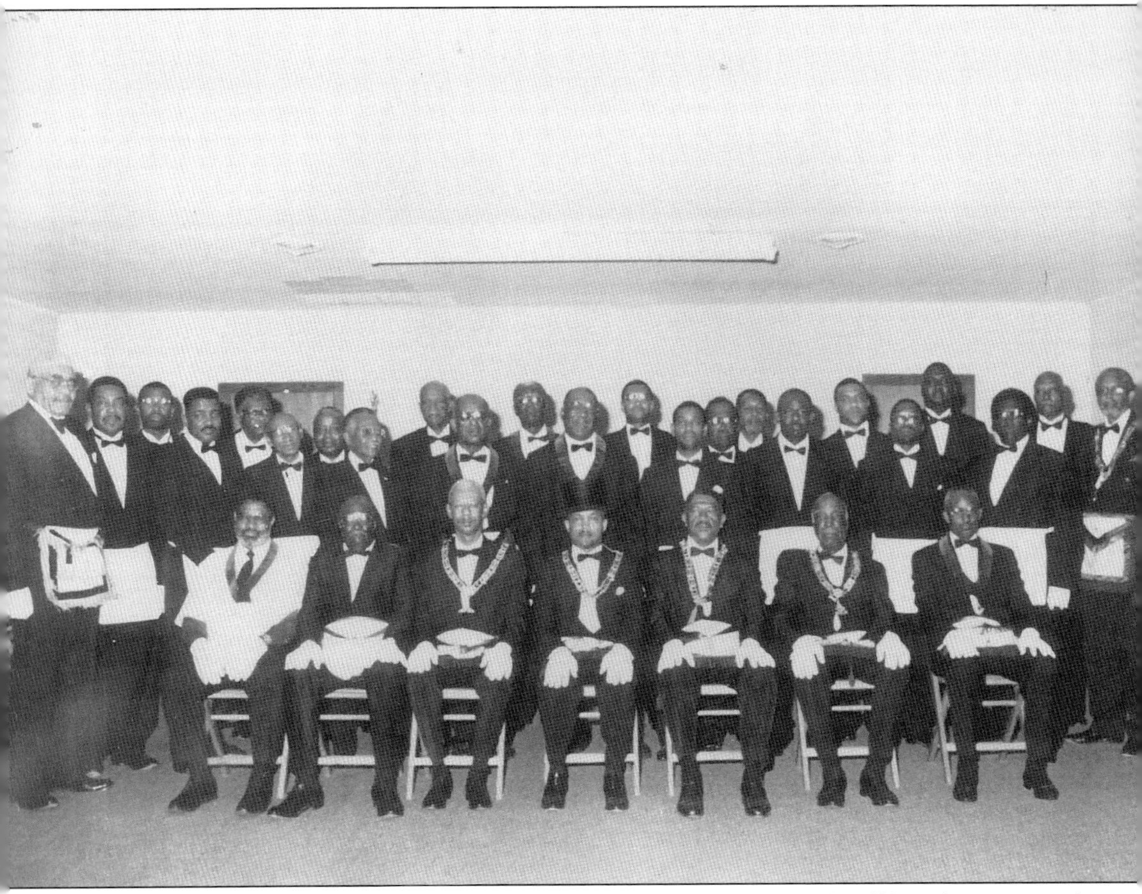

Shown in this late 1980s photo are the brothers of the Prince Hall Affiliated-Beacon Light Masonic Lodge #249, with the Most Worshipful Master Harlan Zachary in the center of the front row. The lodge's existence dates back to almost a century; it was involved in numerous philanthropic efforts in Vance County and the surrounding areas. The Masonic Lodge is located at 1204 West Andrews Avenue and they are the owners and developers of the Beacon Light Goodwill Baxter Apartments, Inc., located on Boddie Street. (Courtesy of Charlie R. Marable.)

ACKNOWLEDGMENTS

Anyone who has ever published a book knows that it is a collaborative work and a joint venture of faith and hope. This book has benefited greatly from the cooperation, assistance, wisdom, and dedication of a committed crew of family members, friends, colleagues, and students.

I am deeply grateful to an entire host of individuals who have gone beyond the call of duty to assist in the completion of this work. I have been supported by colleagues, former professors, librarians, friends, and family members who have sustained me along this journey to create—for the first time—a pictorial history of the African-American presence in Vance County.

I would like to thank many current and past residents of such communities as Mobile, Flint Hill, West End, Standpipe, and Greystone, and such rural areas as Townsville, Williamsboro, and Kittrell. I would like to acknowledge the following individuals who have freely given photographs and treasures from their personal collections: Roosevelt Alston, Valeria Alston, Earl I. Ames, Johnny Ashe, Hattie Yarborough Ballard, Otelia E. Barnwell, Randolph Baskerville, Deborah J. Brown, Thomas Brown, Alice Eaton Bryant, Bessie Bullock, Gertrude Stitt Bullock, Virginia K. Butler, Emeron and Patricia Cash, Gertrude Vaughan Dickerson, Andolia O. Eaton, Courtney Eaton Eisbey, Patty Y. Foster, Gladys Lyons Hawkins, Harry Hedgepeth, Janie Hawkins Hicks, Juanita W. Hicks, Nancy Simpson Hoke, Ruth Hawkins Hughes, Rebecca C. Hunt, , Catherine Vann-Johnson, Ophelia W. Jones, Clarence Knight, Charlie Marable, Sherman G. Parham, Rosa Williams Poole, Sophia R. Ramey, Quentin Ramseur, Ramona Brame Ramseur, Rev. Joseph Ratliff, Andre S. Richardson, Johnnie Y. Sanders, Brian Solomon Simmons, Ethel C.R. Smith, Hurley Taylor, Ernest C. Terry, Tessie Bobbit Vaughan, Hattie B.I. Williams, and Al Wheless.

Special thanks go to the staffs at the *Daily Dispatch*, the H. Leslie Perry Memorial Library, the Vance County Register of Deeds, the Henderson Institute Museum Board, the North Carolina Division of Archives and History, and the Vance County Clerk of Courts Office.

Sources

Caldwell, A.B. *History of the American Negro-North Carolina Edition*. Atlanta: A.B. Caldwell, 1921.

Crow, Jeffrey J., Paul D. Escott, and Flora J. Hatley. *A History of African Americans in North Carolina.* Raleigh: Division of Archives and History, North Carolina Department of Cultural Resources, 1992.

Daily Dispatch. Centennial Edition. Henderson, NC: *Daily Dispatch*, Inc., 1981.

Daily Dispatch. Sesquicentennial Edition. Henderson, NC: Daily Dispatch Company, Inc., 1991.

Edmonds, Helen G. *The Negro and Fusion Politics in North Carolina, 1894–1901.* Chapel Hill : The University of North Carolina Press, 1951.

Henderson City Directories. North Carolina Room, H. Leslie Perry Memorial Library.

Henderson Institute Museum. Henderson, NC.

Henry, Linda Simmons. *The Heritage of Blacks in North Carolina, Vol. I.* Charlotte, NC: The Delmar Company, 1990.

Hughes, Ruth A. *Contributions of Vance County People of Color.* Raleigh, NC: Sparks Press, 1988.

Murphy, Ann Melanie. *An Inventory of Historic Architecture-Henderson, N.C* : Henderson Vance County Chamber of Commerce, 1979.

Peace, Samuel T. *"Zeb's Black Baby" Vance County : North Carolina-A Short History.* Henderson, NC: Harperprints, Inc., 1955.

Vance County Historical Society. *Vance County*. Winston- Salem, NC: Hunter Publishing Company, 1984.

Wadelington, Charles W., and Richard F. Knapp. *Charlotte Hawkins Brown: What One Young African American Woman Could Do.* Chapel-Hill, NC: The University of North Carolina Press, 1999.